The CENTRAL AMERICAN CRISIS

SOURCES OF
CONFLICT AND
THE FAILURE
OF U.S. POLICY

Central America

MEXICO

BELIZE
• Belmopan

GUATEMALA

HONDURAS

Guatemala •

EL SALVADOR
• San Salvador

Tegucigalpa •

NICARAGUA

Managua •

CARIBBEAN SEA

PACIFIC OCEAN

COSTA RICA
• San José

PANAMÁ

Panamá City •

COLOMBIA

The CENTRAL AMERICAN CRISIS

SOURCES OF CONFLICT AND THE FAILURE OF U.S. POLICY

EDITED BY
Kenneth M. Coleman
and
George C. Herring

SR *Scholarly Resources Inc.*
Wilmington, Delaware

First published 1985
Printed and bound in the United States of America
Second printing 1985
Third printing 1986
Fourth printing 1988

Scholarly Resources Inc.
104 Greenhill Avenue
Wilmington, Delaware 19805

Library of Congress Cataloging in Publication Data
Main entry under title:

The Central American crisis.

    Includes bibliographies and index.
    1. Central America—Foreign relations—United States—
Addresses, essays, lectures.   2. United States—Foreign
relations—Central America—Addresses, essays, lectures.
3. United States—Foreign relations—1981– —Addresses,
essays, lectures.   4. Central America—Economic conditions—1979– —Addresses, essays, lectures.
5. Central America—Social conditions—1979– —Addresses, essays, lectures.   I. Coleman, Kenneth M.
II. Herring, George C., 1936–
F1436.U6C46 1985   327.730728   84–27624

ISBN 0–8420–2238–4
ISBN 0–8420–2240–6 (pbk.)

Contents

SECTION III. POLICY OPTIONS

CONCLUSION

Preface

A S THE UNITED STATES involved itself more deeply in Central
America during the Reagan presidency, many citizens
began to feel uneasy about their nation's role in this area.
Some sensed that the prior behavior of the United States had
more to do with current problems in Central America than
public officials were willing to concede, but few could specify
just what had occurred. Wary of the Vietnam experience in
which both Democratic and Republican presidents had argued
that "we can do only what we are currently doing," many
citizens also seemed eager to be exposed to informed discussion of a range of policy options.

The Latin American Studies Program of the University of
Kentucky responded to this public anxiety by sponsoring two
conferences during the 1983–84 academic year. The first was
a series of six lectures given by faculty members from various
disciplines at the university and was entitled "Central America:
Background to Crisis." That series was followed by a two-day
conference entitled "Central America: Policy Options," to
which leading participants in the national policy debate were
invited. Included here are most of the presentations delivered
at both these events, as well as two additional articles.

This volume offers for interested general readers and for
students in a variety of college-level courses a critical explanation of how the United States has become engaged in conflict with Central American revolutions. It also proposes
alternative policies to deal more effectively with those revolutions. We reject the assumptions underpinning existing policy. We do not intend to suggest that the United States is
responsible for all the ills of Central America or that the Reagan
administration can do nothing right. However, many of those
people who are most knowledgeable about the region have
advocated accommodating, rather than confronting, the revolutionary government of Nicaragua and existing revolutionary movements in El Salvador and Guatemala. We believe that

these views should be brought before a wider audience. The spirit of our enterprise is not to foreclose debate by asserting that our arguments are beyond question but instead to make educated debate possible by informing citizens more systematically of ideas that they will not hear from the Reagan administration. Indeed, we recommend that this book be read along with expositions of official thinking such as the Report of the President's National Bipartisan Commission on Central America, the so-called Kissinger Commission Report.[1]

If there is an underlying political bias to this volume, it is toward the social democratic option. Most of the authors believe that accommodation between the rich and the poor, the landed and the landless, or capitalists and industrial workers would have been possible if political systems controlled by the rich, the landed, and the owners of capital had pursued timely and enlightened policies. Furthermore, all of the authors herein agree that certain political systems of Central America failed to do this, and that the United States bears some responsibility for these failures.

Nonetheless, even at this late date many Latin American specialists believe, along with one of our contributors, Daniel Oduber, that "peace is possible" in Central America. To achieve that peace, which is attainable only by striking a social democratic bargain between the propertied and the poor, political systems will have to be opened rather than closed to the political left. By its opposition to power sharing in El Salvador and its support of counterrevolution in Nicaragua, the Reagan administration contributes to the closure of political systems.

We believe that a peace shaped by compromise with Central American revolutionaries would be an honorable peace consistent with the long-term interests of the United States and indeed essential to defending those interests. The United States seeks primarily peace and stability in the area on its southern periphery. To be true to its ideals, however, it must support democratic forces in Central America. Its economic stake in the region is small, moreover, and it should be willing to accept fundamental economic changes if Central Americans desire to make them. It should identify with those political forces that respect their adversaries and should tolerate those

---

[1]This report can be obtained from the Superintendent of Public Documents, U.S. Government Printing Office, Washington, DC 20402.

whose views may differ. In instances where extreme polarization has given rise to revolution, the United States should let the Central Americans settle their own conflicts. It should not attempt to prevent left-wing governments from coming to power. Once such governments have attained power, the United States should remain open-minded and flexible in its policy. If such governments become authoritarian or develop close ties with its enemies, the United States may wish to remain aloof, but it should not lock itself into a policy of confrontation. Initial impressions of implacable hostility by revolutionary governments may be wrong. Those who come to power by attacking the United States may discover in time the utility of maintaining relations. Historical scholarship has suggested that accommodation with revolution is both possible and beneficial to the United States.[2]

Historian WALTER LaFEBER's opening remarks place the Reagan administration's policies in historical perspective by stressing that they are but recent manifestations of a long-standing pattern of U.S. attempts to control social change in Central America through military and political intervention. Section I then focuses on the indigenous causes of the current conflict, with two articles specifically addressing the fundamental economic problems that lie beneath social conflict and political turmoil in the area. First, economist MICHAEL WEBB discusses the history of labor markets in Central America and provides background essential to understanding the current shortage of remunerative employment. Second, anthropologist BILLIE DeWALT presents a detailed examination of how recent agrarian trends have exacerbated employment problems and have generated additional pressure on political systems. Sociologist KATHLEEN BLEE next examines the role of the church, especially the ecclesiastical base communities of lay persons, in stimulating demands for political and economic change. Political scientist KENNETH COLEMAN concludes this section by analyzing the basic structure of political conflict in the area, distinguishing between conventional, reformist, and revolutionary ideologies of change. He attributes recent conflict in three countries—Nicaragua, El Salvador, and Guatemala—to the systematic exclusion of reformist groups from political power.

---

[2]Cole Blasier, *The Hovering Giant: U.S. Responses to Revolutionary Change in Latin America* (Pittsburgh, 1976).

Section II moves more directly into the current policy debate. Since so much public attention has been focused on the analogy with Vietnam, GEORGE HERRING's discussion of the uses and misuses of historical analogy is a helpful beginning to an assessment of President Reagan's Central American policy. ELDON KENWORTHY analyzes the propensity of the U.S. government to define change that it cannot control as a threat to its "vital interests," while DAVID ROSS considers the Caribbean Basin Initiative, an early Reagan policy proposal, as an example of how the United States seeks to maintain control in Central America through bilateral trade relations. Finally, THOMAS WALKER describes the deterioration of U.S. relations with Nicaragua during the first four years of the Sandinista regime, arguing that under President Reagan "the United States was simply not interested in any settlement which would have left the Sandinista revolution intact."

DANIEL ODUBER's analysis of the possibilities for peace initiates the section on policy options. Oduber is a former president of Costa Rica and an early participant in the Contadora process. The editors believe that his discussion of the forces operating in the region warrants special attention. He notes that reform-oriented groups, including both social and Christian Democrats, often have been the target of violence by the political right. Nonetheless, he believes that these groups will eventually emerge as powerful political forces in the area if external forces, including the United States, can be held at bay. In outlining alternative policies, ABRAHAM LOWENTHAL's critique of the Kissinger Commission Report proposes that the United States "should define much more carefully" its vital interests in Central America and should "pursue those interests vigorously, while shying away from unnecessary involvements." Lowenthal identifies those interests as the absence of Soviet bases, offensive facilities, or strategic weapons. However, he also argues that the United States should take a sustained interest in the development of Central American countries "on terms that respect the sovereignty of their nations."

In conclusion, GEORGE HERRING and KENNETH COLEMAN synthesize comments made by each contributor and outline an approach for coping with revolutionary change. The United States should accept revolutionary change when it is inevitable

and should accept Latin regimes that redefine property relations in accord with the traditional Hispanic concept of the
"social function of property."

We hope this book will reach some of the many citizens
who are concerned about the wisdom of current policy in
Central America. If it helps to stimulate public debate, we will
feel that it has served its purpose, however readers may assess
the merits of the views expressed.

Kenneth M. Coleman and *George C. Herring*
Lexington, Kentucky
September 1984

Acknowledgments

A NUMBER OF INDIVIDUALS have made important contributions to the publication of this volume. Four persons warrant special thanks. Otis Singletary, president of the University of Kentucky, listened with interest when first confronted with the idea of inviting a major statesman to Lexington to deliver the keynote address at a conference on Central America. He quickly agreed to finance the proposed conference, thus making it possible in February 1984. The articles in this volume by Daniel Oduber, Abraham F. Lowenthal, and Walter LaFeber are a direct result of Dr. Singletary's commitment to the event.

Kathleen M. DeWalt, associate professor of (Medical) Behavioral Science at the University of Kentucky, as chairperson of the Seminars and Colloquia Committee of the Latin American Studies Program, played a key role in organizing the conference. Without her efforts, it simply would not have happened and this book would not have been published. Dr. DeWalt has published widely on the social determinants of nutrition, based on field work in Honduras and Mexico. Her contributions to understanding Central America, therefore, transcend the organizational, and she has been a valuable sounding board for those contributors from the University of Kentucky.

Abraham F. Lowenthal of the University of Southern California proved extraordinarily helpful at an early stage of our conference planning. He not only agreed to participate in the conference himself but also suggested that Daniel Oduber would be an appropriate keynote speaker. Dr. Lowenthal's advice proved to be sagacious.

Finally, Carol Reardon, doctoral candidate in history at the University of Kentucky, read the proofs and prepared the index with customary skill and efficiency.

We also are indebted to the *World Policy Journal* for the right to reprint the article by Eldon Kenworthy.

Contributors

Kathleen M. Blee is a sociologist at the University of Kentucky who studies migration, family structures, and political activism, as well as the Central American church. She has contributed articles on the political orientation of immigrants to *Social Problems* and to a volume on *Classes, Class Conflict and the State*. She also has published in the area of political theory and historical methodology.

Kenneth M. Coleman is associate professor of political science and director of the Latin American Studies Program at the University of Kentucky. He has published on Mexican and Venezuelan politics in such journals as *Comparative Political Studies, Social Science Quarterly, Latin American Research Review,* and the *Journal of Developing Areas.*

Billie R. DeWalt is associate professor of anthropology and rural sociology, University of Kentucky. A specialist in agricultural systems, he has done field work in Mexico and Honduras. He has published numerous articles in anthropological and ethnological journals and is the author of *Modernization in a Mexican Ejido: A Study in Economic Adaptation* (1979).

George C. Herring is professor of history, University of Kentucky, and editor of the quarterly journal *Diplomatic History*. His recent work has focused on U.S. involvement in Vietnam and includes *America's Longest War: The United States and Vietnam, 1950–1975* (1979) and *The Secret Diplomacy of the Vietnam War: The "Negotiating Volumes" of the Pentagon Papers* (1983).

Eldon Kenworthy is a political scientist at Cornell University. He has written widely on Latin American politics and inter-American relations, contributing to *Comparative Politics,*

Democracy, Bulletin of the Atomic Scientists, and the *New York Times.* His recent work has dealt with Cuba and Nicaragua, after earlier studies of Argentina.

Walter LaFeber is Noll Professor of History at Cornell University. A specialist in the history of American foreign relations, he is the author of *The New Empire* (1963), *The Panama Canal* (1978), *America, Russia, and the Cold War* (5th ed., 1984), and *Inevitable Revolutions: The United States in Central America* (1983).

Abraham F. Lowenthal is professor of international relations at the University of Southern California and executive director of the Inter-American Dialogue in Washington, DC. He previously served with the Ford Foundation, the Council on Foreign Relations, and the Woodrow Wilson International Center for Scholars. His published books include *The Dominican Intervention* (1972), *The Peruvian Experiment: Continuity and Change under Military Rule* (1975), and *Armies and Politics in Latin America* (1976).

Daniel Oduber, president of Costa Rica from 1974 to 1978, previously served his country as ambassador to the United Nations, minister of foreign affairs, head of the Partido de Liberación Nacional (PLN), and presiding officer of the Costa Rican congress. Currently he serves as president of the governing board of the PLN and as vice-president of the Socialist International.

David F. Ross is associate professor of economics, University of Kentucky. He has taught in Puerto Rico and Liberia and has published essays in the *New Republic.* He is the author of *Honduras: A Problem in Economic Development* (1959), *The Long Uphill Path: A Historical Study of Puerto Rico's Development Program* (1966), and *Negro Employment in State and Local Governments in the South* (1973).

Thomas W. Walker teaches political science at Ohio University. A specialist on Nicaragua, he has published *The Christian Democratic Movement in Nicaragua* (1970) and *Nicaragua: The Land of Sandino* (1981) and has edited *Nicaragua in Revolution* (1982). His edited collection, *Nicaragua: The First Five Years* and a much-revised second edition of *Nicaragua: The Land of Sandino*, will be published in 1985.

Michael A. Webb is assistant professor of economics at the University of Kentucky and specializes in commercial policy and economic development. He was a coeditor of *Dimensões do Desenvolvimiento Brasileiro* (1978) and has published in both the *Oxford Economic Papers* and *Journal of International Economics.*

Walter LaFeber

The Reagan Policy in Historical Perspective

SINCE 1979 U.S. officials have changed General Carl Maria von Clausewitz's famous dictum that war is only a "continuation of State policy" (that is, politics) "by other means." In Central America the U.S. approach has been to use war as a substitute for "state policy." Diplomacy has been replaced by warfare; military escalation has been substituted for politics. More specifically, the Reagan administration has used diplomatic discussions as a fig leaf for military escalation. "War," Clausewitz wrote 150 years ago, "is only diplomacy somewhat intensified, a more vigorous way of negotiating."[1] The United States has transformed that postulate to read: war, slowly intensified, is the most important means for negotiating with adversaries in Central America. In dealing with the Sandinista government in Nicaragua or the Farabundo Martí National Liberation Front (FMLN) revolutionaries that attempt to overthrow the government in El Salvador, the Reagan administration has used war, not negotiations, as its state policy.

One example demonstrated the approach with clarity. Since 1981 the State Department twice attempted to modify administration policy to the extent that a so-called "dual track," rather than simply a military track, would be followed. The dual track approach was initially worked out by Thomas O. Enders, assistant secretary of state for Inter-American Affairs (1981–1983). Enders was not a "dove." While stationed in Southeast Asia during 1969–70, he had established his willingness to use force by guiding and helping to cover up the secret bombing of Communist bases in Cambodia. As a top State Department official in early 1983, moreover, he warned that

---

[1] The Clausewitz quotes and a useful commentary are available in Roger A. Leonard, ed., *A Short Guide to Clausewitz on War* (New York, 1968), esp. pp. 11–14.

"it should be made clear to the Soviet Union and Cuba and Nicaragua that the United States may take direct action if they try to destabilize nations in this hemisphere."[2] Behind the scenes, however, Enders had learned that escalating U.S. military involvement was not resolving the central political problems in the region. North American application of force was instead playing a role in causing the Nicaraguan and Salvadoran revolutionaries to escalate their military efforts and the numbers in their armed forces. Enders sought to use the immense U.S. military power as a stick to shape negotiations rather than as a club to drive the Sandinistas and FMLN into oblivion.

His approach ran contrary to the Reagan administration's policy of overthrowing, not negotiating with, the Sandinistas, and its determination to destroy, not discuss power sharing with, the Salvadoran rebels. That policy was being shaped not in the State Department by Enders or Secretary of State George Shultz but in the National Security Council where William C. Clark, the president's National Security adviser, combined little knowledge of and less experience in Central American affairs with an ardent military approach to foreign policy problems; in the United Nations where U.S. Ambassador Jeane J. Kirkpatrick worked out an evolving rationale for the administration's military support of authoritarian regimes in Latin America; and especially in the Pentagon where civilian officials such as Fred Iklé and Nestor Sanchez possessed both an unyielding view of the need to oppose Third World revolutionaries and to assert control over the bureaucratic levers that could create and dispatch armed forces to Central America. Against this range of opponents Enders stood little chance. In May 1983 the White House forced him out of Washington. He became ambassador to Spain, a post that placed him out of the policymaking circles but, in a move that was politically shrewd as well as ideologically necessary, accredited him to a government that agreed with his dual track approach. Enders and the Spanish officials could now console each other while Clark, Iklé, and Kirkpatrick followed the single track military policy back in Washington.[3]

---

[2]Quoted in Allan Nairn, "Endgame: A Special Report on the U.S. Military Strategy in Central America," *NACLA Report on the Americas* 18 (May–June 1984): 39.

[3]Author's interviews, March 1983 and July 1984; *Washington Post*, March 6, 1983.

The State Department, however, did not immediately join the policy consensus despite Enders's departure. The circumstances of the Central American dilemma were too obvious to the professionals who knew the region more intimately and objectively than either Clark or Kirkpatrick. Enders's replacement, Langhorne Motley, had been a real estate speculator in Alaska before becoming a rather widely publicized and outspoken U.S. ambassador to Brazil in 1981. Little evidence existed publicly to indicate that Motley would move contrary to mainstream administration policy; indeed, the evidence (his toughness as ambassador, his closeness to White House advisers, and his apparently simplistic approach to resolving the Nicaraguan-Salvadoran problems quickly) placed him in the Clark-Kirkpatrick circle. But Motley learned quickly. He continued to espouse a tough military approach and agreed with the continuing North American buildup in the region, but, resembling Enders, he came to understand that, unless the United States aimed for some diplomatic settlement, military power could lead to a disastrous dead end. Worse, that power, instead of frightening the revolutionaries into surrender, drove them into more rapidly expanding their military influence. United States military escalation created the opposite results that it had set out to achieve.

Motley also began to explore the dual track alternative, but, in July and August 1983, he and the State Department were dramatically undercut by the White House announcement that the United States would begin massive military maneuvers in the Central American region. The North American forces were to conduct the largest peacetime maneuvers in history around Central America, deploying as many as 30,000 men. The announcement occurred at a time when the United States rapidly built up the military capacity of Honduras as a base for attacking Nicaragua, and as the CIA publicly escalated its supplying and direction of the Contras (Nicaraguan exiles including former military officers from the dictatorial Somoza regime which the Sandinistas had overthrown in 1979 and who were now trying to overthrow the Sandinistas). The White House apparently announced this dramatic step without informing either Motley or Shultz about its decision.

The State Department had simply been cut out of the policy loop. Shultz was reportedly furious. His anger erupted, moreover, at a moment when Congress and knowledgeable private citizens unloosed a barrage of criticism at the Reagan approach. A political crisis of some proportions loomed. The White House staff, this time led by James Baker, brilliantly gained time by arranging the appointment of a bipartisan commission on Central America, chaired by former Secretary of State Henry A. Kissinger. The commission was charged by President Reagan with examining the Central American dilemma in depth and recommending a course of action. The political crisis temporarily passed, but the U.S. military escalation meanwhile continued; it indeed reached new levels during late 1983 and early 1984, just as the Kissinger Commission issued a report that refused to condone any power sharing with the Salvadoran revolutionaries, condemned the Sandinistas, and placed its strongest emphasis on the need to provide military security and not on diplomatic approaches.

The Kissinger Commission thus emerged out of a multi-dimensional threat to Reagan's policy. The first threat was growing public dissatisfaction. The second was congressional criticism that grew so intense that it threatened to cut off North American aid to the Contras and the Salvadoran military. Such aid had become virtually the entire life support system for the Contras and the Salvadoran officers. The third occurred in Central America itself where U.S. military policies spread— not limited—the threat of revolution. This final challenge, its extent and origins, deserves closer study, for it can reveal much about the foundation of U.S. problems in Central America and why Washington's policy is so deeply rooted that not even the State Department can easily push it in a new direction.

By early 1984, after nearly one full term in office, President Reagan had involved the United States in several costly wars. The bloodiest in terms of North American lives lost occurred in Lebanon where 269 U.S. soldiers were killed within one year. In Central America, North Americans were involved in three war fronts, and a fourth threatened to open.

The first war front engulfed El Salvador where about 40,000 governmental soldiers fought 9,000 to 12,000 revolutionaries. In January 1981 the FMLN had launched a "final offensive" to sweep the government from power, but the Salvadoran army inflicted heavy casualties in pushing back the offensive with surprising ease. About 3,500 FMLN troops remained after the defeat; over the next three years their numbers tripled. By early 1984 the military situation reached the point where the

Kissinger Commission believed that the collapse of the Sal-vadoran army was not inconceivable. Despite costly U.S. train-ing and supplies (Washington's aid to El Salvador totaled more than $1 billion between 1978 and mid-1984), the government's troops were often inept. Only one out of every ten trained in the United States reenlisted, officers in some key areas were corrupt and ineffective, and key commanders were more con-cerned with their tasks in brutal terrorist death squads that killed about 40,000 civilians between 1979 and 1984 than with fighting the revolutionaries.

Washington's policy rested on military power. No deal was to be made with the FMLN until it could be made on terms dictated by the U.S. and Salvadoran governments. Such dic-tation could not occur until revolutionary forces were destroyed. But the government in San Salvador lost much of its legitimacy during the early 1980s and found it increasingly difficult to mobilize either its own people, or the U.S. Con-gress on which it depended ever more for survival, to fight a difficult and expensive military campaign. This loss of legiti-macy arose from a number of developments: the transfor-mation of a 1979 *golpe*, which had promised to evolve into a liberal regime, into a conservative, army-controlled govern-ment; the association of that government with horrible human rights violations; the inability of the regime to carry out land and other reforms that could stimulate the economy and rally masses of peasants to its cause; and the continuing domina-tion of Salvadoran politics and economics by wealthy oli-garchs, or the so-called Fourteen (or Forty) Families that had run the country as a personal fiefdom since the nineteenth century and whose exploitation had largely brought about the revolution.

To restore this slipping legitimacy, the United States sponsored elections. The first, in 1982, created a constituent assembly; the second, in 1984, elected a president. Both elec-tions accomplished the North American objective: to provide at least the semblance of legitimacy for the government in Salvadoran and U.S. eyes. That between 16 percent and 25 percent of the 1982 votes may have been fraudulent, or that Washington intervened to ensure that the winning party (a group unfortunately linked to some of the worst human rights atrocities) did not obtain the interim presidency, were results that the Reagan administration understandably did not wish to discuss. In neither election did the revolutionaries participate. A half-dozen of their top leaders had been trapped and murdered in cold blood by the Salvadoran army in 1980 as they prepared to discuss negotiations with the government. No guarantees existed that the personal safety of any politician in the liberal-to-radical part of the political spectrum could be ensured against the death squads' rifles in either 1982 or 1984. The United States controlled the 1984 election. It used public relations devices and front organizations operated by the CIA, which together with the U.S. embassy in San Salvador worked out and supervised the election process.[4]

In this manner, elections became an integral part of U.S. military policy. They were conducted not to create a nationally accepted government but to create a regime that appeared more legitimate and thus more capable of mobilizing North American support to conduct military campaigns.

The second war in the region occurred in northern Nicaragua along the Honduran border. The Contras, with about 10,000 to 12,000 men, attempted to launch invasions from Honduran bases into northern Nicaragua. They particularly wanted to declare the existence of a provisional government on Nicaraguan soil, a regime that the United States could then recognize as an alternative to the Sandinista government. To fight the incursions the Sandinistas built an army of 50,000 troops and reserve militias of about 100,000. By late 1983 the CIA had taken command of the Contras, shoving aside the politically inept leaders who had failed to achieve their military or political goals. By mid-1984 over $70 million of CIA money had flowed to the Contras, but there was little to show for the expenditure other than several hundred who had been killed on both sides and intensified CIA activities in Nicaragua itself, including the bombing of the Managua airport and the destruction of the country's major oil refinery and docks in late 1983.[5]

A third war, one in which the United States was less involved, devastated parts of southern Nicaragua along the

---

[4]*Washington Post*, February 25, 1984; Timothy Garton Ash, "A Tale of Two Countries," *Spectator*, March 31, 1984; *Central America Report*, March 30, 1984; *Washington Post*, May 4, 1984.

[5]*New York Times*, June 11, 1984; Commission on U.S.-Central American Relations, *U.S. Military Intervention in Central America* (Washington, DC, 1984), pp. 4–5, 8–12.

Costa Rican border. An anti-Sandinista group (with the Spanish acronym ARDE) led by Edén Pastora and Alfonso Robelo included about 4,000 soldiers. Pastora and Robelo had been major figures in the Sandinista movement in the late 1970s, but they left Managua when Pastora received no important post in the new regime and when both men perceived that the Sandinistas intended to carry out a social revolution through authoritarian methods with which Pastora and Robelo had little sympathy. The relationship between the two was seldom smooth. Pastora adamantly refused to move closer to the CIA or to form a partnership with the Contras in the north as the United States urged him to do. He charged that the Contras included too many Somocistas whom he had helped throw out of power in 1979. Robelo, on the other hand, proved increasingly open to the idea of cooperating with both the CIA and the Contras. Pastora's troops seized a town along the southern border and held it briefly in 1983–84, but the effects of their "victory" were ephemeral. The Sandinistas, who have never been able to take Pastora very seriously because of his lack of sophistication and see him as an opéra-bouffe character, did not deploy their best troops against the southern rebels. In the spring of 1984, moreover, a bomb planted at Pastora's press conference severely wounded him, killed four journalists, and threw his movement into confusion. No evidence emerged to indicate conclusively who planted the bomb. As Pastora recovered, Robelo and the CIA began reorganizing the southern forces so they could move more aggressively against the Sandinistas. This third front grew in importance as the Reagan administration escalated its military pressure against Nicaragua.[6]

A fourth war also was being fought in Central America, although the United States was much less directly involved than in the other three. The Guatemalan government had been fighting revolutionaries intermittently since 1960. The outbreak changed dramatically in its political complexion during the mid-1970s when significant numbers of Indians joined the revolutionaries for the first time. Holding a bare majority of Guatemala's population, the Indians have been among the most oppressed and politically quiet people in Latin America. The army-controlled government, however, went too far when

---

[6]*New York Times,* June 14, 1984.

it grabbed large areas of land and devastated traditional Indian settlements.

The Guatemalan government was a U.S. creation. In 1954 a CIA-planned and -directed operation overthrew a constitutionally elected regime. The United States undertook the *golpe* because President Dwight D. Eisenhower's administration concluded that large-scale land reforms planned by the Guatemalan government threatened U.S. investments and were being pushed by Communists inside the Central American nation. The CIA operation put into power one of the most oppressive military regimes in the hemisphere, one that even turned on its own president (and the leader of the 1954 invasion forces) and assassinated him in 1957. The army itself split in 1960 to produce the first revolutionaries, a small group of junior officers who had been trained in the United States and consequently knew how to defend themselves against the Guatemalan troops sent out to destroy them. The revolution went through several phases before the Indians finally threatened to give it a mass base in the 1970s. The government responded with such atrocities in 1977 that President Jimmy Carter threatened to cut off military aid unless the Guatemalans stopped the repression. The government warned Carter that it no longer wanted North American assistance and continued slaughtering Indians.[7]

The Reagan administration attempted to reopen military aid channels, but Congress refused to appropriate any money. The chief executive nevertheless scored some small, significant victories including the transfer of some military parts to Guatemala through private channels. The administration also was encouraged by, if it did not play a part in, changes in the Guatemalan government that put into power military leaders who successfully carried out a "beans and bullets" campaign against the Indians: the villages were pacified with food and aid or else their inhabitants were handled with force. As human rights violations disappeared from stories in North American newspapers (although not from the `Indian villages), and as the regime conducted an election in mid-1984 to elect a constituent assembly, the way began to open for the Reagan administration to become more directly involved in Guatemala.

---

[7]There is an extended discussion of these points in Walter LaFeber, *Inevitable Revolutions: The United States in Central America* (New York, 1983), pp. 209–13, 256–61.

The restraint on U.S. involvement was less the limits imposed by North Americans than the Guatemalans' fervent belief that they did not want to become like the Hondurans whose country was being made into a U.S. military base. The Guatemalan military is one of the proudest and most tightly controlled in Latin America. Its members have exceptional loyalty to their institution and do not care for outside advice, even from the nation that initially put them into power in 1954. Because of the Guatemalan army's strength and the nation's influence in the region, and also because of the desire of Pentagon planners to form a Central American military front to deal with the FMLN and Sandinistas (a front that would have to include Guatemalan army forces), the Reagan administration nevertheless pressed in 1983–84 to increase its leverage in Guatemala. It wanted to help that nation's armed forces in every way allowed, and in some cases not condoned, by Congress. Guatemala was being fitted into the larger military policy of the United States. It was becoming the fourth front for North American "state policy," to use Clausewitz's phrase.

In Guatemala, El Salvador, and the Nicaraguan revolutionary conflict, the United States allied itself with the forces of the past: regimes represented by small elite groups that had exploited their own people for a century or more, by military officers who had lived off their countries for decades and now formed death squads to kill suspected critics, and— in the case of the Contras—army officers and political leaders closely associated with dictatorships. Such a perspective on U.S. policy raises two major questions. First, how did North Americans who were once, as John Winthrop (and much later Ronald Reagan) phrased it, to form a "city on a hill" that shined its light of liberty to the world end up in such tragedies? Second, what alternatives to the Reagan policy existed by the mid-1980s?

The United States did not create the conditions that produced Central American revolutions. When the Spanish colonial rulers involuntarily departed amidst the Latin American wars for independence during the first two decades of the nineteenth century, they left behind class-ridden societies, most of which were desperately poor and parochial. Many Central American political leaders were so conservative that they did not want Spain to leave (some feared, correctly, that Guatemala would immediately attempt to extend its power over the area), and they succeeded in killing the nascent Central American union movement of the 1820s and 1830s that might have united the five nations—Guatemala, El Salvador, Honduras, Nicaragua, and Costa Rica—into a more self-sufficient unit. As parochialism triumphed, the oligarch class developed its power in each of the nations except Costa Rica. In that country a more homogeneous racial composition (heavily Spanish with little Indian or black blood that could be found elsewhere in the region) and a relatively equitable land-holding system, which survived into the twentieth century, created bases for a more consensual political system than emerged in the other four nations. With only two major exceptions—the civil wars of 1918 and 1948—Costa Rica developed a democratic and stable political system that set it apart in the region and gave its people, the "Ticos," somewhat of a feeling of superiority that made more difficult later attempts at Central American cooperation.

In El Salvador, Guatemala, and Nicaragua, on the other hand, control of the land was tightly held by relatively few. Masses of peasants sunk to depths of poverty and forms of wage slavery by the late 1920s. The elites exploited the land and laborers to produce plantation crops such as coffee, cotton, and bananas to be exported to industrializing nations. These Central Americans thus became dependent on one or two crops. They were unable to regulate the prices of their products because the exports were sold on a world market, not in domestic markets where some control could be exerted. Domestic markets were too poor and wealth was too inequitably distributed to ensure a more self-sufficient economy.

Honduras underwent a somewhat different development. It had more available land than its neighbors, and consequently its peasants could find areas for scratching out a living. The best land for plantation crops, however, moved into the hands of U.S. banana companies after 1890. Honduras became the prototype of the "banana republic," with its lands, transportation, communications, and government operated directly, or more indirectly in the case of the government, by North Americans. Occupying the key strategic location in the region, and willing to cooperate with those who held dollars for investment, Honduras occupied the role as Washington's staunch and agreeable ally decades before the Reagan administration used it as a base for U.S. military and covert operations in the 1980s.

North American policy worked on two levels until the 1930s. On one, private investors and merchants penetrated the economies until every nation except El Salvador became dependent on the U.S. economy for either markets or food staples or both. El Salvador, which actually had tried to become a state in the North American system during the 1820s, escaped U.S. financial control to work more closely with West Europeans until World War II. On the second level, Washington officials frequently dispatched troops to maintain stability. The objectives were at least twofold: to provide peace of mind for Yankee investors and to ensure that European powers, especially the British and Germans, would not take such police chores into their own hands. United States soldiers and sailors had appeared as peacekeepers in the nineteenth century, but, after Theodore Roosevelt began building the Panamá Canal in 1903 and issued his so-called "corollary" to the Monroe Doctrine in 1904 (a pronouncement in which Roosevelt said that henceforth his country would act unilaterally to suppress civil wars in Latin America), the United States became the supreme military power in the hemisphere.[8]

Most notably the United States used its strength to maintain order when North American forces landed in Nicaragua in 1911–12 and, more particularly, to guarantee that a faction willing to cooperate with Washington would remain in power. Unfortunately, the Nicaraguans did not care for such a regime, and the foreign troops consequently had to remain until 1925 to ensure stability. When they left, civil war almost immediately resumed; the troops returned in 1926 and stayed until 1933. During these later years, however, they signally failed to destroy the guerrilla band of Augusto Sandino who vowed to fight until the Yankees left his country and who found much support among the peasants. By 1933 the intervention was becoming too costly and politically embarrassing for Washington officials. The administrations of Herbert Hoover and Franklin D. Roosevelt pulled out the troops but left behind a new device for maintaining U.S. interests: a native National Guard trained by North Americans and commanded by young Anastasio Somoza. A Nicaraguan who received much of his education in the United States, Somoza promptly used the guard to catapult himself over the nation's more venerable politicians and became dictator. He murdered Sandino, when

---

[8]Ibid., chap. 1.

the guerrilla leader came to Managua to make peace, and controlled the country until an assassin gunned him down in 1956. His sons then took over until they lost power in 1979 to the Sandinistas.[9]

The lessons of the 1912 to 1933 military interventions in Nicaragua were instructive. The first lesson was that by using force it could take a long time to construct viable, pro-U.S. regimes in Central America. A second lesson was that not even a twenty-year occupation could produce equitable political and economic systems, only a dictatorial government whose first commitment was to stability and self-aggrandizement. Finally, a third lesson was that North American military intervention produced a result that had long terrified Washington officials who dealt with the Soviet Union, China, and Mexico: mass-based revolutionaries who fought U.S. interests at every turn and who seemed to prosper even more when fresh foreign troops appeared to fight them. By 1933 U.S. military intervention produced exactly the opposite results intended by Washington policymakers.

Unfortunately, those lessons were not well learned. United States military involvement became less direct and public during the "Good Neighbor" era of President Franklin Roosevelt, but control of the region remained ultimately in North American hands, although it worked through direct economic leverage, through the common cause of World War II, and through the need of the region for North American products and foodstuffs in the 1940s and 1950s. The economic ties, however, did nothing to alleviate the class divisions and inequitable economic situation in the region; indeed, they worsened these problems. Pressures in Central America built toward a series of explosions. One occurred in Guatemala between 1944 and 1954 when a middle-class outbreak overthrew a dictatorship and established a reform government that tried to redistribute wealth and institute fair elections. It was this government that incurred the wrath of the Eisenhower administration in 1954.

The respite gained by this military-CIA action was brief. In 1959 Fidel Castro suddenly appeared as the ruler of Cuba.

---

[9]There is a fine overview in Lester D. Langley, *The United States and the Caribbean, 1900 to 1970* (Athens, GA, 1980); and Neill Macaulay, *The Sandino Affair* (Chicago, 1967) is the standard account.

No nation in Latin America, not even Nicaragua, had been as fully under Washington's control since the 1890s as Cuba. Castro's success, and his ability to maintain his power despite enormous U.S. pressures including an attempted replay of the 1954 CIA operation at Cuba's Bay of Pigs in 1961, raised the specter of other Castros appearing in Latin America. No nations were more ripe for such revolutions than Nicaragua, El Salvador, Honduras, and Guatemala. In 1961 President John F. Kennedy launched the Alliance for Progress to develop an economically just and democratic Latin America that would not need Castro's type of change.

The alliance became a key cause of the revolutions in the 1970s and 1980s. It did so because the economic aid that the United States poured into Central America during the 1960s went to the oligarchs who controlled the distribution points in the economies. As the wealthy profited, the poor multiplied. Even before his death in 1963, Kennedy understood that the alliance was not working as he had hoped; it was even polarizing some of the Latin American societies. To maintain stability and give the alliance time to work, Kennedy and his successor, Lyndon Johnson, launched a series of military policies.[10]

Increased numbers of Central American troops were trained at U.S. bases in the Panamá Canal Zone and in the United States itself. Military aid to these forces roughly doubled during the decade, and much of this North American assistance was directed toward creating counterinsurgency forces that soon preyed on their own innocent people. A policy that aimed to create stability for development too often ended with Guatemalan, Salvadoran, or Nicaraguan officers torturing political suspects for the officers' edification and the perpetuation of their corruption. In 1963–64 the United States even attempted to create a Central American military force (CONDECA) that could act as a unit to provide region-wide stability. CONDECA collapsed under the national antipathies that divided Honduran from Salvadoran (the two peoples actually went to war briefly in 1969), Guatemalan from Nicaraguan, and Costa Rican from everyone else.[11]

---

[10]This argument on the alliance is presented at length in Walter LaFeber, "Inevitable Revolutions," *Atlantic Monthly* 249 (June 1982): 74–83.

[11]Don L. Etchison, *The United States and Militarism in Central America* (New York, 1975), esp. pp. 64–67.

These new policies nevertheless reintroduced a powerful, direct U.S. military presence for the first time since the
early 1930s. In historical perspective, the Good Neighbor era
from 1930 to the 1950s appears as an aberration. As Washington policymakers used troops to maintain stability in much of
Central America before 1933, so they now used force to quiet
the growing unrest ironically developing out of the Alliance
for Progress. By the 1970s President Richard Nixon's Latin
American policy depended almost entirely on military aid given
to regimes controlled by the armed forces. Such an approach
worked only sporadically. By the late 1970s three revolutionary
movements—Guatemalan, Nicaraguan, and Salvadoran—grew
stronger. At the start of the Alliance for Progress twenty years
before, only one small revolutionary group in Guatemala had
threatened Central American oligarchs.

President Carter attempted to deal with this new insurgency through a human rights program that he hoped would
force the oligarchs to make their systems more humane and
open before those systems were overthrown by revolutions.
Carter's policy, however, contained a fatal contradiction. The
oligarch-military complex ultimately had to rule through terror
and oppression; it had no other legitimacy. To force this complex to cease such oppression undermined its own authority.
Carter's human rights program consequently undermined the
status quo, but the president proved not to be prepared to
accept the results, which in all of Central America except Costa
Rica meant leftist forces would take advantage of the oligarch-
military weakness to propel themselves into power. No center
existed, no viable Christian Democratic type of party that could
present an alternative to the leftist factions. The centrists either
had bases too weak to threaten the two extremes, or, as in El
Salvador and Nicaragua, the centrists had been killed, exiled,
or otherwise discouraged from political participation.[12]

Carter's ultimate test came in Nicaragua during 1979. As
the Somoza dictatorship escalated its oppression, including
the bombing of slums where Somoza's National Guard mis-
takenly believed the Sandinistas hid, Carter forced the dictator

---

[12]This argument is derived from the work of Sandy Vogelgesang, *American
Dream, Global Nightmare* (New York, 1980), esp. the sections on El Salvador; and
Lars Schoultz, *Human Rights and U.S. Policy Toward Latin America* (Princeton, 1981).

to act more humanely. Somoza's change of tactics, however, opened new opportunities for the revolutionaries who rapidly gained power in early 1979. Carter then resumed sending some aid to Nicaragua and even tried to work out a hemisphere-wide approach that would block the Sandinistas from obtaining power; the president apparently hoped to put elements of the National Guard in control until at least the 1981 elections. Carter found no support for such intervention. In July 1979 the Sandinistas gained control of Nicaragua.[13]

This brief historical survey is a necessary framework for understanding the Reagan administration's policy since 1981. Its emphasis on military force—the preeminence of Pentagon civilians and National Security Council hard liners willing to use force unilaterally in place of negotiations or a multilateral approach to resolving the Central American outbreaks—puts history on its side. With the exception of the Good Neighbor era, Washington officials have consistently used military force to try to maintain stability and protect their nation's interests in the region, regardless of the changing nature of those interests. In this sense, the Reagan policy is traditional. The history and the tradition it embodies, however, have not been among the happier pages in U.S. diplomacy. Since 1900 Central American nations have become ever more unstable internally, not happier and more stable. Since 1954 (and in Nicaragua since the appearance of Sandino in 1927) revolutionaries in the region have moved to the left, not toward the democratic middle. For at least eight decades the United States has been the most powerful force by far in the Central American area; in some cases, for example, Nicaragua, Honduras, and Costa Rica, the relationship developed into almost total dependency of the smaller nation on the giant neighbor to the north.

It cannot be argued that the United States has paid too little attention to Central America in the twentieth century. The opposite is the case. Nor can it be argued that the United States has been reluctant to use military force, both overtly and covertly, in the region. The opposite is the case. Nor can it be argued that the constant application of force and the

---

[13]Richard R. Fagen, "Dateline Nicaragua: The End of the Affair," *Foreign Policy*, no. 36 (Fall 1979): 178–91; Arnold Levinson, "Nicaraguan Showdown," *Inquiry* 22 (June 11 and 25, 1979): 13.

integration of the North and Central American economies have benefited either side or bought time so that the Central American oligarchs could make their societies more equitable. The opposite has been the case.

This history needs to be studied in order that the historical cycle can be broken. An alternative is the Contadora proposals formulated in September 1983 and then agreed to by the five Central American nations in January 1984. These proposals declare that the signatories will deescalate military fighting, reduce their armed forces, reject foreign military advisers or forces, refrain from intervention in the affairs of other nations, promise to carry out open and fair elections, and commit themselves to equitable economic development plans. The Contadora principles comprise a wish list, and so-called "realists" in Washington and elsewhere dismiss the principles as empty, if not dangerously seductive, promises. But no one can say they will not work until they are tried. To try them requires that the most powerful nation, the United States, agree to the principles, especially the points on military deescalation and the removal of foreign military forces.

No one can guarantee that the Contadora approach will work. Its multilateral emphasis makes it especially unwieldy and, no doubt, frustrating for Washington officials who pride themselves on quick decisions and pragmatism. Their approach already has produced the opposite of what they intended: the increase in the number and the radicalization of revolutionary movements. Their emphasis on North American unilateral action has alienated allies and caused regional Latin American powers to break with U.S. policy. If the integration of the economies, the application of military force, and unilateral decision making have been the three characteristics of U.S. policy toward Central America during the past eighty years, then the results of that history should convince the supposed pragmatists and realists that at least a two-track approach, with the larger and stronger track running through the Contadora process, should become the history of the future. In this case war is not a substitute for state policy.

Indigenous Sources
of Conflict

Michael A. Webb

Economic Opportunity and Labor Markets in Central America

U NEMPLOYMENT AND UNDEREMPLOYMENT have been chronic problems in Central America. Deeply rooted in the region's history, they have persisted even with the tremendous growth of the economies of the individual nations since World War II, exceeding 30 percent in Guatemala, El Salvador, and Honduras in 1970 (see Table 1). Unemployment and underemployment have been major causes of the deep social and political frustration that has stimulated revolutionary movements. To understand the origins of the present unrest in Central America and the difficulty of devising workable solutions, it is essential to analyze the historical sources of these employment patterns.[1]

One useful concept for understanding the economic history of Central America is the dual labor market. A traditional dual labor market consists of a seemingly infinite supply of laborers whose only alternative to employment in the export sector is in near subsistence agriculture. As a result, wages in the export sector are determined solely by supply conditions, an upper limit being created by the unattractive alternatives. The numerous laborers in the Central American economies did not share in the prosperity resulting from increasing exports. Rather, their real wages stayed at the near subsistence level, while the incomes of those owning the land used for export crops rose substantially.

This review of the evolution of the Central American economies explores the causes of dual labor markets and inequitable income distribution. The characteristics of the economies today can be traced to the terrain and climate of the

---

[1]For a detailed account see Murdo MacLeod, *Spanish Central America: A Socioeconomic History, 1520–1720* (Berkeley, 1973), pp. 52–55.

Table 1. Unemployment in Central America, 1970

	(1) Percentage of Central American Agricultural Work Force	(2) Percentage of Estimated Agricultural Unemployment[a]	(3) Percentage of Population in Rural Areas	(4) Estimated Minimum Percentage of National Unemployment[b]
Guatemala	38.5%	52.3%	68.9%	36.0%
El Salvador	21.4	58.3	62.1	36.2
Honduras	17.7	42.5	72.3	30.7
Nicaragua	13.3	21.5	60.0	12.9
Costa Rica	9.1	14.7	60.0	9.7
Central America	100.0	44.4[c]	66.0[c]	29.6[c]

[a]A full-time job was considered as the equivalent of 280 days employment per year. Those working less than 280 days are treated as employed for a portion of the year.

[b]This entry represents the estimated agricultural unemployment (column 2) multiplied by the percentage of the national population found in rural areas (column 3). The cross-product represents the minimum possible level of unemployment in the country, given the existing level of agricultural unemployment.

[c]A weighted average for the Central American region which takes into account the population of each country.

SOURCE: Max Alberto Soto, "The Labor Markets in Central America," in Juan Buttari, ed., Employment and Labor Force in Latin America: A Review at National and Regional Levels (Washington, DC, 1979), Tables 2.4, 2.12, pp. 32, 50, respectively.

region and to the economic system imposed by the early Hispanic settlers in the sixteenth and seventeenth centuries. For a variety of reasons, conditions have worsened in most of the countries since the early nineteenth century, leading to the present labor unrest.

The economic history of Central America can be divided into three stages. The first lasted from the Hispanic colonization until the coffee boom of the mid-1850s. During this time dual labor markets were established in El Salvador and Guatemala, the two westernmost countries of the region; the seeds for a much less severe form of duality also were planted in Nicaragua and Honduras; and a relatively egalitarian economy emerged in Costa Rica as a result of market and non-market forces. The second period lasted roughly from the 1850s through the 1930s and was marked by increasing specialization in the production of coffee and bananas. An intensification of the dual labor markets occurred in El Salvador and Guatemala, while the economy of Nicaragua began to take on some of the same characteristics. During the third phase, labor market pressures increased in all five countries, becoming especially severe in those with labor market duality, and conditions in Honduras grew closer to those in the two western countries.

Before Bananas and Coffee:
A Pattern Develops

The Hispanics settling Central America in the sixteenth and seventeenth centuries encountered a scarcity of good land and an abundance of indigenous labor. The western areas, now Guatemala and El Salvador, offered a larger supply of fertile land and consequently the largest concentration of indigenous peoples, most of them engaged in farming. The quality and quantity of cultivable land deteriorated to the southeast. The Indian population was consequently less sedentary and declined steadily in this region. Bloody revolts and maltreatment of the indigenous population in the earliest years took their toll. Large numbers of Indians were exported as slave labor, especially to Peru and to the larger Caribbean islands which had lost almost their entire indigenous populations. This slave trade continued until about 1550, almost depleting the indigenous populations of Nicaragua and Honduras. Estimates at the time of Spanish arrival show 600,000 for Nicaragua and 500,000 for Honduras, while a Spanish census in the late 1540s found only about 11,000 in Nicaragua and 36,000 in Honduras.[2] In addition, severe epidemics and pandemics occurred in the late sixteenth and throughout the seventeenth century, one pandemic eliminating virtually the entire Indian population of the Costa Rican highlands.[3] Costa Rica was populated by relatively small numbers of nonsedentary Indians, estimated to be approximately 80,000 upon arrival of Spaniards in 1563. The Indians were almost decimated upon

---

[2]Robert S. Chamberlain, *The Conquest and Colonization of Honduras, 1502–1550* (New York, 1967); Richard Millett, "Historical Setting," in James D. Rudolph, ed., *Nicaragua: A Country Study* (Washington, DC, 1982), p. 33.

[3]For an in-depth account see MacLeod, *Spanish Central America*, pp. 43–55, 98–100, 205–06.

early contact with the Spanish, their numbers falling to 3,200 by 1645.[4]

Although the primary activity in the region was subsistence agriculture, the Hispanic settlers were involved in the production and merchandising of exports such as wood, cocoa, indigo, and livestock. Because of the availability of exploitable land, the Hispanic migration gravitated to the west. Further southeast the land was less suitable for these early exports and hence attracted fewer Hispanics. A crucial result of these differences, which was to have a continuing influence on the Central American economies over the next centuries, was the granting of large holdings of land in the western regions to immigrants of aristocratic origin. Middle-class farmers, not unlike the English settlers of North America, later settled the less profitable southeastern lands, especially in Costa Rica but also in Honduras and Nicaragua.

By the 1770s, then, a dichotomy had developed between El Salvador and Guatemala in the west and Costa Rica in the southeast, with Honduras and Nicaragua somewhere in between. Western migrants engaged in commerce or held large tracts of land sufficiently profitable to warrant the use of slave labor. Less profitable land, such as in the eastern region of Central America, would not yield a surplus sufficient to justify slaves. Export crops were grown almost exclusively in the western regions and western Nicaragua, while migrants to Costa Rica and Honduras produced primarily for subsistence or for sale to the western markets.

By the 1700s the extremely large Indian and emerging Ladino populations provided an excess of labor in the west. The land tenure system established by Spanish settlers exacerbated this problem. For example, an estimated one-third of the land in El Salvador was appropriated by Spain for private use.[5] While much of the Indian population in the west had been sold into Peruvian slavery or killed, many Indians were retained as slave labor under a draft system for export activities. The scarcity of land for export activities limited the supply of major Central American exports. Thus, the substantial international demand for such exports as indigo and cocoa resulted

---

[4]Mitchell A. Seligson, *Peasants of Costa Rica and the Development of Agrarian Capitalism* (Madison, WI, 1980), pp. 4–5.

[5]David Browning, *El Salvador: Landscape and Society* (Oxford, England, 1971), p. 84.

in high prices, making the preferred lands extremely valuable.[6] The lack of profitable exports from the southeastern regions, including Costa Rica, precluded the import of slaves. Virtually the entire population of Costa Rica remained ethnically European and middle class.[7] The burgeoning Ladino population, composed of former landowners who had experienced misfortune, some of the less wealthy Hispanic settlers, and Indians who entered the Hispanic culture, aggressively pushed the Indians back onto poorer and poorer lands as they themselves were pushed back by the large Hispanic estates. Ladino migrants from the western areas provided a rural labor force in western Nicaragua and Honduras and supplied labor for the Honduran mines.[8] By the early 1800s, Ladinos were a prominent group in terms of numbers in all but Guatemala, which still had a large Indian population, and Costa Rica. For Central America as a whole, the population is estimated to have been 65 percent Indian, 31 percent Ladino, and 4 percent white by 1820. Approximately 84 percent of the Nicaraguan population was Ladino, and the population of El Salvador consisted of 54 percent Ladino, 43 percent Indian, and 3 percent white.[9]

By the late 1700s the far-flung Spanish Empire was under severe strain and rebellion broke out in many colonies. The success of the revolution in Mexico brought independence for the Central American states in 1821.[10] Even with the elimination of Spanish rule in Central America, struggles among the provinces continued. An abortive union fell apart in 1838, leaving a group of independent republics.

The emergence of independent nations in Central America effected important economic changes. The influence of the western merchant class declined considerably in the absence of Hispanic rule. The monopsony-monopoly power of the Central American importers and exporters depended solely on appointment by, and protection from, the crown, and the end of Spanish control resulted in a significant redistribution of profits which otherwise would have gone to the owners of prime agricultural land. Struggles over economic

---

[6]MacLeod, *Spanish Central America*, p. 49.
[7]Seligson, *Peasants of Costa Rica*, p. 8.
[8]Ralph Lee Woodward, Jr., *Central America: A Nation Divided* (New York, 1976), p. 77.
[9]Ibid., p. 79.
[10]Ibid., pp. 80–91.

policy persisted between liberals, largely landowners favoring free trade, and conservatives, mostly urban merchants. The wealthy landowning class was now distinct from the others, but its composition was not entirely static; many of its members perished from economic misfortune or the political struggles. Economic policy, especially in El Salvador and Guatemala, was determined primarily by the banana booms of the late nineteenth century, as will be discussed in the next section.[11]

Demand for commodities and different endowments of natural resources thus determined the labor supply and land tenure conditions which would shape the labor markets of the Central American republics for centuries to come. The profitability of export agriculture in the west resulted in a large pool of unskilled labor and an extremely skewed distribution of virtually the only available form of wealth—land that could be cultivated profitably. The wealthy few utilized their resources to secure the political and financial power necessary to maintain and improve their positions. Their political power produced vagrancy laws and laws concerning land titleship which helped to maintain the character of the labor markets. Their wealth also allowed them to profit from new opportunities resulting from the high demand for indigo, cochineal, cotton, coffee, and bananas.

Unable to compete for loans with the large landowners, the landless could not take advantage of such opportunities. The initial inequality was most pronounced in the two western republics where conditions today remain the most extreme. The relatively weak political power of colonial and nineteenth-century elites in Nicaragua, where inequality of wealth was initially less pronounced, provides a middle ground, while at the other end the distribution of wealth was initially more equal in Honduras and Costa Rica. Widespread access to land was a necessary condition for attaining human welfare in colonial Central America. Where land was available to many people, other factors such as personal skills—or human capital, in the language of economists—also came into play in determining variations in the level of well-being attained by individuals. This was the case in Costa Rica and Honduras

---

[11]For an in-depth analysis of the liberal-conservative struggles, and eventual move toward liberal policies by conservative regimes and general ascendancy of liberal rule, see Woodward, *Central America*.

where the economic opportunities available to individuals were greatest. However, in Guatemala and El Salvador, the poor were poor primarily because they had been excluded from access to the land.

Impact of Banana and Coffee Production on Labor Markets

The labor markets that were altered by the growth of the banana and coffee industries were already characterized by an abundance of poor and economically vulnerable farmers. However, labor market conditions varied substantially between countries, and existing differences were exaggerated by public policy choices. Those choices were often made in response to the opportunities that public officials perceived for their countries to benefit from international agricultural trade between 1850 and 1930. The consequences of some policy choices, made in response to the desire for international trade, were to reinforce existing trends toward labor market dualism. The consequences of public policy were particularly negative in the cases of El Salvador and Guatemala, much less so in Costa Rica and Honduras, and intermediate in Nicaragua.

Labor markets were influenced initially by institutions such as slavery, labor drafts, and debt peonage. Although slavery was officially abolished throughout Central America upon independence, it had been prominent solely in the western regions, while in other areas it had been gradually replaced by a seasonal draft system. Upon independence, this was legally replaced by debt peonage in most countries, although the draft system persisted in some parts of the two western states.[12] Like the draft system, debt peonage kept indigenous labor in Guatemala and El Salvador effectively enslaved for part of the year. This system declined and largely disappeared in El Salvador in 1881, but it survived legally until 1931 in Guatemala, after which it was replaced by vagrancy laws in each country.[13]

---

[12]See, for example, Thomas P. Anderson, *Politics in Central America* (New York, 1982), p. 51.

[13]The draft and debt peonage systems were based on relations between estates and villages. As the indigenous people of El Salvador lost their land and the village life weakened, a more efficient manner of acquiring labor, by enforcement of vagrancy laws, was used.

Coffee production began in Central America in the early 1800s but was insignificant until Costa Rica promoted plantings in the 1830s. The coffee boom of the 1850s and 1860s yielded a new class of enriched landowners, benefiting some Ladinos, Costa Rican farmers, local merchants, and immigrants, but especially the large landowners who had ready access to financial markets.[14] Primarily through land concentration and loss of untitled holdings, it also led to increasing impoverishment of a substantial class of rural people.

The coffee boom had varying effects on the Central American economies. In Guatemala and El Salvador land suitable for coffee production was confiscated from farmers without titles by landowners and merchants, most of them Hispanic. As a result of language, cultural, and legal barriers, Indians were excluded from title to any land, much less that on which coffee might be produced. Communal land owned by the indigenous peoples of El Salvador, which accounted for most of the best coffee-producing land, was systematically taken from them by a series of government decrees.[15] The first, enacted in 1856, required that two-thirds of the communal land be planted in coffee or relinquished to the state. Although some of this ground was subsequently planted in coffee, in 1881 the government went further, requiring that all communal lands be divided among owners. These lands were abolished the next year, however, and massive evictions of Indians followed.[16] In Guatemala, Indians were excluded from a government program, under which free coffee trees were given to all who would plant them.[17]

While policies undertaken by Guatemalan conservatives in the early to mid-1800s ensured that the large Indian population in the cold and dry western highlands would be somewhat isolated as a distinct group, the already small Indian population of El Salvador dwindled rapidly as Ladinos and big landholders took more and more land. This confiscation led

[14]See, for example, Tommie Sue Montgomery, *Revolution in El Salvador: Origins and Evolution* (Boulder, CO, 1982), p. 40.

[15]Ibid., p. 40.

[16]Ibid., p. 42.

[17]John Dombrowski et al., *Area Handbook for Guatemala* (Washington, DC, 1970), p. 28.

most of the indigenous peoples to work for the large land-owners, resulting in their incorporation into the Ladino population.[18] The Indian and Ladino labor supply also was artificially increased by the introduction of the vagrancy system in El Salvador in 1881 and the reaffirmation of the debt peonage system in Guatemala in 1894.[19] Rather than tightening labor markets in the two western republics, the boom in coffee, and resulting alterations in land tenure and labor laws, produced a seemingly infinite supply of unskilled labor at wages not far above subsistence.

Scarcity of labor and the labor-intensive nature of coffee production resulted in less coffee yield in Nicaragua, but it still became a significant export in the 1870s, leading to a shortage of labor for the planters.[20] Hence, in certain parts of the country, a series of post-1875 reforms were enacted including vagrancy laws, debt peonage, and the prohibition of subsistence agriculture. Increased concentration of the already moderately concentrated western agricultural lands followed. Coffee production in Nicaragua tended to complement, rather than replace, traditional agriculture. Along with the great availability of land in Nicaragua, this allowed many Ladino farmers to share in the new prosperity.[21] Thus, while concentration took place in Nicaragua, it was less extensive than in the two western republics.

Coffee production did not become a major activity in Honduras because the land was not well suited for it.[22] Export production remained insignificant in the 1860s, except for the bananas grown along the coasts. Cultivation of bananas, however, increased the amount of land that could be made productive and provided an additional demand for labor. Land

---

[18]Woodward, *Central America*, pp. 76–77.

[19]The coffee boom directly created a scarcity of labor as more and more lands were being cultivated. As an alternative to raising wages to attract labor to the coffee estates, laws were passed to increase the supply of available labor. As village life continued in the Guatemalan highlands, the debt peonage system was an effective way to ensure an adequate labor supply. However, this system had declined prior to the coffee boom, and until the new law was passed there was some question about its legality.

[20]John A. Booth, *The End and the Beginning: The Nicaraguan Revolution* (Boulder, CO, 1980), pp. 20–22.

[21]Ibid.

[22]J. Mark Ruhl, "Agrarian Structure and Political Stability in Honduras," *Journal of Interamerican Studies and World Affairs* 26 (February 1984): 36.

for subsistence and local market agriculture was readily available throughout the nineteenth century, ensuring a higher wage for those Ladinos who chose to work for the larger farms or banana plantations.[23] Without an available supply of unskilled Ladino or indigenous labor, Costa Rica was characterized by smaller coffee farms and less labor-intensive production than in the other three coffee-producing nations.[24]

These differences led to varying economic situations in the Central American countries. An early impetus for tariffs and other measures to promote industrialization had waned; therefore, free trade policies were largely pursued until the 1940s. Certainly the small size of the region's population, along with its poverty, precluded the existence of a domestic market for industrial products. Central America's own modest endowment of resources, lack of proximity to resources held by others, limited potential markets for industrial goods, and minimal transportation all meant that early measures designed to promote industrialization would fail.

Against a common background of limited industrialization, labor policies became crucial governmental choices that determined the nature of economic growth. In Guatemala and El Salvador, labor policies favorable to large landowners were adopted. While similar, although less extreme, policies were adopted in Nicaragua, these were not implemented in either Honduras or Costa Rica. Indeed, expropriation of private lands for communal use was legally sanctioned in Honduras in the 1880s for localities whose growth had led to landlessness. Such a policy was in direct contrast to those in Guatemala and El Salvador.

The differences between the two western republics and the three southeastern ones were significantly widened by agricultural changes in all of them. The southeastern republics experienced a banana boom in the late nineteenth century, while cotton became a major crop in Guatemala and El Salvador and, to a lesser extent, in Nicaragua. The introduction of cotton in Guatemala, and in the littoral plains along the Pacific coasts of El Salvador and Nicaragua, tended to displace the production of traditional crops for a brief time,[25] especially

[23]Ibid., p. 37.
[24]Seligson, *Peasants of Costa Rica*, p. 19.
[25]Alastair White, *El Salvador* (New York, 1973), p. 128.

exacerbating labor market conditions brought about by the rapid coffee growth in the two western countries. The banana boom significantly increased the abundance of profitably cultivable land in Nicaragua, as well as in Honduras and Costa Rica, since bananas thrived in the formerly unused hot and humid lowlands of these three countries. At the same time, it provided a significant boost in demand for labor, requiring labor-intensive care all year round.[26]

A peculiar form of labor market duality thus evolved in Guatemala and El Salvador and, to a lesser extent, in western Nicaragua as a result of the availability of a large supply of workers and unequal distribution of land. These workers severely reduced the economic worth of unskilled labor and rendered land virtually the only asset in which to hold wealth. The overabundance of workers, combined with the initial unequal distribution of wealth in the form of profitably cultivable land, left workers few alternatives. Unskilled and with virtually no wealth, they were denied access to the financial markets for loans and earned little more than subsistence, which limited their ability to save. They were denied opportunities to purchase land, engage in entrepreneurial activities, or increase their skills through formal education or training. Government intervention, reflecting the disproportionate political power of those groups in possession of wealth, reinforced this labor market duality. Central American duality, unlike that in other places, appears to have been deliberately created and maintained by those in power.

A second peculiarity of labor market duality stemmed from the seasonal nature of labor movements between the two sectors. In Guatemala, El Salvador, and western Nicaragua, laborers worked part of the year on very small, mainly untitled farms, or as tenants or sharecroppers on land leased from the large estates. They also worked seasonally for the large coffee and cotton farms.

Labor market duality did not develop in Honduras and Costa Rica. In Honduras the supply of unskilled labor was limited by a relatively small population and the availability of land from which incomes significantly above subsistence could be earned. Demand for labor was generated by the banana

---

[26]Woodward, *Central America*, p. 181.

plantations. The supply of and demand for unskilled labor in Costa Rica were both reduced by widespread land tenure.

Increasing specialization in banana and coffee production continued through the 1920s, at which point over 70 percent of the region's export earnings, and over 90 percent of those for Costa Rica, El Salvador, and Guatemala, resulted from the sale of these commodities. Increasingly, untitled Guatemalan and Salvadoran farmers were driven from their lands, becoming sharecroppers or relocating in less productive lands or in the emerging urban centers.[27] A decline in coffee prices in the late 1920s led to widespread defaults on loans and debts; for example, an estimated 28 percent of coffee holdings in El Salvador changed hands, with these losses hitting the small growers hardest.[28] Increasing exports led to the rising importance of communication and transportation services and of government bureaucracies and merchandizing services. Growth in these latter two areas, in turn, produced urban centers inhabited by small middle classes and a growing number of urban laborers.[29] Unions began developing in the 1920s and through the mid-1930s as urban centers and labor supply continued to expand. With the depression of the 1930s, land titles continued to be traded, and production for agricultural export fell in response to a 60 percent decline in export prices for Central American products. While less was produced and demand for labor in the agricultural sector dropped, the amount of land under title did not change. Large owners simply took land out of production. All these factors produced declining incomes for seasonal laborers and a consequent flow of migrants to the small but crowded urban labor markets.[30]

The depression of the 1930s resulted in rising labor unrest and led to the ascendancy of such military figures as General Jorge Ubico in Guatemala and General Maximiliano Hernández Martínez in El Salvador. Although military coups and governments had played prominent roles in all countries except

---

[27]Montgomery, *Revolution in El Salvador*, pp. 46–47.

[28]William H. Durham, *Scarcity and Survival in Central America* (Stanford, 1979), p. 56.

[29]Woodward, *Central America*, pp. 165–66.

[30]V. Bulmer-Thomas, "Central American Economic Development Over the Long Run—Central America Since 1920," *Journal of Latin American Studies* 15 (November 1983): 274.

Costa Rica since independence, they essentially served the interests of the dominant landowners in the western republics.[31] Labor unrest increased the value of repressive force and thus the power of the military, especially in the western republics. The weakness of the landed oligarchy in Nicaragua permitted the military to gain even more power and finally in the 1930s gave rise to the Somoza regime, under which the large growers had little voice. The lack of any significant oligarchy in Honduras, on the other hand, permitted rule by relatively powerful military leaders who took care not to alienate the large class of small farmers.

Increasing Labor Pressures and Responses: Central America Since World War II

Central American economies have become increasingly diversified since World War II and generally have experienced impressive income growth, with real per capita income doubling between 1950 and 1976. Export earnings grew to eighteen times their 1950 level by 1980, yet the basic structures of labor markets were not significantly altered except in Honduras. There the land tenure system and labor markets more and more began to resemble those of El Salvador, although never quite reaching the same extremes.

The prices of Central America's major exports improved immediately after World War II, but the trend was reversed by the mid-1950s.[32] This decline in the relative prices of coffee, and especially bananas, resulted from rapidly rising incomes throughout the world, and, in the case of coffee, from increased Asian and African competition. The relatively income-inelastic

---

[31]The role of the military in the nineteenth century is reviewed in Woodward, *Central America,* pp. 169–72. The importance of the military in the twentieth century followed the economic trouble of the period and the ensuing labor unrest and development of local Communist parties (ibid., pp. 215–17). The decline in coffee prices after the crash of 1929 worsened living conditions for small farmers and farm workers and led to the election of Arturo Araujo in El Salvador. His announcement that the Communist Party would be allowed to participate in elections in late 1931 resulted in his dismissal by the military, whereupon military rule was established. A brief insurrection followed in 1930 but was crushed. The free election of General Jorge Ubico in 1931 was swiftly followed by his emergence as dictator and by the launching of war against the Communists there in 1932.

[32]Bulmer-Thomas, "Economic Development," p. 274.

demand for these commodities combined with rising incomes in the consuming nations to yield a decline in demands relative to other commodities and hence lower relative prices.[33] On the other hand, with infrastructure improvements and an increasing supply of labor, especially in Honduras, the production of coffee in Central America continued to expand. Diversification of agriculture occurred naturally, with the production of alternative commodities becoming relatively more profitable. Timber, cacao, and abaca production rose in Costa Rica, as did sesame production in Nicaragua. Coffee growing finally began in Honduras as lands became accessible.

During the latter 1940s and 1950s greater production of cotton and sugar took place throughout the region. Cotton production began on a commercial scale in the 1920s, but acreage remained modest until the late 1930s. The tremendous growth of cotton production in the late 1930s and 1940s resulted largely from its high price during World War II. The elimination of malaria along the plains and the improvement in insect control provided an impetus to cotton production during the postwar period. Expansion was further boosted by the building of roads in cotton-producing areas, especially the littoral road in El Salvador.[34] From 1952 to 1967 land planted in cotton in Nicaragua more than quadrupled,[35] while that in El Salvador rose almost sevenfold.[36] Cotton-producing areas in Guatemala increased almost tenfold between 1952 and 1962,[37] and by more than that in Honduras,[38] although Honduras and Costa Rica never became significant exporters. By this time cotton was Guatemala's second major export, accounting for 20 percent

---

[33]The income elasticity of demand for a commodity is defined as the percentage change in quantity demanded resulting from a 1 percent increase in income of consumers holding prices constant. A commodity with an income-inelastic demand, that is, with an elasticity less than 1, will account for a declining share of a growing community's budget in the presence of unchanged prices.

[34]For a detailed account of the development of cotton production and its ramifications for local economies, see White, El Salvador, pp. 127–30; and Browning, El Salvador: Landscape and Society, pp. 226–48.

[35]Peter Dorner and Rodolfo Quirós, "Institutional Dualism in Central America's Agricultural Development," in Stanford Central American Action Network, eds., Revolution in Central America (Boulder, CO, 1983), p. 229.

[36]Browning, El Salvador: Landscape and Society, pp. 231–35.

[37]Shelton H. Davis, "State Violence and Agrarian Crisis in Guatemala: The Roots of the Indian-Peasant Rebellion," in Martin Diskin, ed., Trouble in Our Backyard: Central America and the United States in the Eighties (New York, 1983), p. 160.

[38]Ruhl, "Honduras," p. 40.

of its export earnings, while Nicaragua became the major cotton exporter of the region, supplying 46 percent of Central America's exports in the late 1960s.[39] The expansion of cotton production in Guatemala, El Salvador, and Nicaragua, despite low population densities in the Pacific coastal regions where it was grown, displaced many settlers producing staple crops. Such expansion exacerbated labor market conditions, as did the expansion of cattle production. The resulting contraction of economic opportunity was especially severe in El Salvador.

Cane sugar production rose substantially in all five countries (see Table 2), following the elimination of the U.S. sugar quota for Cuba. Honduras reached self-sufficiency in sugar cane in 1962 and almost tripled exports between 1967 and 1976.[40] Exports of sugar from the other four countries also increased.

In addition, a beef production boom (see Table 3) took place in the 1960s and the 1970s,[41] although production in the

Table 2. Percentage Increases in Areas Planted in Sugar Cane, 1950–1980

Costa Rica	El Salvador	Guatemala	Honduras	Nicaragua
130%	154%	392%	279%	131%

SOURCE: V. Bulmer-Thomas, "Central American Economic Development Over the Long Run—Central America Since 1920," *Journal of Latin American Studies* 15 (November 1983): 288.

Table 3. Central American Exports of Meat (Millions of U.S. Dollars)

	Guatemala	El Salvador	Honduras	Nicaragua	Costa Rica
1972	18	5.1	16	38.7	28.3
1979	38.3	14	61.2	95.1	81.6

SOURCE: Edelberto Torres-Rivas, "Central America Today," in Martin Diskin, ed., *Trouble in Our Backyard: Central America and the United States in the Eighties* (New York, 1983), p. 31.

---

[39]Millett, "Historical Setting," p. 33.

[40]White, *El Salvador*, pp. 130–32; Ruhl, "Honduras," p. 40.

[41]For an extensive analysis of the negative effects of the rise in beef production in Central America, see Billie R. DeWalt, "The Agrarian Bases of Conflict in Central America," in this volume.

region already had been on the rise earlier. For example, on large farms in Honduras it rose 66 percent between 1952 and 1965 and more than doubled in Costa Rica between 1963 and 1970.[42] The introduction of Brahman cattle in the late 1950s and 1960s, the elimination of coastal diseases, and rising foreign demand made the cattle business attractive. Rising incomes in the United States and Europe, due to the income-elastic demand for beef products, led to higher prices. The sudden jump in beef production followed the decline of cotton in the latter 1960s. With the fall of cotton prices, leading producers were forced to seek alternative uses of land. Much of the cotton-producing land went to pasturage to support cattle, although beef production also displaced that of agricultural commodities for subsistence in some areas. This effect was mitigated by the fact that beef production was slightly more labor-intensive than cotton growing, and some land formerly used for cotton was reverted to food production.[43]

One familiar effect of this diversification in the two western republics was the taking of lands from untitled farmers. The tremendous rise in cotton and sugar production along the littoral plains of El Salvador displaced thousands of tenant and untitled farmers and added to the pool of unemployed and underemployed labor.[44] Production of neither commodity absorbed all the labor displaced, and this was exacerbated by the beef boom. Landlessness in rural El Salvador rose from 11.8 percent in 1961 to 29.1 percent in 1971 and to 40.9 percent by 1975, by which time many Salvadoran emigrants had been returned by the government of Honduras.[45] Real income of farm units measuring less than one hectare actually declined between 1961 and 1975.[46] As a result of these natural changes and the introduction of a minimum wage law in 1965, which discouraged tenancy and farm employment, already crowded labor markets in El Salvador were characterized by 20 percent

[42]Ruhl, "Honduras," p. 40; Seligson, *Peasants of Costa Rica*, p. 164.

[43]Durham, *Scarcity and Survival*, p. 33.

[44]For a precautionary analysis of unemployment and underemployment concepts used here and elsewhere, as well as their trends, see Peter Gregory, "Employment, Unemployment and Underemployment in Latin America," *Statistical Bulletin of the OAS* 2, no. 4 (1980): 1–20.

[45]Melvin Burke, "El sistema de plantación y el proletarización del trabajo agrícola en El Salvador," *Estudios Centroamericanos* 31, nos. 335–36 (September–October 1976): 473–86.

[46]C. Samaniego, "Movimiento campesino o lucha del proletariado rural in El Salvador?" *Estudios Sociales Centroamericanos* 9 (1980): 125–44.

unemployment and 40 percent underemployment rates in the early 1970s.[47]

The leftist governments of Juan José Arévalo and Jacobo Arbenz did not alter the structure of the labor market in Guatemala; a peonage system was merely replaced with a similar vagrancy system. In any case, the Arbenz regime was overthrown in 1954, and the status quo was not significantly upset. Cotton production subsequently mushroomed in Guatemala, accounting for 4 percent of the country's exports in 1956 and 20 percent by the mid-1960s, although its share later fell.[48] The rise in cotton production did not displace food production by smaller farmers to the same extent as in El Salvador,[49] since the Indians already were located in the cool, dry western highlands and poorer Ladino farmers in the lower eastern hills. Yet land centralization and rural underemployment did exist. It has been estimated that in Guatemala in 1966 there were 70,000 permanent residents and laborers on large farms and about 400,000 seasonal workers, Ladinos, and Indians migrating to the lower lands of cotton, coffee, and sugar production.[50] In 1970 approximately 2 percent of the farms in Guatemala held 72 percent of the farmland.[51] Landlessness in rural Guatemala stood somewhere around 60 percent in the late 1970s.[52]

Significant changes in the agricultural sector, and subsequently in the labor market, did take place in Honduras. Less than one-half its farmland was in private hands in 1950, and landlessness had become a major problem by 1965 as a result of two forces.[53] First, the growing worldwide demand for cotton and beef led to an increase in income to be earned from land to which title was not formerly held. A land enclosure movement in the 1950s and 1960s by the larger beef and cotton producers caused the ejection of untitled farmers from public lands, especially as cotton production expanded in the

---

[47]Pedro Vuskovic, "Economic Factors in the Evolution of Central American Societies," in Richard R. Fagen and Olga Pellicer, eds., The Future of Central America: Policy Choices for the U.S. and Mexico (Stanford, 1983), p. 37.

[48]Dombrowski, Guatemala, p. 254.

[49]Ibid., p. 278.

[50]Ibid.

[51]Ibid., p. 28.

[52]Anderson, Politics in Central America, p. 51.

[53]Ruhl, "Honduras," pp. 35–49.

most densely settled agricultural region of Honduras.[54] Since considerable capital was required to produce cotton, this resulted in expansion being undertaken by a relatively few large enterprises. It was estimated that only 10 percent of the country's farmers were able to guarantee loans and thus have access to credit.[55]

Public policy addressed these issues in the late 1960s and early 1970s. The land enclosure movement was halted in 1966 because of peasant resistance, and illegal enclosures were eventually returned. Considerable public, and a little private, land was distributed to the poorer peasants beginning in 1962 and increasingly in the mid-1970s. Approximately 8 percent of the total farmland and 12 percent of the total rural families of Honduras were involved in the Honduran land reform.[56] Simultaneously, cotton production decreased with the fall in cotton prices, and an estimated 60,000 illegal Salvadoran immigrants were expelled in order to relieve land pressures in the southern and western areas of Honduras.[57] All of these changes eased conditions for the poorer farmers and rural laborers. Still, the Honduran population increased so rapidly that the number of farms grew 25 percent, while the amount of farmland expanded by only 5 percent from 1952 to 1974.[58]

The growing impoverishment of farmers in Honduras was less severe and more widespread than in the western countries. No effective agricultural oligarchy developed primarily because the banana industry provided a sustained demand for labor and the unionization of banana workers generated greater political power for some peasants. The expansion of larger farms was thus limited. The poverty of the Honduran economy, in the meantime, restricted city growth and supported a miniscule middle class in urban areas.

With the experience of the 1930s fresh in their minds, Central American leaders attempted to industrialize in order to diversify and insulate their economies from fluctuations of

[54]M. Posas, "Política estatal y estructura agraria en Honduras 1950–1978," *Estudios Sociales Centroamericanos* 8 (1979): 37–116.

[55]Howard I. Blutstein et al., *Area Handbook for Honduras* (Washington, DC, 1971), p. 142.

[56]Ruhl, "Honduras," p. 53.

[57]Stephen Volk, "Honduras: On the Border of War," in Martin Diskin, ed., *Trouble in Our Backyard: Central America and the United States in the Eighties* (New York, 1983), pp. 215–16.

[58]Ruhl, "Honduras," p. 49.

the world market. These attempts were initially made by individual governments, but they failed because of the extremely small sizes of the Central American economies.[59] This led in 1960 to the formation of the Central American Common Market (CACM), complete with designated "integration industries" to be developed in each country. Even in combination the attempt to industrialize did not provide relief. In a sophisticated econometric study of the CACM through 1966, Jeffrey B. Nugent found that the difference in growth of exports by CACM members to CACM members and to the rest of the world was on average 2.3 percent for the entire period.[60] Moreover, the common market resulted in a once-and-for-all increase in per capita income of .6 percent, or $1.60 per head using current dollars, while private investment was not even significantly affected. Hence, the effects of CACM were exceedingly modest.

There are several reasons for this failure. The countries each produce similar products so that little gain from regional free trade can be expected; limitations of land, labor, and capital plague industrialization; and the natural resources and labor skills provide the region with a distinct comparative disadvantage in manufacturing in the world market. Further, producing goods for the home market was not sufficient to stimulate overall development. In 1982, for example, the combined gross domestic product of the five Central American countries remained less than that of the state of Mississippi. As a result of the war between El Salvador and Honduras in 1969;[61] the subsequent expulsion of Salvadoran immigrants from Honduras; the perception of an uneven distribution of gains from union; and especially, as a result of disappointment with the total benefit of the CACM to the region, the experiment in economic integration had disappeared by the early

[59]Gary W. Wynia, "Setting the Stage for Rebellion: Economics and Politics in Central America's Past," in Howard Wiarda, ed., *Rift and Revolution: The Central America Imbroglio* (Washington, DC, 1984), pp. 54–56.

[60]Jeffrey B. Nugent, "A Study of the Effects of the Central American Common Market and of the Potential Benefits of Further Integration," Guatemala, Secretaria de Integración Económica Centroamericana and U.S. Agency for International Development, 1971.

[61]The "Soccer War" between Honduras and El Salvador in 1969 had its roots in a lingering border dispute and series of bitter soccer matches between the two national teams, but it was especially due to the treatment and expulsion of Salvadorans as part of a land reform program in Honduras. See Thomas P. Anderson, *The War of the Dispossessed* (Lincoln, NE, 1981), pp. 167–75.

1970s. Even so, an industrial sector virtually nonexistent at the end of World War II averaged an 8.5 percent yearly growth between 1950 and 1980. Industrialization proceeded to levels well beyond those existing after World War II (see Table 4), although in El Salvador, one of the two most industrialized of the Central American republics, this led to the presence of no more than a few dozen factories located in the capital city.[62]

While industrialization was expected to alleviate the unemployment and underemployment problems of the countries, the industrial sector was less labor-intensive than agriculture. The most heavily promoted industries were petroleum, basic metals, metal products, paper, oilcloth, textiles, and chemicals, which were capital-intensive, not labor-intensive. With the movement of available investment capital away from the rural sector toward the urban industrial sector, many workers were "released" from the countryside as well as from less capital-intensive traditional industries. Those released from traditional forms of employment frequently did not find jobs in industry.[63] The poor and lower-middle class laborers already located in the cities were simply forced to compete for scarce jobs in an expanded labor pool. The gains from industrialization went, not surprisingly, mainly to those able to raise the financial capital needed to take advantage of opportunities provided by industrial growth—the large landowners—primarily located in the two western republics.

The lot of the rural and urban poor worsened, and the increasing competition for work began to affect seriously the

Table 4. Share of Manufacturing Industry
(Gross Domestic Product, 1970 Prices)

	Guatemala	El Salvador	Honduras	Nicaragua	Costa Rica
1950	11.1%	12.9%	9.1%	10.8%	11.5%
1960	11.7	13.9	11.4	12.6	11.5
1970	14.6	17.6	14.1	19.2	15.1

SOURCE: Economic Commission for Latin America, *Statistical Yearbook of Latin America, 1980* (New York, 1980), p. 70.

---

[62]Anderson, *Politics in Central America*, p. 63.

[63]This is because modern industries such as petroleum, chemicals, basic metals, and mass-produced textiles generate fewer jobs per unit investment than agriculture or such traditional industries as clothing or footwear manufacturing and furniture-making.

lower-middle classes in the cities. Economic pressures on all social classes were exacerbated by the oil shock of 1973 and by the subsequent raising of world oil prices (see Table 5).

Revolutionary activities have appeared in both western countries, supported by manpower from the urban lower-middle class and the poor from both rural and urban areas.[64] The policies of the Somoza regime in Nicaragua, moreover, alienated virtually the entire populace including lower-, middle- and upper-class groups.[65] Widespread disaffection led to a popular and successful revolution and to the leftist Sandinista regime. By contrast, the strong rural labor movement in Honduras resulted in the adoption of some preemptive social programs,[66] similar in spirit but not as extensive as those later undertaken in Nicaragua.

Conclusion

The present structure of the labor markets of Central America is attributed here to the early distribution of population and to the system of land tenure established in the various economies upon the arrival of Hispanic settlers. Economic patterns were established early, sustained over centuries, and became progressively extreme. Land was allocated

Table 5. Change in Working Class Real Wage Indexes, 1967–1977

Nicaragua	−40%
Guatemala	−34%
El Salvador	−17%
Honduras	− 8%
Costa Rica	+17%

SOURCE: Roland Ebel, "The Development and the Decline of the Central American City-State," in Howard Wiarda, ed., Rift and Revolution: The Central American Imbroglio (Washington, DC, 1984), p. 95.

---

[64]For specific incidents see Lars Shoultz, "Guatemala: Social Change and Political Conflict," in Martin Diskin, ed., Trouble in Our Backyard: Central America and the United States in the Eighties (New York, 1983), pp. 194–95; and Enrique A. Baloyra-Herp, "Reactionary Despotism in Central America," Journal of Latin American Studies 15 (November 1983): 295–319.

[65]Booth, Nicaraguan Revolution, pp. 97–126.

[66]Ruhl, "Honduras," pp. 49–56.

and labor was distributed primarily by nonmarket forces. Variation in the availability of labor and in systems of land distribution determined the distribution of wealth in the countries of the region. These factors, in combination with changing international markets, produced varying economic conditions in the different countries.

In particular, the relative scarcity of profitably cultivable land resulted in the high value of such land in most countries. Combined with relatively large endowments of labor, this resulted in low wages in Guatemala and El Salvador. Wealth in these two countries, then, was in land and was held by relatively few. These people used their wealth to gain access both to incomplete financial markets and to political power in order to maintain and even increase the gap between themselves and the rest of the population. Those without land and without wealth and access to financial markets were often kept in that position by the rich. Changes in production of agricultural or manufactured goods altered neither the basic structure of wealth-holding nor the labor markets. Instead of diminishing with a rising national income, the extent of the labor market duality widened in the two western republics. This generated severe unemployment and underemployment among the unskilled and ultimately contributed to similar phenomena among the lower-middle class as labor competition became increasingly fierce.

This pattern was not as prevalent in Honduras and Nicaragua where exports were less profitable in the early years when labor was relatively mobile and land tenure patterns were being established. The extremes in wealth were not so evident, although at times those with greater affluence attempted to exploit their nonmarket power and access to financial markets in ways that increased inequality. Consequently, inequality in the distribution of income occurred in these two countries as well. Lacking the extreme conditions found initially in El Salvador and Guatemala, however, large landowners were precluded from concentrating land as extensively in response to the changing profitability of potential exports. Costa Rica provides the illuminating contrast. The early distribution of wealth was more egalitarian, and that has not changed appreciably. Labor markets, as a consequence, are much less dualistic.

The Central American economies rarely have been able to provide a sufficient level of economic opportunity to guarantee widespread popular satisfaction. The closure of opportunities to most of the populace not only reduces employment directly but also thwarts economic development, thereby impeding additional job creation. Political conflict is most severe today in El Salvador where chances for economic and employment growth are most limited. It is least severe in Costa Rica where economic opportunity is greatest and labor markets are thus less saturated.

Since the lack of economic opportunity for most Central Americans is the result of long-standing historical factors, not the least of which is inequality in land tenure, solutions to the present conflict are not easily found. If economic advancement is to be extended beyond the fortunate few, bringing with it additional jobs and more dynamic economies, structural adjustments are required. The redistribution of land and wealth, however, is always politically controversial. As Kenneth Coleman notes in this volume, political discord is often based on conflicting visions of how best to develop Central American economies. Such dissension can become especially serious when the issues concern distributions of wealth and income.

Billie R. DeWalt

The Agrarian Bases of Conflict in Central America

THE CURRENT HEADLINES on Central America have provoked many questions concerning the causes of political upheaval in the region. A revolution has succeeded in Nicaragua, revolutions continue in El Salvador and Guatemala, and Honduras is being turned into an armed camp. Even Costa Rica, the only one of the five Central American republics with a significant democratic tradition, has become embroiled in conflict with its neighbors and has experienced internal unrest.

Presented in this essay are some comparative data on the agrarian systems of Central America. The principal objective is to demonstrate that recent agricultural trends, especially the concentration of land ownership resulting from the growth of the cattle industry, have contributed to the conflicts occurring in Central America. Four major points will be emphasized:

1) that the agricultural sector is extraordinarily important in the economies and to the people of Central America;
2) that the agrarian sector of these societies has historically been marked by an emphasis on export commodities;
3) that the export orientation and associated processes have helped to cause an extremely unequal distribution of land and a lack of employment opportunities in Central America; and
4) that these in turn have had a significant role in creating the social, economic, and political instability in the region.

It is difficult to obtain accurate current information on the agricultural sector; therefore, the author has relied largely

43

on data before 1979, a time that predates the Nicaraguan Revolution and the latest outbreak of civil war in El Salvador. As
we will see, the agrarian processes described here have developed over a long period of time and are still continuing in
several of the republics. In other countries the changes that
are now occurring are direct consequences of the current
revolutionary ferment in the region.

The percentage of the population directly involved in
agriculture is still an important segment in all of the countries.
In 1980 it ranged from a low of 29 percent in Costa Rica to a
high of 63 percent in Honduras, and was over 50 percent in
El Salvador and Guatemala. The percentage contribution of
the gross domestic product made by agriculture was also substantial, ranging from a low of 18.5 percent in Costa Rica to a
high of 33.5 percent in Nicaragua.[1]

While all of the Central American countries have been
devoting substantial effort to industrialization, agriculture has
been an important part of their attempts to finance this industrialization. Throughout Latin America, countries count on the
agricultural sector to produce staples to feed their rapidly
growing and urbanizing populations. Price policies have generally been structured to keep the costs of basic foodstuffs to
a minimum. These policies are presumed to serve the needs
of urban dwellers and factory workers. However, these "cheap
food" strategies have often served as disincentives for production because it is simply not profitable enough for farmers
to cultivate basic staples. As Alain de Janvry has shown, the
effect of cheap food policies has been increasingly to reduce
small farmers to the margin of existence as they are generally
the producers of basic commodities. They continue to try to
produce enough for their own subsistence but do not find it
worthwhile to try to produce a surplus for the market.[2]

Another way in which agriculture is used to finance industrialization is that a substantial part of the Central American
countries' foreign exchange is earned from agricultural exports.

---

[1]The percentages of the population involved in agriculture in 1980 may be
found in Table 2. Percentages for the contribution of agriculture to the gross domestic
product were 18.5 in Costa Rica, 27.5 in El Salvador, 28.3 in Honduras, 28.4 in Guatemala, and 33.5 in Nicaragua. These data may be found in J. W. Wilkie and S. Haber,
eds., *Statistical Abstract of Latin America*, vol. 22 (Los Angeles, 1983), pp. 291, 293–
95.

[2]Alain de Janvry, *The Agrarian Question and Reformism in Latin America* (Bal-
timore, 1981), pp. 157–73.

In 1978 agricultural products comprised well over 50 percent of the total exports in all of the countries, and almost 70 percent in Guatemala and Honduras. This percentage had increased since 1971 in all of the countries except for El Salvador and Honduras where it had declined slightly.[3] At the same time that the governments of Central America have been implementing cheap food policies, they have generally provided subsidies and credit for the capitalist sector of agriculture to try to stimulate the production of export commodities such as bananas, coffee, sugar cane, beef, and cotton. The goal of such policies is to earn scarce foreign exchange.

Cheap food policies and an emphasis on export agriculture are both based on a belief in comparative advantage, the idea that a country should produce those products for which it is most favorably endowed in terms of natural resources, labor skills, cost advantages, or other factors. The concept of comparative advantage is an essential element of the free trade policies advocated by liberal economists since Adam Smith.[4] As will be seen, these policies have not been kind to Central America.

Export agriculture has been a significant part of Central America's linkage with the world market since it was colonized by the Spanish. In many areas of Central America, cacao was a vital export crop as far back as 1540. Indigo was another early export commodity until it was replaced by synthetic dyes in the middle of the nineteenth century.[5] This was around the time that coffee became important. Bananas and other tropical fruits were added around the turn of the century and have been supplemented in more recent times by cotton, sugar

---

[3]The actual percentages of exports contributed by agriculture for 1978 were 53.4 for El Salvador, 58.1 for Costa Rica, 58.9 for Nicaragua, 68.2 for Honduras, and 68.9 for Guatemala. See Wilkie and Haber, *Statistical Abstract of Latin America,* pp. 402, 406–07, 409, 411.

[4]See Joan Robinson, *Aspects of Development and Underdevelopment* (Cambridge, MA, 1979), pp. 102–03. In her critique of free trade and comparative advantage, Robinson notes that this idea is dependent upon two assumptions, neither of which holds in the modern world. First, the argument is made in terms of comparisons of static equilibrium conditions in which each trading nation is characterized by full employment of resources and balanced payments. Second, because all countries are treated as having the same level of development, unequal exchange is not part of the model.

[5]Murdo MacLeod, *Spanish Central America: A Socioeconomic History, 1520–1720* (Berkeley, 1973). This is an excellent source for the early history of agricultural exports in Central America.

cane, and beef cattle.[6] The region has followed policies designed to make use of its comparative advantage—its tropical location—to export products to the rest of the world.

One major problem for Central America has been that these agricultural exports are extremely vulnerable to "boom and bust cycles"; that is, depending on world demand, prices fluctuate wildly. When demand rises the prices for agricultural products also rise, giving more individuals in more countries an incentive to plant them. This often results in overproduction that will sometimes cause prices to drop precipitously. Because demand for these products is relatively inelastic (as prices drop, consumption does not rise significantly), low prices continue for several years until supply decreases. Further contributing to the instability of demand is that many of these crops are subject to substitution effects. Just as indigo was replaced by synthetic substitutes, the demand for cotton declined as synthetic fabrics were increasingly used in clothing (a process that began to reverse after the steep rises in oil prices after 1973). High sugar prices several years ago led to the increasing use of corn sweeteners, and the world sugar market has been slack ever since.

These bust cycles reduce the profits of the landowners, leading to three economically rational responses on their part. First, those who can afford to do so attempt to expand their holdings still further so that they maintain their profits by earning smaller margins on greater production. Second, they diversify to spread their risks over a larger number of crops. The expansion into cotton, sugar cane, African palm, melons, beef cattle, and other crops may be seen as part of this strategy.[7] Finally, they seek to reduce their costs of production, most typically by attempting to reduce labor costs through the

---

[6]A very good general reference, particularly on the importance of coffee and bananas in Central American history, is Ralph Woodward, *Central America: A Nation Divided* (New York, 1976), esp. pp. 149–202. More in-depth accounts of the significance of agricultural export commodities may be found in Tommie Sue Montgomery, *Revolution in El Salvador: Origins and Evolution* (Boulder, CO, 1982), esp. pp. 34–46; John A. Booth, *The End and the Beginning: The Nicaraguan Revolution* (Boulder, CO, 1982), esp. pp. 20–26; Mitchell A. Seligson, *Peasants of Costa Rica and the Development of Agrarian Capitalism* (Madison, WI, 1980), esp. pp. 14–72; Jefferson C. Boyer, *Agrarian Capitalism and Peasant Praxis in Southern Honduras* (Ann Arbor, MI, 1983), esp. pp. 62–95; and Richard N. Adams, *Crucifixion by Power: Essays on Guatemalan Social Structure, 1944–1966* (Austin, TX, 1970), esp. pp. 353–79.

[7]See Montgomery, *Origins and Evolution*, p. 45 for an account of this in El Salvador in the 1920s.

use of increased technology, such as machinery or herbicides, or by shifting to less labor-intensive crops.

A good example of such processes comes from southern Honduras, the region in which I have been working periodically since June 1981. This area is inhospitable. The coastal plain around the Gulf of Fonseca is not extensive. There is a dry season from December until May, and there is usually another extended dry period during the rainy season that makes agriculture risky. During the colonial period, indigo and sugar cane were cultivated in this region and some scrub cattle were raised, but the area was a backwater compared with other regions of Central America. Although some coffee was grown in the south, agrarian capitalism and an emphasis on export agriculture did not penetrate this region until after 1950. After this date, sugar cane, cotton, and especially cattle production for the international trade began to change the region's agrarian systems.[8]

Sugar cane and cotton are both crops that, while cultivated by large landowners, provide significant labor opportunities for the small farmers and landless people. The cane is cut by workers using machetes, while the cotton is picked by hand. During the past several years, however, the world market for both of these commodities has been in a bust cycle. The two large sugar cane mills are in danger of closing because of heavy debts, and cotton cultivation has become more and more unprofitable because production requires increasing amounts of pesticides to control insects. This has caused many farmers to continue a trend—the conversion of their lands to pasture for cattle production—which was begun in the late 1950s and early 1960s. Under current conditions, the main requirement for cattle production is having large extensions of pasture land. The expansion of production thus requires clearing all available land for pasture, and, when possible, purchasing and/or renting more land.

The change in land use patterns is dramatic. Between the 1952 and 1974 agricultural censuses in southern Honduras, the amount of land in pasture increased by 50 percent, reaching over 60 percent of the total land area in 1974. This has occurred

---

[8]See Boyer, *Agrarian Capitalism*, pp. 59–61; Billie R. DeWalt and Kathleen M. DeWalt, *Farming Systems Research in Southern Honduras*, Report No. 1, Department of Sociology, University of Kentucky, Lexington; Billie R. DeWalt, "The Cattle Are Eating the Forest," *Bulletin of the Atomic Scientists* 39 (1983): 18–23.

in both lowlands and highlands. One of the ways in which the process is facilitated is that many landholders rent forest land to the poor who clear it to produce subsistence crops. Pasture is interplanted with these crops so that after a year or two of cultivation the landholder is left with a permanent pasture. The poor have only the option of attempting to rent the increasingly scarce areas of forest land.[9]

Why are landowners so interested in cattle and pasture? One landowner in southern Honduras explained her reasons. She reported that in the past she had grown cotton on her lands. In recent years, with the unpredictability of prices on the world market, the high costs of chemicals, fuel, machinery, and the problems associated with hiring workers, she has decided that the crop is too risky and unprofitable. With just three or four hired hands, she can effectively manage a herd of several hundred cattle. Input costs are lower, and, while prices are still unpredictable, it is common practice to hold on to the animals when prices are too low.[10]

The conversion of land to pasture is going on all over Central America. Land utilization patterns for Honduras and Costa Rica show that only a little over 6 percent of the land in both countries is used for export crops like bananas, coffee, cotton, and sugar cane. While some may criticize the multinational corporations that control the production and/or marketing of these commodities, at least their production employs a substantial amount of labor. However, at present, over 50 percent of the land in both countries is devoted to pasture for cattle, an export commodity that employs relatively little labor.[11]

The growth of cattle production in the five Central American countries has been phenomenal. Between 1959 and 1979

---

[9]See DeWalt, "The Cattle Are Eating the Forest," pp. 20–21.

[10]Although this landowner did not mention it, another advantage of cattle is that they are quite maneuverable. Estimates are that 200,000 of Nicaragua's cattle were smuggled out of the country into Honduras between the beginning of the revolution and mid-1981 (see Joseph Collins, *What Difference Could a Revolution Make?* [San Francisco, 1982], p. 45). It is also common for Hondurans to smuggle their cattle into El Salvador or Guatemala where prices are higher.

[11]These data were obtained by the author from the following sources: for Costa Rica, unpublished accounts from Proyecto de Información Agropecuario del Istmo Centroamericano, Instituto Interamericano de Cooperación para la Agricultura, San Jose, Costa Rica; for Honduras, compiled from various volumes of the Censo Nacional Agropecuario, Dirección General de Estadistica y Censos, Republica de Honduras, Tegucigalpa, 1977 and 1978.

the number of cattle increased by 80 percent, from 6.9 million to 12.4 million head. While meat production in these countries increased by over 185 percent, consumption has barely increased, and per capita consumption actually declined in Honduras and Costa Rica. The reason is that exports of beef have risen even faster (about 500 percent in the last twenty years) than production.[12] The United States is the biggest consumer of exported beef, using it for hamburger, pet foods, and other processed meats.

The effects of turning Central America into a large cattle ranch are profound. Many people have noted the ecological costs, especially the destruction of forests as more and more land is cleared for pasture. In addition, as small farmers and agricultural laborers are displaced from good lands, they are forced into using marginal, often steep-sloped lands in order to produce their subsistence crops. Increased soil erosion is the result. There are no nutritional benefits for the majority of local people; in fact, cattle are competing with poor people for scarce land and food. The pastures to feed cattle replace land that people could use to feed themselves. There are no employment benefits; the main reason for the expansion of cattle production is precisely because so little labor is required. Finally, because cattle production requires extensive amounts of land, larger landholders continue to try to expand their holdings, thus exacerbating inequalities in access to land.[13]

The result of the concentration on export agriculture, especially beef, is that these Central American agrarian systems are now plagued by the dual problems of extreme inequities of land distribution and decreasing employment opportunities.

---

[12]Between 1959 and 1979 the number of cattle increased by 44.4 percent in El Salvador, 60 percent in Nicaragua, 69.2 percent in Honduras, 100 percent in Costa Rica, and 125 percent in Guatemala. These data are reported in Billie R. DeWalt, "Microcosmic and Macrocosmic Processes of Agrarian Change in Southern Honduras," in Billie R. DeWalt and Pertti J. Pelto, eds., *Microlevel/Macrolevel Linkages in Anthropological Theory and Research* (Boulder, CO, n.d.) These percentages are derived from data presented in several U.S. Department of Agriculture foreign circulars entitled "Livestock and Meat" and published between 1959 and 1983.

[13]Other discussions of these processes may be found in Douglas Shane, *Hoofprints of the Forest: An Inquiry into the Beef Cattle Industry in the Tropical Forest Areas of Latin America* (Washington, DC, 1980); James Nations and Daniel Komer, "Indians, Immigrants and Beef Exports: Deforestation in Central America," *Cultural Survival Quarterly* 6 (1982): 8–12; Seligson, *Peasants of Costa Rica*, p. 164; and DeWalt, "The Cattle Are Eating the Forest."

Table 1 indicates the concentration of landholdings that existed in Central America before the Nicaraguan Revolution. Although in several cases agricultural censuses have not been carried out for many years and the data are now quite old, in most countries land concentration is growing rather than declining.[14] A small percentage of the landholders has had control over a large part of the land, while the majority of

Table 1. Concentration of Agricultural Landholdings in Central America

Country	Percentage of Landholders	Percentage of Land Controlled
NICARAGUA (1963)[a]		
< 5 hectares	50.8%	3.5%
>100 hectares	5.0	58.8
EL SALVADOR (1971)[a]		
< 5 hectares	86.9	19.6
>100 hectares	.7	38.9
GUATEMALA (1970)[b] (estimates)		
< 4 hectares	83.3	12.3
>350 hectares	.5	42.4
HONDURAS (1974)[c]		
< 5 hectares	63.8	1.8
>100 hectares	9.1	44.1
COSTA RICA (1973)[d]		
< 4.76 hectares	35.0	1.5
>100 hectares	8.4	67.0

[a]J. W. Wilkie and S. Haber, eds., *Statistical Abstract of Latin America*, vol. 22 (Los Angeles, 1983).
[b]World Bank, *Guatemala: Economic and Social Position and Prospects* (Washington, DC, 1978). While these are estimated figures, they generally agree with the data from the 1964 agricultural census, presented in Wilkie and Haber, *Statistical Abstract of Latin America*.
[c]*Censo Nacional Agropecuario 1974, Tomo II, Tenencia de la Tierra* (Tegucigalpa, 1978).
[d]These data were computed from Table 11 of Mitchell A. Seligson, *Peasants of Costa Rica and the Development of Agrarian Capitalism* (Madison, WI, 1980). The data in Seligson's table were originally expressed in terms of *manzanas*, a unit of land that is equivalent to .69 hectare. For this reason I have used lands that are under 4.76 hectares for my comparison.

---

[14]For Costa Rica see Seligson, *Peasants of Costa Rica*, p. 148; for Honduras see Boyer, *Agrarian Capitalism*, pp. 85–96; and for El Salvador see Martin Diskin, "Land Reform in El Salvador: An Evaluation," *Culture and Agriculture* 13 (1981): 1–7.

landholders has had access only to small plots of land. For example, at the time of the last census in El Salvador only .7 percent of the population controlled almost 39 percent of the land. Meanwhile, almost 87 percent of the landholders were owners of plots of less than five hectares that comprised only 19.6 percent of the cultivated land. In addition, almost 41 percent of the population was completely landless.[15]

A similar pattern prevailed in Nicaragua until the Sandinista Revolution. Anastasio Somoza's family owned one-half of all the farms over five hundred hectares and controlled about one-quarter of all industry. This concentration of land and wealth, and the corruption and abuse of power that went along with it, was one of the principal reasons why so many segments of the populace united to overthrow his regime.[16] The data for the other Central American countries are similar. Guatemala, Honduras, and Costa Rica also have been characterized by an extremely skewed distribution of landholdings.

The revolution that took place in Nicaragua and those in process in El Salvador and Guatemala have roots that go beyond the agrarian issue. Yet the inequalities in the agrarian system are among the most critical stimuli to revolution. One of the rallying cries of the Sandinista Revolution was "land for whoever works it!" and agrarian reform is still a major issue there.

Although a proposal of agrarian reform set in motion the CIA-directed coup that toppled the democratically elected government of Jacobo Arbenz in Guatemala in 1954, the U.S. government apparently perceives the necessity of agrarian reform.[17] To try to correct some of the gross inequalities in Central America and to take some of the pressure off friendly

---

[15]Diskin, "Land Reform in El Salvador," p. 1.

[16]It is interesting to note that in the United States there is a similar pattern of landownership, with about 1 percent of the owners controlling 40 percent of the land. Over 78 percent of the landholders have access to only about 3 percent of the land. The major difference is that in this country there are many more alternative employment possibilities for those who do not have access to land. See Ann Mariano, "A Homesite is a Lot," *Washington Post National Weekly Edition*, February 13, 1984, p. 21.

[17]On Mexico's continuing agrarian problems see Gustavo Esteva, *The Struggle for Rural Mexico* (South Hadley, MA, 1983); on Nicaragua see Collins, *What Difference Could a Revolution Make?* p. 79; and on Guatemala see Stephen Schlesinger and Stephen Kinzer, *Bitter Fruit: The Untold Story of the American Coup in Guatemala* (Garden City, NY, 1982), pp. 75–77.

regimes, the United States has been providing funds for agrarian reform efforts. This is being attempted in El Salvador despite right-wing opposition which has extended to the murder of two U.S. government advisers and the head of the Salvadoran Institute of Agrarian Transformation in January 1981. Even in Costa Rica, which thus far has remained an island of democracy in a sea of military dictatorships, agrarian reform has been promoted with the assistance of the U.S. government. As Mitchell A. Seligson has said, "land reform is seen as an imperative for the future stability of the Costa Rican countryside."[18]

The reason why land reform is so crucial is that jobs are not being created in the industrial sector fast enough to absorb either the increasing population or the people who are being pushed out of the rural areas. This is because the process of industrialization in Central America has followed a path similar to that of agriculture, emphasizing capital-intensive rather than labor-intensive development. As Harley Browning and Bryan Roberts have shown for Latin America as a whole, the percentage of the population employed in industry barely increased, from 18.6 percent in 1950 to only 21.2 percent in 1979.[19] Table 2 demonstrates the same trend for the Central American countries. The percentage of the population engaged in agriculture is declining, and the industrial sector has not expanded at nearly the same rate. In the past twenty years, the percentage of the population in agriculture has dropped

Table 2. Percentage Change in the Distribution of the Labor Force in Central America[a]

	Agriculture		Industry		Services	
	1960	1980	1960	1980	1960	1980
Honduras	70%	63%	11%	15%	19%	23%
El Salvador	62	50	17	22	21	27
Nicaragua	62	43	16	20	22	37
Guatemala	67	55	14	21	19	25
Costa Rica	51	29	19	23	30	48

[a]World Bank, World Development Report, 1983 (New York, 1983), pp. 188–89.

[18]Seligson, Peasants of Costa Rica, p. 123.
[19]Harley Browning and Bryan Roberts, "Urbanization, Sectoral Transformation, and the Utilization of Labor in Latin America," Comparative Urban Research 8 (1980): 86–103.

as little as 7 percent in Honduras and as much as 22 percent in Costa Rica. The percentage employed in industry in the five countries has increased only between 4 and 7 percent. As a result, the rural landless and the small farmer are caught in a squeeze. They are increasingly pushed out of the countryside into the urban areas in which few decent jobs await them. There they either join the ranks of unemployed or, more typically, become engaged in the informal service sector of the economy as shoeshine boys, servants, or street vendors. This has been the true sector of growth in Central American economies, especially in Nicaragua and Costa Rica.

The agrarian processes described above have created greater numbers of underemployed urban poor and continue to exacerbate the already glaring inequalities existing in these countries. The agrarian problems of Central America suggest that hundreds of millions of dollars of military assistance, the training of thousands of troops, and the presence and even participation of U.S. troops are not likely to quell for long the revolutionary fires burning in the region.

Much more fundamental social and economic reforms are needed to provide a permanent solution. These include meaningful agrarian reform; price policies that are not antithetical to the production of basic grains; improved distribution of services such as health, education, and water and sanitation; more widespread participation in government and planning; and elimination of corruption and abuse of power. Without such reforms first, the $8 billion in economic assistance recommended by the Kissinger Commission is only likely to worsen the problem. Walter LaFeber recently has argued that one of the effects of the immensely popular Alliance for Progress during the Kennedy administration was to make revolutions inevitable. The alliance did result in unprecedented economic growth rates in Latin America, but the growth occurred along the lines of capital-intensive strategies, thus creating fewer jobs for the poor who were and still are the most needy beneficiaries. In addition, the economic benefits were largely usurped by the oligarchs who controlled banks and mercantile businesses. Consequently, economic growth created greater inequality and fed revolutionary sentiment.[20]

---

[20]Walter LaFeber, *Inevitable Revolutions: The United States in Central America* (New York, 1983), pp. 148–55.

Given the prevailing conditions in the four Central American republics to which the $8 billion in economic assistance would flow, there is a strong likelihood that, even if the money were to be used for its intended purposes, it would not help. These funds would most likely go into developing capital-intensive industries and into expanding export agriculture. For the agricultural sector, this is likely to continue to engender the concentration of landholdings and the investment in commodities and technologies that minimize labor costs. These developments have a greater likelihood of further lining the pockets of the rich and ignoring the fundamental needs of the poor for land and/or jobs with which to earn a decent living.

Kathleen M. Blee

The Catholic Church and Central American Politics

RECENT EVENTS in El Salvador and Nicaragua have underscored the changing role of the Catholic church in Central American political life. A church whose hierarchy has been traditionally allied with ruling classes and center/right politics now faces persecution from rightist forces allied with the agrarian elite in El Salvador. The revolutionary left, long hostile to Christian principles of faith and morality, now proclaims these as the foundation of revolutionary transformation in Nicaragua. Long-simmering splits within the Catholic church, along lines of authority and region, have erupted into the secular political realm. In the latest of these the Vatican is involved in a bitter public dispute with several Latin American theologians and clergy over the "theology of liberation" and the role of the church in conflicts between social classes. Such contradictions within the Catholic church in Central America have made its powerful political role increasingly contentious.

The movement of some sectors of the Central American Catholic church to the political left and the ensuing ruptures within that institution are the product of changes internal to the church as well as historical changes in the relationship of church to state throughout Latin America. The historical process that redefined the role of religious values in secular politics will be examined here by tracing the impact of doctrinal and organizational changes within the Catholic church. Also discussed will be the way in which changes in the global Catholic church were implemented in the Latin American context. Finally, a comparison will be made of the church's role in El Salvador and Nicaragua today.

In Latin and Central America the Catholic church has long played an influential but contradictory role. As a product of European colonialism, the Latin American church often reflected and reinforced the interests of the colonial land-owning classes against native peoples and the peasantry. The church encouraged the poor in the virtues of patience and obedience, values based in spirituality and clericalism but with a clear message in the world of economics and politics. Yet, even during the colonial period, the Catholic church played other roles in Latin American society. A paternalist church preserved aspects of indigenous cultures by incorporating them into a new religious framework and protected Indians and African slaves from the rawest excesses of the colonial system.[1] Such contradictions were the product not only of differing interests and perceptions within the church hierarchy (between priests and bishops, for example) but also reflected the complex and uneven nature of colonialism in Latin America.

In the twentieth century the mission of the Latin American Catholic church changed as a result of external economic and political forces and internal pressure. The political independence and industrialization of many Latin American nations undermined the viability of the agrarian sector as a primary church constituency. Agrarian elites, tied to colonial powers, increasingly faced challenges by new elites based in manufacturing and commerce who favored political nationalism. At the same time, rapid urban expansion eroded the peasantry and created large working classes in cities that offered insufficient employment opportunities and underdeveloped education, health, and social service systems.[2] This combination of wide disparities in living standards between elites and non-elites and a legacy of successful political movements against colonial domination left twentieth-century Latin America in crisis and increased the likelihood of class-based revolutions. These changes within Latin American societies coincided with movements within the church for greater ecumenical cooperation and a broader interpretation of church doctrine, which further directed the church's attention toward social problems, secular political movements, and urban cultures.

In Latin America the church became interested in economic development models and political reforms which might alleviate the plight of urban migrants, undermine the appeal

---

[1]Penny Lernoux, *Cry of the People* (New York, 1982): p. 18.
[2]See André Gunder Frank, *Latin America: Underdevelopment or Revolution* (New York, 1969), pp. 3–17 for a history of the "development of underdevelopment" in Latin America.

of left-wing political movements, and retain the church's influence in the political arena. This led to an array of Christian
social services, trade unions, youth organizations, universities, and radio schools throughout Latin America which were
heavily financed by direct appeals from the Vatican to Western
European churches. In parts of Latin America the church allied
itself with Christian Democratic parties as the framework for
injecting Christian values into a program of reform and development.[3] Christian Democracy stressed collaboration between
rich and poor in the pursuit of economic growth, democratic
political participation, and state support for selected ventures
in the private sector.[4]

Even as the Latin American Catholic church appeared to
act as one body, serious political and theological disputes
simmered below the surface. Priests and nuns were often critical of the Christian Democratic models of development backed
by the church hierarchy, seeing these as doing little to narrow
the gap between rich and poor and as blocking concerted
political action on behalf of changes in the concentration of
land and industrial ownership. Some Latin American clergy
and theologians took this disillusionment with Christian
Democracy further and invoked Catholic thought as a foundation for popular opposition to capitalist social systems.[5]
These internal divisions began to assume an institutional form
and became public in the 1960s as the consequence of the
world ecumenical council of Catholic bishops known as Vatican II.

Vatican II opened against a background of theological
and doctrinal changes developed by Pope John XXIII in a series
of encyclicals which declared as basic human rights the right
to a decent standard of living, education, and political participation. In the years of Vatican II, changes in the church's
political perspectives were accompanied by a fundamental shift
in the perception of the role of the church in twentieth-century

---

[3]Daniel Levine, "Religion and Politics," in Levine, ed., *Churches and Politics
in Latin America* (Beverly Hills, 1980), p. 23.

[4]On the case of Christian Democracy in Chile see James Petras, *Politics and
Social Forces in Chilean Development* (Berkeley, 1969), pp. 197–255.

[5]Cornel West, "Religion and the Left: An Introduction," *Monthly Review* (July–
August 1984): 13–16. The conversion of Camilo Torres, a Colombian priest, to the
guerrilla movement and his subsequent death is the most noted and most extreme
example. See Maurice Zeitlin, ed., *Father Camilo Torres: Revolutionary Writings* (New
York, 1969), passim.

society. Rather than viewing the church as a fixed body which transmitted dogma from one generation to the next in an unchanging form, Vatican II declared it to be a social institution based on a living and changing community.[6] Such doctrinal change opened the door to a general reinterpretation of society. If social institutions were always in flux, then they must be understood as historical entities which have possibilities for development and transformation. If social institutions, governments, and economies could develop in various ways, then the church had no interest in maintaining any existing social structure.[7] Further, the notion of the church as a living community, together with a lessening of the doctrine of clerical obedience, meant that analysis of societies need not be taken from church dogma or hierarchical proclamations alone but could be derived as well from the daily life of priests, nuns, and laity.[8]

Despite the implications of such change for the church as a whole, the initial repercussions of Vatican II were largely experienced within the North American and European churches. The primary Vatican II theologians were Western European and the scope of discussion was centered around church issues, while social issues had become more pressing in the Latin American nations.[9] The application of the changes of Vatican II to the Latin American church awaited the 1968 meeting of Latin American bishops, the second convention of the Latin-American Episcopal Conference (CELAM) at Medellín, Colombia.

CELAM II was a major turning point of modern Latin American church history. It was held at the juncture of sweeping internal changes from Vatican II and widespread dissatisfaction over the role of the church in Latin American political life. The 1964 military coup in Brazil and disappointment over

---

[6]See Gustavo Gutiérrez, *A Theology of Liberation* (Maryknoll, NY, 1973), p. 8 for a discussion of *Gaudium et spec*, no. 1 which details the position of Vatican II that the church "does not 'find itself' except when it 'loses itself,' when it lives 'the joys and the hopes, the griefs and the anxieties of men of this age.' "

[7]Levine, "Religion and Politics," p. 21.

[8]The theological basis for such change is found in Vatican II's *Gaudium et spec*, no. 44, discussed in Gutiérrez, *A Theology of Liberation*, pp. 8–9. See also Michael Fleet, "The Church and Revolutionary Struggle in Central America," *Social Text* (Spring–Summer 1983): 106–14; Lernoux, *Cry of the People*, p. 31; and Levine, "Religion and Politics," pp. 22–23.

[9]Phillip Berryman, "Basic Christian Communities and the Future of Latin America," *Monthly Review* (July–August 1984): 32.

the progress of Christian Democratic reforms in Chile had provoked political strife within the church. Traditionalists remained committed to moderate reform movements, while others like Bishop Dom Helder Camara of Brazil pushed for the creation of a "church of the poor."[10]

The CELAM II meetings—the forum for political divisions within the hierarchy—resulted in a victory for those forces pushing for dramatic change. Documents of CELAM II reveal a broadening of the concept of "sin" to include an entire social system that inhibits a fully moral life, an analysis of poverty as a problem of societies rather than individuals (thus a problem amenable to political change rather than personal reform), and a sense that Latin American nations had not been well served by either capitalist or Communist models of development.[11] CELAM II backed a political process based not on the importation into Latin America of preexisting development models but on new society models created through the active participation of the masses of people. CELAM II therefore served to popularize a model of participation developed in Brazil by Paulo Freire in which education and change resulted from a dialogue between teacher and student on the conditions of daily life and the possibilities for changing oppressive structures.[12] Throughout Latin America, in the aftermath of CELAM II, this model was drawn upon by priests, nuns, and lay workers who fused the religious and political implications of the everyday experiences of their impoverished constituency.

Despite these changes the CELAM II documents might have remained a footnote in theological history except for two developments within the church which institutionalized the message of the conference. The first was the development of the "theology of liberation," based on the work of Latin American theologians such as Gustavo Gutiérrez of Peru. This theology started from the principle that history should not be an intellectual exercise but should reflect the spiritual and cultural perspectives of the majority of people in a society. In

---

[10]Michael Dodson, "The Christian Left in Latin American Politics," pp. 114–16, as well as Brian Smith, "Churches and Human Rights in Latin America," pp. 156–57, 162–67; and Levine, "Religion and Politics," pp. 23–25, all in Levine, *Churches and Politics.*

[11]Levine, "Religion and Politics," p. 24; Lernoux, *Cry of the People,* p. 38.

[12]Lernoux, *Cry of the People,* pp. 40, 372–75; Berryman, "Basic Christian Communities," pp. 29–31.

this view the history of Latin America could not be read as a history of development and progress but as a history of injustice and repression. On this scale neither capitalism nor colonialism could be judged successful in Latin America.[13]

Liberation theologians expanded ideas developed in Vatican II to argue that all history should be seen as a history of change and movement. Change does not arise from external sources; rather, people change and create themselves and their societies in every social action. The role of the church, then, should not be to lead people toward a predetermined economic or political goal but to ensure that people are free to determine their own course of change. The church should facilitate the movement of societies toward liberation and choice.[14] Although liberation theology is a political theology, it is not a partisan or ideological theology since its practical application has been developed not through political parties but through vehicles of popular participation known as "base communities."[15]

These base communities were the second structure to institutionalize the doctrines of CELAM II. Although base communities differ in structure and ideology across and within countries, all have certain fundamental characteristics. They tend to be relatively small, tight-knit communities of people who share similar levels of income, employment, and education. They are focused on adults as opposed to the usual church emphasis on youth. They discourage individualism in favor of a pooling of experience and a sense of unity and equality among members.[16] Base communities, often located in rural areas or in poor neighborhoods on the outskirts of cities, have been a vehicle whereby the doctrines of CELAM II have been popularized among poorly educated and illiterate populations. Further, these communities have provided a structural framework through which people are encouraged to reflect on their experiences and to envision possibilities for

---

[13]José Miguel Bonino, *Doing Theology in a Revolutionary Setting* (Philadelphia, 1975), passim; Gutiérrez, *A Theology of Liberation*, pp. 21–42.
[14]Levine, "Religion and Politics," pp. 28–30; Tommie Sue Montgomery, "Cross and Rifle: Revolution and the Church in El Salvador and Nicaragua," *Journal of Inter-American Affairs* 36 (Fall–Winter 1982–83): 209–21.
[15]Berryman, "Basic Christian Communities," pp. 27–40.
[16]Lernoux, *Cry of the People*, pp. 40–41.

the future. As such, they have been the catalyst for local movements of agrarian and political reform.[17] In El Salvador, for example, base community movements in rural areas helped provide peasant mobilization for land reform in the mid-1970s. In Nicaragua, base communities were active in the anti-Somoza movement.[18]

The base community and liberation theology movements coincided with other structural changes in the Latin American church. Over the past few decades there has been a move away from foreign-born clergy and the training of native-born clergy in European seminaries and toward indigenous development of clergy.[19] Popular religion or "folk Catholicism," based on a synthesis between Indian and African culture and Catholicism, has been rediscovered. It is reflected in the incorporation of popular images such as suns and moons into the liturgy and the use of liturgical vehicles such as baptism to express both Catholic and native meaning systems.[20]

While the message of CELAM II was spreading throughout a portion of the base of the Latin and Central American church, there were increasing signs of discontent with its message in other sectors of the church. In the late 1970s this discontent broke into open political battle, as the Latin American bishops prepared for their next meeting at Puebla, Mexico. By this time—ten years after CELAM II—the implications of its documents had become clear. Conservatives in the church base as well as the hierarchy were unhappy with the church's implicit criticism of development models in Latin America.[21] Further, they were opposed to the democratization that had occurred within the church, fearing that it would undermine unity, the basis of the church's moral strength.

In preparation for CELAM III, a series of documents and counterdocuments was drawn up by various competing factions. Conservative forces, led by the Colombian bishops and representatives of the Curia (the Vatican Senate), produced

---

[17]Berryman, "Basic Christian Communities," pp. 27–40; Fleet, "Church and Revolutionary Struggle," pp. 106–14; Smith, "Churches and Human Rights," pp. 162–77.

[18]Berryman, "Basic Christian Communities," pp. 34–37.

[19]Lernoux, *Cry of the People*, p. 381.

[20]Ibid., pp. 18, 382.

[21]Michael Fleet, "Neo-Conservatism in Latin America," *Concilium* 161 (January 1981): passim; César Jerez, *The Church in Central America* (New York, 1981), passim.

working papers which explicitly rejected the principles of CELAM II. The working papers focused on "secularization" of Latin American life as a critical problem. They called for increased attention to the preservation of the tradition of faith through religious education, individual prayer, and liturgy. The mission of the church within this conservative perspective was to strengthen institutional religion to provide a moral foundation from which a range of political programs could be drawn. Such a mission would not forsake concern with poverty and injustice in Latin America, but neither would it propose a specific Catholic agenda to alleviate these problems.[22] In response to these papers, Brazilian bishops and liberation theologians issued counterdocuments which reaffirmed the message of CELAM II and argued that the practice of faith required recognition of social "sins" existing in secular society. Christian theology, according to this perspective, can provide a symbol of justice and a sign of hope but only if the church positions itself on the side of the poor and oppressed masses of Latin American society. The substitution of secularization for poverty and injustice as the primary issue for the Latin American church, then, is a step away from the true mission of Catholic faith.[23]

In the two years of preparation for the Puebla conference, the regional discussion of these documents made public the deep and multifaceted division within the Catholic church. Conflict was evident not only between conservatives and liberationists but also between the religious base and hierarchy and between the Vatican and substantial elements of the Latin American church. In recognition of the serious internal problems within the Latin American church, Pope John Paul II flew to Puebla to open the conference. In his address, he argued that it was not possible to reread the Gospel from an ideological viewpoint without destroying the essence of the church's mission, a message heralded by conservatives. However, in a public address to an Indian group, he also noted that, while rights to private property are essential, so too are

[22]Fleet, "Neo-Conservatism," passim.

[23]Phillip Berryman, "What Happened at Puebla," in Daniel Levine, ed., *Churches and Politics in Latin America* (Beverly Hills, 1980), pp. 61–62; Lernoux, *Cry of the People*, pp. 412–25. See also "Reflections and Problems of a Church Being Born Among the People: Popular Church Challenge to Puebla, Mexico, Meeting" (Washington, DC, 1978), passim.

rights to be free from exploitation by property, a message proclaimed by liberationists.[24]

Pope John Paul II's conflicting political messages were repeated throughout the conference proceedings.[25] The bishops praised popular participation but not lay leadership in the church or base communities. They gave subtle approval to the theology of liberation while denouncing the influence of Marxist analysis within this theology. Liberation theology allowed the church to "live liberating evangelization in its fullest" but was overideological "when it uses as a point of reference a praxis with recourse to Marxist analysis."[26] Further, the conference refused to engage in direct political actions such as a proposed denunciation of the Somoza government in Nicaragua. What the Puebla conference affirmed, and what continues today, is the message of a Catholic church split deeply along many lines.

The consequences of this split are seen in the peculiar roles that the church plays in Nicaragua and El Salvador. In El Salvador serious conflict between the Catholic church and the government dates from the 1970s when Archbishop Luis Chavez González encouraged the development of base communities in rural areas. Within a few years hundreds of these communities were established, led by a largely native-born clergy and lay leaders who urged peasants to become agents of change in their lives and social world.[27] Not surprisingly, the first serious attack on church members resulted from issues on agrarian reform. In the mid-1970s there was a series of kidnappings, fires on church properties, and expulsions of foreign missionaries.[28] This initial cycle of repression had a major influence on many base religious workers who increased their

[24]Lernoux, Cry of the People, pp. 425–32. Such seeming contradictions in ideological perspective reflect the complex mission of the papacy, which translates dogma and tradition for contemporary issues while attempting to reconcile the various conflicting goals and issues within the church. Papal pronouncements, therefore, are rarely categorizable along a simple ideological spectrum. For example, see Pope John Paul II's 1983 discourses on economics and labor published as "Work and Unemployment" and "Man and His Values: The Aim of Economics," in The Pope Speaks: The Church Documents Quarterly 28 (1983): 259–68.

[25]Gary MacEoin and Nivita Riley, Puebla: A Church Being Born (New York, 1980), passim.

[26]"La Evangelización en el Presente y en el Futuro de América Latina" (Puebla, February 13, 1979): pp. 1–232, quoted in Lernoux, Cry of the People, p. 442.

[27]Fleet, "Church and Revolutionary Struggle," passim; Montgomery, "Cross and Rifle," passim.

[28]Lernoux, Cry of the People, pp. 61–80.

attempts to organize peasants for social reform. Such organizing led to still another cycle of repression, and by 1977 sectors of the church in some rural areas believed that they were identified targets of right-wing death squads.[29] Such perceptions were not altered by rumors which targeted all Jesuit priests under the slogan "be a patriot, kill a priest."[30]

It was in this tense atmosphere that Oscar Arnulfo Romero was appointed Archbishop of San Salvador. Although known as a conservative at the time of his appointment, Archbishop Romero, as a consequence of continual persecution of the church, moved quickly to the center, adopting a sense of the Salvadoran church as an institution under attack from the right.[31] Romero flew to Rome to complain to the Vatican about government repression of the church and, in so doing, provoked a further division between the church and the government as well as within the church hierarchy between himself and the conservative caucus of bishops.[32] However, Romero did not ally himself with the leftist forces of El Salvador, and he alienated a segment of base community priests in 1979 by continuing to legitimate a middle ground as he insisted that a new rightist civilian-military junta should be supported.

By the following year Romero decided that his position in the political middle had become untenable since it was neither reuniting the church nor lessening political repression. He wrote to President Jimmy Carter, calling for an end to U.S. military and economic aid to El Salvador. Moreover, seeing negotiation and compromise as largely futile in this divided society, Romero increasingly gave sanction to those who opposed the government by violent as well as nonviolent means.[33] In March of 1980 he was assassinated while saying Mass.

Any hope that the split within the church could be healed was broken by Romero's assassination. From 1980 on many laity and lay leaders, and even some clerics, entered antigovernment revolutionary organizations. The persecution of the

---

[29]National Assembly of Women Religious, "Crucifixion and Resurrection in El Salvador," *Probe* (March 1981): passim.

[30]Lernoux, *Cry of the People,* pp. 61–80.

[31]Berryman, "Basic Christian Communities," pp. 35–36.

[32]Fleet, "Church and Revolutionary Struggle," pp. 111–12.

[33]Jon Sobrino, "Archbishop Romero: A Powerful Prophet," *Maryknoll* 75, no. 3 (March 1981): 26–29.

church continued, and local church leaders held up the popular church as a symbol of resistance. In contrast, the conservative hierarchy, valuing preservation of the institution of the church, became increasingly removed from a large portion of the base which identified with liberation theology, either as a pastoral or as a political message.[34]

The Salvadoran church today continues to reflect this schism, with another moderate archbishop, Arturo Rivera y Damas, attempting to mediate the factions of church and state. Increasingly, however, this mediation has become untenable. The split between church hierarchy and base has become so serious in some regions of the country that church leaders refer to "parallel churches." Relations between church and state also continue to be bitter. Death threats not only have been made against Archbishop Rivera y Damas and another Salvadoran bishop but also against nuns at a girls' school where a songbook contained hymns commemorating the slain Archbishop Romero. Such public threats against church officials have mounted as members of the clergy continue to denounce rightist violence and to call for a government dialogue with the insurgents.[35]

The repeated attacks on the church in El Salvador have taken their toll. Since 1972 eleven priests have been assassinated and sixty have been exiled or forced into exile.[36] Despite the defeat of presidential candidate Roberto D'Aubuisson, whose rightist ARENA party is reputed to have been involved in Romero's assassination and other death squad activity, rightist attacks on church members and clerics continue. The office of the archbishop, by tabulating civilian and religious abductions, disappearances, and murders, is seen as an opponent of the government. Any reconciliation between rightwing forces within and outside the government and critical elements of the Catholic church of El Salvador remains unlikely.

In Nicaragua the church has moved in a different direction. Until the 1960s there was little conflict between the hierarchy of the Nicaraguan Catholic church and the Somoza

---

[34]Fleet, "Church and Revolutionary Struggle," passim.

[35]"Church in El Salvador Gaining Role as a Mediator," *New York Times,* June 12, 1984; "Salvadoran Official Hints Church 'Oversteps Role,' " *National Catholic Reporter* (December 3, 1982): 3; "El Salvador Archbishop Warned U.S.: 'Negotiate or Make a Fatal Mistake,' " ibid. (February 17, 1984): 7.

[36]Montgomery, "Cross and Rifle," p. 218.

government. With the impetus of Vatican II and CELAM II, however, some challenge to the Somoza government was mounted by the church in the 1970s. Nicaraguan bishops issued a pastoral letter condemning Somoza's violation of human rights in 1972. In 1974 no Nicaraguan bishops attended the inauguration of Somoza.[37] Unlike in El Salvador, government attacks on the church were sporadic and directed at the lower levels of the church rather than at the hierarchy.[38]

Nevertheless, as popular dissatisfaction with Somoza grew, the church became an important vehicle for organizing the opposition. Within much of the church the common goal to end the Somoza regime in fact masked a variety of political positions as to the nature of a post-Somoza government.[39] The conflict in Nicaragua has not been a simple division between church and state. As in El Salvador, in Nicaragua the church itself is internally divided. Unlike in El Salvador, where much of the division is over theological questions of the role of the church in society, in Nicaragua political and partisan lines divide church members. These differences between El Salvador and Nicaragua reflect the greater repression of the church in El Salvador, which has unified the church internally; the cataclysmic effect of Archbishop Romero's assassination on the church in El Salvador; differences in leadership style and personal ideology between the archbishops of Nicaragua and El Salvador; and the varying levels of incorporation of the church into guerrilla movements in El Salvador and postrevolutionary government organizations in Nicaragua.[40]

Conflicts within the church began in the first months after the overthrow of Somoza. Base community priests, bolstered with assistance from clergy in other Central American nations, built an infrastructure of "people's churches" allied with the revolutionary forces but strongly opposed by the Nicaraguan church hierarchy. Nicaragua's bishops, in their first pastoral letter after the revolution, criticized the new government for curbing legal due process and freedom of expression.[41]

---

[37]"The Church in Nicaragua," *El Salvador Bulletin* 1 (October 1982): 1.
[38]Montgomery, "Cross and Rifle," p. 218.
[39]Fleet, "Church and Revolutionary Struggle," pp. 112–13.
[40]Montgomery, "Cross and Rifle," passim; "Church and Revolution in Nicaragua," *Central America Update* (November 1982): passim.
[41]"The Church in Nicaragua," pp. 1, 5–6.

The early years of the Nicaraguan revolution sharpened these lines of political division within the Catholic church. Base clerics saw the mobilization of the poor through base communities and lay minister programs as central to the implementation of wide-ranging social reforms and literacy education. These progressive forces within the church instituted formal channels of communication and joint work between church workers and leaders of the revolution. Some religious leaders even accepted top posts in the government. The hierarchy of the Catholic church in Nicaragua reacted with greater caution toward the revolutionary government. Although Archbishop Obando y Bravo supported social reform, he labeled the massive 1980 literacy campaign as "indoctrination" and worried about the proliferation of mass organizations supportive of the Sandinistas.

Between 1980 and 1982 hostility between the increasingly Sandinista-dominated government and the church hierarchy deepened. In 1980 the bishops ordered four priests to resign their posts in the government. When the priests refused, they were stripped of their right to perform sacraments. Such incidents of conflict among the Sandinistas, the church hierarchy, and portions of the church base grew more serious.[42] The Sandinistas in 1981 insisted that television coverage of Sunday Mass cover not only the service of the archbishop (an enemy of the government) but also services by local priests friendly to the Sandinistas. In response, the archbishop canceled all filming.[43] In 1982 the junta refused to allow the publication, in the influential newspaper La Prensa, of a letter from Pope John Paul II which encouraged the church base to be more obedient to the hierarchy. Although this policy was later reversed, it also widened the gulf between church and state.[44] By mid-1982 tensions were public and sharp. The Nicaraguan bishops continued to stress a traditional, mystical form of religion and, together with media opposed to the government, publicized several "miracles" which were said to demonstrate God's displeasure with the direction of the revolution.[45] In

[42]Ibid.; "Are Nicaragua's Churches Free?" Christianity and Crisis 42 (September 20, 1982): 250–53.

[43]The history of many of these early conflicts is detailed in "Are Nicaragua's Churches Free?" pp. 250–53; and "Church and Revolution in Nicaragua," passim.

[44]"Church and Revolution in Nicaragua," pp. 1–5.

[45]Thomas W. Walker, "Nicaragua: Catholic Unity Dissolves in Revolutionary Nicaragua," Mesoamericas (September 1982): 8.

February of that year the bishops issued a statement criticizing the government for what they claimed to be violations of the human rights of Miskito Indians when the Indians were relocated from a zone on the Nicaraguan-Honduran border. In response, some Sandinistas verbally attacked the bishops for failing to substantiate their claims and for repeating U.S.-initiated charges against the Sandinistas.[46]

These tensions came to the surface once again during the 1983 visit of Pope John Paul II to Nicaragua. The pope demanded the resignation of five priests from the government as a precondition of his visit. When this demand was rejected by the priests, the order was dropped.[47] Yet, during his visit, the pope made clear his dissatisfaction with the Sandinista government as well as with sectors of the Nicaraguan church. The pope attacked what he called the "people's church" and told the masses that they must obey their bishops lest they undermine the unity of the church: "It is absurd and dangerous . . . to imagine alongside—not to say against—the Church built up around the bishop another Church conceived only as 'charismatic' and not institutional, 'new' and not traditional, alternative and, as lately announced, a popular church."[48]

The pope's visit to Nicaragua set a tone of hostility for the Sandinista government which is carried on to the present by the church hierarchy. The Nicaraguan Episcopal Conference, representing all nine of the country's bishops, issued a pastoral letter in April 1984 which urged peace talks with the rebels. Sandinista junta member Sergio Ramírez Mercado denounced the letter at a public meeting as "a document which is not only totally against the national interest, but which favors the United States." The junta coordinator, Daniel Ortega Saavedra, said the letter was "conceived, calculated and structured by the C.I.A." and charged that "some of the bishops have received orientation at the American Embassy in Managua."[49] The role of the archbishop, in particular, is controversial. Archbishop Obando y Bravo has characterized the

[46]Ibid.

[47]"Pope Says Taking Sides in Nicaragua is Peril to Church," New York Times, March 5, 1983; "Truce Between Nicaraguan Catholics and Junta Discussed," Christian Science Monitor, December 17, 1982.

[48]Pope John Paul II, "Unity of the Church: Homily at Mass in 'July 19 Square' During Visit to Managua, Nicaragua," The Pope Speaks: The Church Documents Quarterly 28, no. 3 (Fall 1983): 206–10.

[49]"Archbishop Denounces Sandinistas," New York Times, May 22, 1984.

government as "capable of any barbarity," and he has become central to a movement of opposition to the Sandinistas. Enrique Bolanos Geyer, president of the Supreme Council of Private Enterprise, claims that "the church is the most important source of encouragement for those of us who don't like what is happening . . . Monsignor Obando is by far the most important leader we have."[50]

Tensions between church and state are not only a matter of national political battles within Nicaragua and El Salvador. Conflict within the church also has erupted within theological circles. In March 1984 a right-wing Italian Catholic lay magazine carried an article on liberation theology by Joseph Cardinal Ratzinger, the West German who heads the influential Vatican office, Sacred Congregation for Doctrine of the Faith. The article accused several Latin American liberation theologians of flirting with Marxism and class warfare. In response, the Vatican issued a statement claiming that the document was intended as a "working paper" and had been published without the cardinal's consent. Nonetheless, many within the church regarded this publication as an attempt to influence the meeting in Bogotá between the Sacred Congregation and CELAM which considered the issue of liberation theology.[51]

Ratzinger's attacks on liberation theology as "a fundamental danger for the faith of the church" recently resulted in the Sacred Congregation's interrogation of Leonardo Boff, a Brazilian liberation theologian. Boff was called to the Vatican to answer charges of doctrinal error in his book *Church: Charisma and Power*, which analyzes the hierarchical church from a Marxist perspective.[52] The Vatican also issued a document entitled "Instructions on Certain Aspects of the 'Theology of Liberation,' " prepared by the Sacred Congregation and issued by Pope John Paul II which criticized liberation theology for identifying religious salvation with human liberation.[53]

The response from liberation theologians has been strong and public. In response to Cardinal Ratzinger's initial attack,

---

[50]Ibid.

[51]T. M. Pasca, "Church of the Poor: A Wafer the Vatican Can't Swallow," *The Nation* 238 (June 2, 1984): 657, 672–75.

[52]"Church's Activist Clerics: Rome Draws Line," *New York Times*, September 6, 1984; "Brazilian Faces a Vatican Inquiry Over Support for Social Activism," ibid., August 20, 1984.

[53]"Vatican Censures Marxist Elements in New Theology," ibid., September 4, 1984.

a group of prominent theologians including Gutiérrez, Edward Schillebeeckx of the Netherlands, and Hans Kung of West Germany issued a statement defending liberation theology and attacking its critics: "There are tensions necessary to the life of the church, but today these are exacerbated by integrist and neo-conservative groups. Resisting all social change and holding that religion has nothing to do with politics, they fight against movements of liberation and make choices that constitute an offense against the poor and oppressed."[54]

What is the likely scenario for the church in Central America based on the experiences of Nicaragua and El Salvador and internal strife in the church? Such prediction is necessarily tentative and speculative since regional and national church alignments are often the product of shifting global church politics. However, some trends do emerge from this historical analysis of Central American Catholic church history.

First, in countries where official and quasi-official repression targets significant portions of the clergy or lay leadership, the hierarchy of the church is likely to be drawn into at least verbal confrontation with the government. The pattern of El Salvador is currently being repeated in Guatemala where intense repression of lay workers, the expulsion and withdrawal of foreign priests and nuns, and the murder of thirteen priests since 1974 have caused the country's bishops to protest to the government.

Second, although the years since Vatican II have seen the rise of a counterreform movement within the Catholic church to moderate or reverse the process of liberalization, this movement is not likely to be successful. The theological, liturgical, and political reforms of Vatican II were institutionalized in many forms throughout the global church. In Central America, they gave rise to theological and political movements of a Christianity from the perspective of the poor and oppressed and to structural links between secular reform movements and the church in the base communities. Despite the desire of some within the church to move away from confrontation with right-wing governments, these reforms, once widespread and institutionalized, are not likely to be reversible within the immediate future.[55]

---

[54]"Text of Statement Issued by Catholic Theologians," ibid., June 25, 1984.
[55]Fleet, "Neo-Conservatism," passim.

Third, the conflict in Nicaragua shows little signs of abating. As the country becomes more polarized in political goals, it will be more difficult to unify the church around either secular or religious issues. It is possible that this schism is not reparable as long as Nicaragua is torn by internal and external strife.

Finally, the continuing struggle for and within the Central American Catholic church has had ramifications outside the region as well. In the United States and Western Europe the church hierarchy and laity have become politically active in Central American issues, largely in opposition to Western intervention. Church members have been the major impetus in the movement to provide sanctuary to Salvadoran and Guatemalan refugees and have been vocal in their opposition to U.S. policies in the region.[56]

In Central America the Catholic church fundamentally shapes the nature of political conflict and possibilities for political change. Since the colonial period the Central American Catholic church has been a powerful actor. This influence is not likely to be eroded substantially in the near future. Yet, political processes are not molded in a simple way by the power of the Catholic church. The church is a complex and dynamic institution whose political agendas do not always correspond to secular political divisions of right and left. Thus, the hierarchy may support revolutionary movements of the left in some countries and oppose leftist governments or parties in others. Moreover, the Catholic church, especially in Central America, does not speak with a single voice. Internal divisions, reflecting differences of authority and political analysis, are seen in the contradictory views which members of the church hierarchy and laity espouse in secular politics. The future results of Catholic church influence in Central American politics will be determined not only by the relations of church and state in each country but also by the shifting balance of power within the larger institution of the Catholic church.

---

[56]"Churches and U.S. Clash on Alien Sanctuary," *New York Times*, June 28, 1984.

Kenneth M. Coleman

The Consequences of Excluding
Reformists from Power

As ONE LOOKS at Central America late in the first Reagan presidency, six different political systems seem to have
responded to similar economic and social problems in strikingly different fashions over the course of the twentieth century. One revolution has succeeded in Nicaragua; a
revolutionary insurrection is well under way but currently
stalemated in El Salvador; another revolutionary struggle is
occurring but remains in an earlier stage in Guatemala; in
Honduras revolutionary movements have yet to make much
headway, but they will surely be attempted in the next decade.
In two polities, Panamá and Costa Rica, revolutionary struggles
are unlikely to make any appreciable progress in the next
decade. Most important, there is a correlation between political systems and the degree to which revolutionary struggle
has advanced (see Table 1). The more thoroughly that reformist elements have been excluded from power over the first
seventy-five years of this century, the more likely that revolutionary struggle will succeed in the last quarter century. The
other side of this equation is that the more important the role
that reform elements have played in the political process the
more likely that revolutionaries will be seen as irrelevant. There
is truth to the assertion, made over twenty years ago by John F.
Kennedy, that those who make peaceful change impossible
in Latin America will make violent revolution inevitable. One
need not be an uncritical believer in the myth of Camelot to
find that description apt. Where is the "reformist political center" that the United States purports to support? And, if absent,
where has it gone?

Let us consider for a moment the world view of those
individuals whom I have called reformists and contrast their
orientation with two alternative outlooks commonly found in

Table 1. Apparent Relationship Between Extent of "Revolutionary Success" in 1984 and Historical Tendency Toward Exclusion of Reformists from Political Power

Low ———→ Exclusion ———→ High

	Reformists define the state	Strong military reformism	Weak military reformism	Lengthy reform era (1944–1954) followed by systematic exclusion	Brief periods of modest reform followed by exclusion of reformists	Systematic exclusion of reformists from political power
HIGH DEGREE OF "REVOLUTIONARY SUCCESS"						
Revolutionaries in power						Nicaragua
Revolutionaries control territory; can wage fixed battles with national army					El Salvador	
Revolutionaries can disrupt economic and government operations but do not control territory and avoid fixed battles				Guatemala		
Occasional revolutionary skirmishes or terrorist acts; no sustained revolutionary activity			Honduras			
No serious revolutionary threat	Costa Rica	Panamá				
LOW DEGREE OF "REVOLUTIONARY SUCCESS"						

Central America. To do so, I will borrow from the terminology of Charles Anderson who has written one of the truly definitive books on Latin American politics.[1] Anderson distinguishes between what he calls the conventional strategists of development—the reformist strategists—and the revolutionary strategists, or abstract models that can serve as bench marks for comparison.

The conventionalists assume that development consists of the elaboration of an existing modern sector of "still imperfectly modernized" economies. Conventionalists acknowledge that there is a distinction between a capital-intensive, skilled-manpower employing sector of the economy and a sector seen as traditional, labor-intensive, and premodern. It is typically assumed that the fruits of growth will eventually reach the "premodern community" if only the existing modern sector were allowed to expand. For the conventionalist, as Anderson puts it,

> Capital and technology are the twin keys to the processes of growth. The greatest obstacles to development lie in the inadequacy of investable savings and the fund of technical know-how. Those who hold or could make available such resources must be protected and encouraged.
>
> The role of public policy, for the conventional strategist of development, is to support, stimulate, and protect industry, commerce and market agriculture . . . government is to establish a climate propitious for further investment and to provide appropriate . . . services within the modern sector. However, government need not self-consciously concern itself with bringing change to the community defined as premodern. Gradually, the fruits of productivity will 'filter down.'[2]

Obviously, industrialists, financiers, and agriculturalists in a position to expand because they are "credit worthy" are among those who stand to profit from such a vision. So are individuals fortunate enough to be employed in an expanding modern sector, including a sizable number of middle-class managers,

---

[1]Charles Anderson, *Politics and Economic Change in Latin America: The Governing of Restless Nations* (New York, 1967).
[2]Ibid., pp. 163–64.

white-collar employees such as bank tellers, and factory workers in industries large enough to be unionized. But many are excluded from short-term benefits in this vision of change. The article by Billie R. DeWalt in this volume suggests whose interests are left out.[3]

Surely in most of Central America those excluded by the conventional vision of economic transformation as short-term beneficiaries would have to include: 1) the vast numbers of descendants of indigenous communal landholders whose lands were historically gobbled up through reallocations of land by the state to those who promised to become export commodity producers[4]; and 2) those landless peasants today who are driven onto poorer and poorer land by the expansion of the cattle industry, or by other export commodities. These people have lacked political power and have been excluded from the process by which public policy was determined. There has been no effective articulation of their interests. No case has been presented and argued effectively for such individuals. No one has been forced to listen to those made landless by public policy over the past century. Nor has there been an attempt where the conventionalists have dominated the making of public policy to seek out the opinions of the landless. Anderson again suggests the reasons why:

> In formulating an approach to that part of the society whose demands are largely uncommunicated to decision-makers, the upholders of the conventional approach usually assume a compatibility between the interests and

---

[3]Specifically, Professor DeWalt discusses how the expansion of the cattle industry in Central America has served the interests of a small elite of agrarian capitalists, while impinging on the ability of a large number of peasants to subsist through traditional forms of agriculture. Since those individuals cannot be well employed in cities, given the characteristics of late capital-intensive industrialization, they are left essentially without options. For a good discussion of how similar processes have negatively affected peasants in even the most "successful" of Central American states, see Mitchell A. Seligson, *Peasants of Costa Rica and the Development of Agrarian Capitalism* (Madison, WI, 1980).

[4]One might wish to contrast the cases of El Salvador, where the traditional communal lands, or ejidos, were effectively stripped from indigenous peoples in the initial coffee booms of the 1850–1880 era, with neighboring Honduras where some semblance of ejidal communities remained. See Tommie Sue Montgomery, *Revolution in El Salvador: Origins and Evolution* (Boulder, CO, 1982), pp. 27–53; and J. Mark Ruhl, "Agrarian Structure and Political Stability in Honduras," *Journal of Interamerican Studies and World Affairs* 26 (February 1984): 33–68.

assumptions of the 'invisible sector' and their own. The interest of the 'silent' individual is in improving his standard of living. He would live and act as an effective consumer and producer within a modern economic context. He will understand that he can achieve this goal *only by* the linkage of his own efforts with the gradual extension of the productive capacity of the existing modern sector, *unless he is 'misled' by irresponsible agitators who would use the accumulated savings of society not as the wherewithal of productivity, but as a juicy plum to be distributed to their own advantage.* Prosperity must gradually filter down.[5]

Such is the political and economic vision of the conventionalist. No extraordinary efforts must be undertaken by governments on behalf of the landless, the urban poor employed in the service sector, or other economically marginal groups. The vision of the conventionalist is that the rich serve the poor best by putting their resources to work in investments. Such investments will work eventually to the benefit of the poor via the diffusion effect implicit in economic growth, which is never bad for anyone and can be produced only by allowing the rich to do that which they do best—invest. Those who argue otherwise are demagogues who would squander national resources. Indeed, in some variants of the argument, the demagogues may well be Communists. Such is the logic of those conventionalists not inclined to make subtle distinctions, a genus we shall encounter in our discussions of El Salvador, post-1954 Guatemala, and in Somoza's Nicaragua. Not all conventionalists are red-baiters, to be sure. Indeed, the vast majority are not. Nonetheless, the politics of at least three Central American states have been structured tragically by such political extensions of a vision of economic change, political inferences that have led to massive violations of basic human rights.

The next group, the reformists, are individuals preoccupied with the discrepancy between the existing modern sector and the traditional sectors. Reformists do not believe that such discrepancies will automatically disappear with the diffusion of modernity. Indeed, they see some of the features of economic progress as tending to generate or exacerbate

---

[5]Anderson, *Politics and Economic Change,* pp. 167–68 (emphasis added).

existing inequalities. Yet, they also see hope, if economic change could be guided by public authorities in the proper direction. Anderson puts it this way:

> The fundamental problem for the reformer is the poverty of the greater part of the nation, the glaring contrast between the standard of living of the modern sector and the rest of society. . . . The democratic reformer would 'incorporate' those heretofore only marginally affected by the modern political economy 'into the life of the nation.'[6] This approach to economic change is not so much one of specifying the critical factors in the development process (such as the lack of capital and technical know-how that conventionalists specify). It is rather one of seeking the *terms of compatibility* of the various interests and demands in society under the general rubric of development. The style is essentially *aggregative*. There is a faith that *all* sectors of society have a role to play in the development effort . . . even those groups that have been most reticent . . . have a part to play in the process of change. . . . From his point of view, he would save the recalcitrant from the disaster of revolution which would befall them if change were not wrought, save them, to some extent, in spite of themselves.[7]

In essence, the reformer seeks a process not of diffusion but of sequential change. He begins by inducing one segment of society to undertake a change that may be only partially desired. Then, after that first change, other segments of society may be persuaded, often reluctantly, to make sacrifices for the long-run collective good of society. The reformer runs the risk of displeasing everyone over time but tries to induce those who are presumed to be somewhat myopic to make the changes necessary to permit everyone to benefit eventually.[8] These changes often involve redistribution of resources and privilege downward toward the poorest elements in society. Certain expenditures by government, which conventionalists

---

[6]This would typically involve organizing the previously unorganized to make them effective participants in the political process.

[7]Anderson, *Politics and Economic Change*, p. 177 (emphasis added).

[8]The classic discussion of these tactics can be found in Albert O. Hirschman, "Models of Reform-Mongering," *Journeys Toward Progress: Studies of Economic Policymaking in Latin America* (New York, 1963), pp. 227–97.

would define as uneconomic and inefficient, are essential to the reformist vision of change. Reformers hope that the initial reluctance and displeasure of the privileged can be overcome in time, as the wider, long-term benefits of reform become apparent to those who first opposed change.

The economic argument of reformers is that growth can only be sustained when greater purchasing power is put in the hands of the poor so that the effective national market increases. The reformist judges that a very sizable portion of the potential market, often up to 50 or 60 percent, cannot afford the consumer durable purchases that could stimulate national industrialization. State action to enlarge the effective market is required. That implies instituting social welfare and public works programs, providing credit to small producers, and creating other activities to be paid for by taxing the rich at a higher rate. Sometimes reformists even dare to address the question of property ownership, pursuing land reforms that take over lands not in production or those over a maximum size, often set at the level of 500 or so hectares (1,235 acres). Not surprisingly, therefore, reformists can generate intense hostility in their efforts to induce the recalcitrant propertied to go along with schemes for change that the propertied, as natural conventionalists, are not inclined to accept.

The revolutionary shares the preoccupation of the reformist with the discrepancy between the modern and traditional sectors. But the revolutionary differs in two crucial ways. First, he rejects the assumption of the reformist that a process of sequential change can be identified that will lead to developmental outcomes, believing instead that a set of disjunctive, simultaneous changes are necessary for bona fide development to occur. The assumption is that the existing social structure is exploitative; that it functions to concentrate land, income, and opportunity upward; and that for the poor existing structures are harmful and cannot be otherwise. The revolutionary is inclined to the belief that sequential changes are piecemeal and inadequate; what is needed is a coordinated effort to break through structures of economic and political interaction that oppress human beings.

Second, the revolutionary denies that all elements in society can be induced to participate in activities leading to the common good. The revolutionary, much like the philosophical conservative, has a rather pessimistic assessment of human nature, or at least of human nature under capitalism. Reformists believe that all segments of society can be made to contribute to the developmental effort, while revolutionaries believe that local capitalists will always subvert modest sequential reforms, if only because of their contacts with outside agents of world capitalism who can intervene to defend property. Therefore, in order to make real progress, political leaders need to break through the limits imposed by local capitalists on national development. The relationships of the nation with the world of external capitalism must be restructured. If this involves incurring the wrath of the capitalist powers, so be it. The revolutionary would look at the development of the cattle industry in Central America and would say:

> Look, it is no accident that such a pattern has emerged. The capitalists will obviously follow the logic of capital accumulation. They will never willingly alter their behavior to accommodate the interests of the poor peasants, whom they exploit as renters to clear pasture land, then whom they cast off their land. Those who attempt a piecemeal reform, such as that of limiting landholdings, or reorienting credit or water toward the poor, will probably provoke violence against the intended beneficiaries, who are not in a position to defend themselves. And if the reformists succeed in the short run, they will induce the propertied to launch an international campaign to oppose their reforms, summoning up a frenzy among the metropolitan capitalist powers, principally the U.S. Hence, why bother with piecemeal reform? What you need is *una ruptura*.

So, quite the opposite of the conventionalist, the revolutionary sees the modern sector of the economy as the source of the problem, rather than as a potential solution. Obviously, political compromise between revolutionaries and conventionalists is most difficult since they see the world in such totally different terms.

Political compromise can occur, however, if the reformist center comes to play a major political role. Indeed, the probability of political compromise is determined by the size and political impact of reform-oriented groups. Since only reformists seek a role for everyone in the development policymaking process, their role as brokers is essential to the process of forging political agreement. Conventionalists would exclude revolutionaries, and revolutionaries, if successful, would exclude at least some conventionally oriented capitalists. Only reformists entertain the belief that the assets of the rich can and should be employed in the short term to improve the lives of the poor. For different reasons, both the left and the right reject that reasoning.

Turning to specific cases at opposite ends of the spectrum, first let us examine Costa Rica where the reformist vision has reigned since 1940.[9] In contrast to other Central American states, Costa Rica witnessed the development very early in the postindependence era of a class of small free-holding yeoman farmers, resembling somewhat those of the United States. In both cases the emergence of the yeoman farmer resulted from the inability of indigenous peoples to offer resistance.[10] Eventually, Costa Rica experienced an upward concentration of land since it was unable to resist the seductive siren of export agriculture.[11]

However, Costa Rica started from a different base of land tenure, one that was fundamentally more equal at the time when independence was achieved. While rural landlessness became a social problem that occasioned divisiveness in Costa Rica, the divisiveness was more manageable. In the 1940s, first under President Rafael Calderón Guardia, then later under President José (Pepe) Figueres, a series of reformist governments has ruled Costa Rica, motivated by the social democratic vision that the Partido de Liberación Nacional (PLN), the party of Pepe Figueres, has claimed for itself.[12] With an electoral process more respectable than others in Central America, the PLN forces established after 1949 a system of meaningful electoral competition in which the incumbents, including the PLN, are frequently voted out of office only to return later. There

---

[9]A good recent survey of Costa Rica can be found in Charles Ameringer, *Costa Rican Politics* (New York, 1983).

[10]In Costa Rica other factors were involved such as the lack of extractable resources. This meant that those who settled in Costa Rica were forced to work their own lands.

[11]This evolution is chronicled in Seligson, *Peasants of Costa Rica*. Costa Rica's experience with land concentration, resulting from the expansion of export agriculture, is similar to that of other Central American states.

[12]Daniel Oduber, president of Costa Rica from 1974 to 1978 and whose essay is included in this volume, represents that vision.

is, however, a broad consensus on the outline of public policy, on the need for an activist state that seeks to mitigate social conflict by mildly redistributive activity. That consensus has held up for more than forty years, since before the coming to power of the PLN. It has been severely tested in recent years when the Costa Rican state, now heavily in debt, has presided over an economy in which the gross national product is contracting, rather than expanding.[13] But most Costa Ricans continue to agree on the general direction of public policy. They do not regret that Figueres nationalized the banking system in 1949, immediately upon coming to power, nor that the PLN decreed an immediate one-time only 10 percent tax on assets over 50,000 *colones*. These were seen as limited acts not necessarily leading toward total socialization of the economy, nor toward total confiscation of large private fortunes. And, indeed, they were not. They were actions undertaken to launch social reforms necessary to benefit a wide segment of Costa Ricans.

The Costa Rican state is today an activist one. To take only one example, it devotes $28 U.S. yearly per rural inhabitant for health care, compared to $4 in Honduras and $2 in Guatemala.[14] While the per capita income of Costa Rica is higher than neighboring Honduras and Guatemala, the ratios of investments in such activities, once adjustments are made for the available gross national product per capita, are still highly favorable to Costa Rica.[15] This represents the reformist and social democratic vision of this state. Costa Ricans see some real benefits from their government: they have had a measure of electoral choice for decades such that those who lose elections actually give up office; they have no formal military establishment to exhaust budgetary resources; and they have an extensive governmental apparatus, employing one out of every five of their working population, often in decentralized state agencies that have considerable autonomy from centralized direction. In short, were it not for the lack

---

[13]For two rather pessimistic assessments of Costa Rica in the 1980s, see Flora Montealegre, "Costa Rica at the Crossroads," *Development and Change* 14, no. 2 (April 1983): 277–96; and Juan del Aguila, "The Limits of Reform Development in Contemporary Costa Rica," *Journal of Interamerican Studies and World Affairs* 24, no. 3 (August 1982): 355–74.

[14]See Thomas John Bossert, "Can We Return to the Regime for Comparative Policy Analysis? or The State and Health Policy in Central America," *Comparative Politics* 15, no. 4 (July 1983): 424.

[15]See Bossert's figures on gross domestic product per capita, ibid., p. 426.

of petroleum, it might be argued that Costa Rica has functioned rather well over the twentieth century, both politically and economically. If so, that may well be because the reformist vision—the vision of the social democrats—has been most fully implemented there.

By contrast, the reformist vision in El Salvador has been quashed, and the red-baiters have controlled the political process for decades, polarizing political life between those who would use violence to defend the conventionalist vision of economic change (and thereby the status quo) and those who would use insurrection to overthrow it. Polarization came fifty years ago to El Salvador and has never departed. Stephen Webre describes the origins of polarization in the 1930s:

> General Martínez had no sooner assumed the presidency in 1932 than he faced a crisis whose legacy continues to weigh heavily upon the Salvadoran political consciousness. On January 22, 1932, Indian and ladino peasants in the country's Western zone rose in rebellion under nominal Communist leadership and swept through the district looting, pillaging, and on occasion killing local officials and landowners. Government troops . . . quickly suppressed the movement. Retribution following the restoration of order was swift and brutal. Local civilians lynched some leaders before they could be taken by authorities, but those who fell into official hands fared little better; execution was generally immediate. . . . In most areas it was apparently sufficient proof of guilt to be noticeably an Indian or peasant. . . . The most reliable study concludes that . . . between eight thousand and ten thousand . . . suspected rebels died, probably more than 90 percent of them in the repression, rather than in the fighting itself. By contrast, victims of rebel violence amount to perhaps one hundred, most of whom were soldiers or local officials.[16]

While one need not justify the taking of life in the original uprising, it should be clear that on balance the famous *matanza*, or slaughter, of 1932 involved disproportionately more indiscriminate violence by the political right than by peasants who

---

[16]Stephen Webre, *José Napoleón Duarte and the Christian Democratic Party of El Salvador, 1960–1972* (Baton Rouge, LA, 1979), pp. 7–8.

rebelled on the left. The ratio, according to Thomas P. Anderson, the definitive U.S. historian of this event, was about one hundred killings by rightists to every one by a leftist.[17]

The very audacity of rebellion by the poor in 1932 structured the terms of discourse of Salvadoran politics for the remainder of the twentieth century. Since then the allegation of communism has been employed frequently to discredit those who have advocated reform in El Salvador. The case of the much-maligned José Napoleón Duarte is instructive. Duarte is the Christian Democrat who served as an appointed president of a civilian-military junta between 1980 and the elections of 1982 and who was elected president in 1984. He was portrayed by segments of the U.S. press in the early 1980s as a tool of the Salvadoran military, yet he ran as a coalition candidate opposing the military's choice for the presidency in 1972. In the end, that election was apparently stolen from Duarte when early returns showed him clearly in the lead. But how was that campaign conducted? According to Webre, "throughout the campaign, Duarte was the subject of numerous accusations and innuendos that appeared to have two major objectives: 1) to portray Duarte personally as dishonest and incompetent; and 2) to identify him and the coalition in the minds of voters as Communists."[18]

These verbal attacks were launched because the Christian Democratic Party was bold enough in 1972 to propose for the first time a serious land reform program. The campaign platform departed sharply from earlier party proposals by advocating a legal limit to the size of landholdings and the breaking up of *latifundios*, that is, large underutilized rural estates. Even this program manifested the traditional Christian Democratic caution, however. The government would fix the permissible size of landholdings only after carefully considering in each case the nature of the land, type of crops being produced, and the efficiency of land use. In fact, only the largest landowners with great tracts of unused land were in danger of expropriation.[19]

To what did the Christian Democratic land reform proposals lead? According to Webre, red-baiting was the initial

---

[17]Thomas P. Anderson, *La Matanza: El Salvador's Communist Revolt of 1932* (Lincoln, NE, 1971), pp. 134–37.
[18]Webre, *José Napoleón Duarte*, p. 164.
[19]Ibid., p. 157.

response. Ultimately, however, electoral fraud was committed against Duarte's candidacy. On the first point he notes:

> Opponents of Duarte's coalition waved the 'bloody shirt' of the 1932 peasant uprising, charging that false demagogic promises of agrarian reform (presumably like those the Duarte coalition was now making) had caused that tragic outbreak. The general theme of these attacks was that left-wing deceit of the masses, not oppression or exploitation, led to social violence.[20]

Duarte was attacked in anonymous advertisements in the press as being the "puppet of the opportunistic and deceitful leaders of the Salvadoran Communist Party." Nonetheless, despite such red-baiting in the 1972 campaign, Duarte seemed well on his way to victory on election night. The truth will probably never be known, but it was announced by the electoral commission early in the evening, after the compilation of the vote in San Salvador, the capital city and home of 30 percent of the national electorate, that Duarte had a two-to-one lead over his major opponent. Shortly thereafter the military government banned any further broadcasting of the election results. The next morning Salvadoran residents awoke to hear that Duarte had been defeated by a margin of 22,000 votes. The *Economist* of London noted "how coincidental it was the government's position began to improve only when the results stopped being announced on radio and television."[21]

This was the reality of Salvadoran politics from 1932 through 1980 when the United States began its deep involvement. The electoral process was fraudulent; reformist elements, such as the Christian Democratic Party, were systematically excluded from power. Only in the late 1970s and early 1980s, when human rights violations increased markedly, did major elements of the Salvadoran center give up all hope of reform and begin to drift toward the revolutionary movement. Increasingly, leaders of the reformist center concluded that just two options remained: 1) to join with the

---

[20]Ibid., p. 166. For an example of how little things have changed in El Salvador, see "On Salvador Hustings: Two Old Foes in Rematch," *New York Times*, March 1, 1984, wherein Lydia Chavez quotes a campaign worker for Roberto D'Aubuisson: "[the] ARENA campaign worker said Mr. D'Aubuisson's message could be distilled into a single sentence: 'He is against Communism and Duarte is a Communist.' "

[21]*Economist*, February 26, 1972, cited in Webre, *José Napoleón Duarte*, p. 171.

military that actually governed El Salvador, hoping to institute change from within; or 2) to join the revolutionary insurrection because all expectation of change from within was destroyed. Duarte chose to join a civilian-military junta in 1980. A group of military officers purporting to favor reform had come to power in 1979. Guillermo Ungo, a social democrat, and Rubén Zamora, another Christian Democrat, first served the junta and later made the choice for revolution. In one sense, neither Duarte nor Zamora nor Ungo was happy with his options. Duarte knew he did not control the military. The others initially preferred reform to revolution, but, given the choice between maintaining a social order they considered devoid of moral authority for its human rights violations and insurrection, they opted for revolution.

What human rights violations, one might ask? Let us consider the case of Mario Zamora, brother of Rubén, who was the attorney general for welfare in the military-civilian government that promised reform in 1979. Yet he was assassinated in his own house by a government-backed death squad linked to Roberto D'Aubuisson, later the speaker of the Constituent Assembly in El Salvador and still later a presidential candidate. The killing was seemingly linked to D'Aubuisson's televised allegation that Zamora was working for the guerrillas, a charge immediately and heatedly denied by Zamora. Thomas Anderson describes subsequent events in the following terms:

> On 22 February 1980, while the PDC leader was conducting a meeting at his house, with such persons as Napoleón Duarte and Héctor Dada, another cabinet member, they were raided by masked right-wing vigilantes. . . . Mario Zamora was singled out, taken into the bathroom, and shot dead. As a result of this incident, both Rubén Zamora, brother of the murdered and a member of the PDC Central Committee, and Héctor Dada resigned from the party and the government, which they criticized for not even being able to protect its own members and for its failure to arrest D'Aubuisson for Zamora's murder.[22]

Not surprisingly, Rubén Zamora soon joined the guerrilla movement. He is now one of the major spokesmen for the FDR/FMLN, with which former U.S. Senator Richard B. Stone

---

[22]Thomas P. Anderson, *Politics in Central America* (New York, 1982), p. 83.

was attempting to negotiate in 1983. Needless to say, Zamora was not easily convinced that human rights would be guaranteed by a government in which D'Aubuisson played a leading role as presiding officer of the Constituent Assembly.[23] It is somewhat comprehensible that Zamora would like to see power shared between the guerrilla movement and the existing authorities before he would recommend that the guerrillas participate in any electoral process.

The point here is not necessarily to endorse Zamora's decision to join the guerrilla movement. Nor is it to suggest that Duarte made the better choice by staying within the system. Rather, it is to suggest that there were no good choices for reformists in Salvadoran politics. The situation has been tragically limited. The center has been effectively excluded from the political process up until 1984. That, I would submit, is the fundamental cause that revolution has gone as far as it has in El Salvador. The range of choice has been reduced to two options: 1) no meaningful attack on the social problems of El Salvador,[24] or 2) revolution. Given that harsh reality many, but not all, Salvadorans choose revolution. The country remains tragically divided, with approximately a 50-50 split between those who prefer no change and those who do, defined either as reform or revolution.[25] There is still no clear consensus for revolution, but, if the choice were to stay the same, that consensus might yet emerge. Duarte's election in 1984 appears

---

[23]The election of Duarte as president in 1984, thereby eliminating D'Aubuisson as a major political figure, may have created a possibility for dialogue with the guerrilla opposition, if Duarte can demonstrate control over the military.

[24]Whatever the law says, and the new 1983 constitution of El Salvador speaks with some boldness of agrarian reform, there will be no effective change until the death squads opposing such reform have been brought under control.

[25]This is a contentious assertion that not all analysts accept. The author assumes that the Christian Democrats enjoy the support of about 43 percent of the voting electorate, as they proved in 1982 and in the first round of the 1984 general elections, but that the nonvoters would vote primarily for the left. Adding the two groups together would probably produce a change-oriented faction of 50 percent to 55 percent. The 1984 runoff resulted in a Christian Democratic victory, with 53.6 percent of the vote. This was seemingly because the Party of National Conciliation (PCN), once the preferred party of the Salvadoran military, refused to endorse the candidacy of Roberto D'Aubuisson in the runoff election. PCN supporters presumably abstained or voted for Duarte, therefore accounting for the Christian Democratic victory. That support may have been circumstantial, however, and it is not necessarily support that will stay with Duarte's party in future elections. Hence, the author infers that the Salvadoran electorate remains fundamentally divided. It is still possible though that Duarte's performance in office will generate new support for the reform-oriented center.

to indicate a resurrection of the reformist option, but it remains unclear whether he will be allowed to implement reformist policies.

Let us examine, more anecdotally, one other case of the exclusion of reformists.[26] In 1981 I was invited to lecture in Guatemala at an institute sponsored by the U.S. Information Agency. On that visit I had occasion to meet Vinicio Cerezo, secretary general of the Christian Democratic Party, and his wife, Raquel, a linguist who works with indigenous languages such as Quiché. Both are charming, humane, and reasonable persons, but they live under great duress, as repeated assassination attempts have been made on them by right-wing death squads. This was under the government of General Romero Lucas Garcia, but Guatemala has not changed dramatically since that time, as best I can infer from various sources and from academics who have traveled there more recently.[27]

The negotiations leading to my meeting with Cerezo were interesting in themselves. A young free-lance journalist who attended my lectures approached me after four days, having concluded that my political views were not those of the extreme right. He inquired if I would be willing to meet with Cerezo, who had been his classmate at the Universidad San Carlos. I said that I would like to do so but had little time, suggesting that perhaps Saturday morning before I left town would be convenient. I invited the Cerezos to meet me at my hotel. Pedro,[28] the journalist, called Cerezo who demurred that he would rather not meet me at the hotel as there might be "a bit of a security problem." Pedro then relayed this news to me. As I reflected upon the wisdom of going through with this meeting, I wondered: "Am I being set up?"

Nonetheless, I walked across Guatemala City with Pedro on Saturday morning to the house of Cerezo's friends. As we

---

[26]For an introductory survey of recent Guatemalan politics, see Anderson, *Politics in Central America*, chaps. 1–3. For an understanding of the tragic U.S. role in bringing about the political stalemate that yields so much violence today, see Stephen Schlesinger and Stephen Kinzer, *Bitter Fruit: The Untold Story of the American Coup in Guatemala* (Garden City, NY, 1982); or Richard Immerman, *The CIA in Guatemala* (Austin, TX, 1982).

[27]See, for example, the report of a massacre, assembled in Shelton H. Davis and Ricardo Falla, *Voices of the Survivors: The Massacre at Finca San Francisco, Guatemala* (Boston, 1983); "Death and Disorder in Guatemala," *Cultural Survival Quarterly* 7, no. 1 (Spring 1983); or various reports of Amnesty International.

[28]This is a pseudonym.

walked, Pedro explained that very recent attempts had been made on the lives of the Cerezos so they were in hiding. Our pace quickened a bit, and I began to exhibit extraordinary interest in all passing vehicles and pedestrians. We arrived and knocked on a solid iron gate with an iron sliding window. The window opened and a guard with a submachine gun peered out: "Ah, estás tú, Pedro . . . y el otro?"

"No, ombre, está bien, Vinicio ya sabe que un profesor norteamericano viene a entrevistarse consigo."

We entered and I nervously saw the second guard, also with a submachine gun. Then came Cerezo. We greeted. Coffee was offered. The gunmen disappeared, and we talked with considerable candor for over two hours.[29]

Cerezo told me the details of the attacks on his person; he was most convincing. He also told me that over seventy leaders of the Christian Democratic Party had been killed in the past three years.[30] Cerezo expressed the belief that all these deaths were the responsibility of government-linked death squads,[31] adding that the government wanted to destroy the center by driving it into rebellion along with the incipient guerrilla movement. If they can prove that some Christian Democrats have joined the guerrillas, they can more easily justify attacking all Christian Democrats.

"The government is having some success because some of our people are doing just that . . . joining the guerrillas," lamented Cerezo. "But I am not about to give up that easily," he said; "I am not certain that we ought to run candidates in the upcoming elections [of 1982],[32] because our people would be targets for the death squads, but I would like to see us endorse the least objectionable of the military candidates.[33]

---

[29]The conversations reconstructed below are not verbatim transcripts of our encounter but rather represent selected highlights of a conversation that lasted much longer. As best my memory serves me, they capture the flavor of our meeting.

[30]Cerezo told a similar story to others at this time. See "Guatemala: Christian Democrats Seek US Support for Election Guarantees," *Latin America Weekly Report* 20 (May 22, 1981), wherein similar figures are cited.

[31]A U.S. embassy official in Guatemala City, in charge of estimating the origins of political killings in the country, estimated that "80% are the work of government-linked death squads." Personal interview, June 1981.

[32]The results were subsequently overturned by the military before the new officials could take office.

[33]This decision prompted a negative assessment of Cerezo by many observers of Guatemala who share my values. These individuals see Cerezo as having made a "pact with the Devil." For reasons noted below, I cannot judge him so harshly.

In addition, by way of response, we are doing other things."
He continued:

> It is lamentable but we have had to arm ourselves. We
> are not going to go easily, we will take some of them with
> us . . . that is why we have added the machine guns.
> Moreover, we have had to plan for the long run. I must
> assume that by the time democracy returns to Guatemala,
> and I believe it will, I will not be here. Hence, the party
> cannot be overly dependent on me, or on any other leader.
> We have got to adopt something more akin to a cell orga-
> nization that is not fully public, so that there will always
> be someone ready to step in and fill the void.

"Why do you continue?" I asked. "Isn't this fundamentally hopeless?"

"I love my country," answered Cerezo, "and I believe it
can happen . . . that out of a tradition of violence and repression can come democracy . . . such as happened in Venezuela."

We debated the replicability of the Venezuelan experience, and then my time was up. As I flew back to Miami, I
thought about Cerezo and his beliefs and concluded that they
were fundamentally irrational, that the odds of democratic
reformism emerging out of the current carnage of human rights
violations in Guatemala were truly slim or nil.[34] I also concluded that I had just met a patriot, a man who loved his
country in spite of its flaws and was determined, against all
reason, to set it right. The man was irrational, but I respected
him immensely.[35]

I had been on an Eastern Airlines flight. Every day that
flight left Miami in early morning for Guatemala City and then
made the return flight in the afternoon. Within weeks after
my trip, a bomb exploded on the apron at the Guatemala City
airport, killing a luggage handler who was sitting on a cart

---

[34]This is especially so as long as Washington continues to define the problems
of the area as susceptible to solution via military means.

[35]The reasoning is that, while Cerezo pays some moral costs by trying to position his party in order to profit should the military ever relinquish power, there are
also moral costs to revolution. Once power has been seized by violence, the capacity
to compromise with one's political opponents, even those who disagree only moderately, may be eroded. Since respect for other human beings is a value fundamental
to democracy, the revolutionary route to power may impede the subsequent attain-
ment of a culture of democratic compromise. The choice is not an easy one. Both
reformists and revolutionaries may warrant some respect.

with the luggage waiting for the Eastern flight, which had been delayed, to arrive from Miami. The bomb had been timed to explode while the plane was in the air. As it turned out, Cerezo had been booked on that flight. It is quite possible that the bomb had been intended for him.[36] Miraculously, as far as I know, Cerezo is still alive, but the chances for democratic reform in Guatemala continue to atrophy, if not to die.[37]

There are, or have been, three political systems in Central America where the reformist center has been excluded from the political process. Nicaragua, under the tutelage of three Somozas between 1934 and 1979, witnessed unrivaled corruption and the systematic exclusion of the political center.[38] In the end, business people, trade unionists, peasants, schoolteachers, and twelve-year-old children rebelled in unison. The Nicaraguan Revolution was a genuinely popular one. Like all such multiclass mass movements, the participants had dramatically different visions of what would happen after the Somozas were gone, and disagreements emerged early in the new era of government by the Sandinista National Liberation Front. The point is, however, that the revolution succeeded because Anastasio Somoza Debayle provided no place for the political center and drove the vast majority of the population, including the hierarchy of the church, into at least tacit acceptance of the armed insurrection. The situation has not been quite so dramatic in El Salvador, but it tends toward that direction; likewise in Guatemala. As Richard Fagen and Olga Pellicer recently have observed,

> The politics of reform, at first deeply wedded to electoral strategies, increasingly embraced oppositional strategies of other sorts (strikes, mass protests) and finally was forced to choose between ineffectiveness and possibly physical opposition on the other. By the 1980s, the choice for many

---

[36]It is certain that Eastern Airlines no longer flies into Guatemala.

[37]In July 1984 elections were held for a constituent assembly to write a new constitution. Cerezo's Christian Democratic Party was one of two parties receiving the largest number of votes in that election. Whether a consensus can be built that will induce the Guatemalan military to return to the barracks and to rein in death squads that have operated with impunity remains to be seen. From the vantage point of July 1984, that scenario seems improbable.

[38]The literature on Nicaragua has mushroomed since the success of the revolution. Two particularly useful volumes are John Booth, *The End and the Beginning: The Nicaraguan Revolution* (Boulder, CO, 1982); and Thomas W. Walker, *Nicaragua in Revolution* (New York, 1982).

ex-reformists had become relatively stark: death, exile, alliance with guerrilla movements, or a devil's pact with the military.[39]

In between these situations, in which the reformist center has been excluded, and Costa Rica, where reformists govern, fall Honduras and Panamá where military governments have tolerated, or even encouraged, experimentation with reform. Space limitations preclude an extended analysis of the likelihood of revolution in each case. In Honduras the signs are mixed. Civilians have exercised nominal political control since 1981. At least one informed commentator, Thomas Anderson, argues that instances of political repression are more frequent in Honduras than the North American press reports.[40] Yet, he also notes that there are elements of political pluralism in Honduras that are exceptional by Central American standards: the press is freer than in most of the isthmus; the university has a measure of genuine academic freedom and moral authority; unions are more fully accepted and less subject to bloody repression; and some agrarian reform occurred in the 1970s, providing relief to pressures on the land.[41] Perhaps for these reasons, then, revolutionary movements have not spread in Honduras as rapidly as in the three more repressive cases. There is a bit of space in which the reformist center can operate, even though the military remains a powerful force behind apparent civilian rule.

The same is true in Panamá. Recently established trappings of democracy have not yet been put to the test.[42] What emerged under the reign of General Omar Torrijos from 1968 to 1980 was a sustained attempt at preemptive reformism undertaken by a military government.[43] An accommodation was reached between the reformists and the military government. While it is too soon to claim that this alliance will last,

---

[39]Richard R. Fagen and Olga Pellicer, eds., *The Future of Central America: Policy Choices for the U.S. and Mexico* (Stanford, 1983), pp. 3–4.

[40]Anderson, *Politics in Central America*, p. 137.

[41]See Ruhl, "The Influence of Agrarian Structure."

[42]The election of a civilian president, Nicolás Ardito Barletta, in 1984 initiated a new period of governance that appeared to be democratic, but it remained unclear that the military had really ceded power. The proof will come when Ardito Barletta seeks to do something with which major factions in the military disagree.

[43]See Steve C. Ropp, *Panamanian Politics: From Guarded Nation to National Guard* (New York, 1982).

it does seem to have postponed the initiation of revolutionary movements.[44] The absence of revolutionary fervor in Panamá may have less to do with the long-standing presence of U.S. forces there than with the performance of the Panamanian military.

Consideration of the six major polities of the isthmus reveals a pattern.[45] Where the reformists have been most systematically excluded from power, revolution seems to have advanced the furthest. I commend to readers, then, the writings of Walter LaFeber, Eldon Kenworthy, Thomas Walker, and other contributors who examine in this volume the role that the United States has played in supporting governments that exclude reformists from power.

---

[44]Indeed, in 1983 and 1984 there were disturbing signs of growing militarization by the most antichange elements of the armed forces. See, for example, "Panama Lurches Right," *Washington Report on the Hemisphere* 4, no. 2 (October 18, 1983): 1.

[45]These polities exclude English-speaking Belize, which heretofore has not been caught up in the political turmoil of the area.

The Reagan Policies: A Critique

George C. Herring

Vietnam, El Salvador, and the Uses of History

M ORE THAN TEN YEARS AGO, toward the end of the Vietnam War, the Harvard historian Ernest May examined a series of case studies from World War II through Vietnam. He concluded that, in responding to foreign policy crises, policy-makers and the public were invariably guided by history, especially by their memory of the recent past. May went on to say that equally invariably they used history badly. Their historical knowledge was at best superficial. Their historical reasoning was "thoughtless and haphazard." Indeed, he specifically argued that such reasoning had been a major cause for American involvement in Vietnam.[1]

Similar to the case studies May considers, from the time El Salvador became a major national issue it has been inextricably linked to Vietnam. It is instructive, therefore, to consider the ways in which Vietnam and El Salvador have been compared, to analyze the extent to which and the reasons why they are in fact analogous, and, proceeding from there, to discuss how history can be useful in dealing with the problems of today. In general, it should be noted that history is no better used now than in the instances May studied a decade ago, and this is true of those who oppose U.S. involvement as well as those who support it.

Looking first at how Vietnam and El Salvador have been joined in public discussion in recent years, no matter what one's point of view, analogies have been discovered, memories evoked, and lessons drawn. To start at the beginning, and at the top, there are indications that the Reagan administration, in undertaking its initial, firm commitment to El Salvador, thought that it could win a quick victory and in so doing

---

[1]Ernest R. May, *"Lessons" of the Past: The Use and Misuse of History in American Foreign Policy* (New York, 1975), pp. x, xi, 190.

erase the stigma of defeat in Vietnam and exorcise the so-called Vietnam syndrome, the perceived public reluctance in the wake of Vietnam to take on commitments in the Third World.[2]

When the quick victory turned into an illusion and President Ronald Reagan's commitment aroused the popular apprehensions it was supposed to dispel, the president and his advisers immediately sought to distance themselves from Vietnam. Then Secretary of State Alexander M. Haig, Jr., went to great lengths to show that Vietnam and El Salvador were drastically different. The United States had clear-cut, indeed obvious, vital interests in El Salvador, he insisted, something which had not been the case in Vietnam (a statement that must have come as a shock to the generation of policymakers which had based an escalating commitment in Vietnam on precisely the opposite grounds).[3] Since early 1981 President Reagan has repeatedly stated that there is "no comparison with Vietnam and there's not going to be anything of that kind [in El Salvador]."[4] Reaganites like Ernest Lefever have echoed this refrain, arguing that the United States failed in Vietnam because it did not act decisively and at least implying that Reagan will not make that mistake in El Salvador. The more apt analogy, Lefever insisted, was Greece where, under the Truman Doctrine, the United States turned back an insurgency between 1947 and 1949. Other Reagan supporters insist that the Dominican Republic, where Lyndon Johnson successfully intervened in 1965, is more relevant.[5]

American conservatives have supported the president's commitment in El Salvador, but, where Reagan has attempted to evade the Vietnam issue, his conservative brethren have pronounced numerous lessons from Vietnam that should guide policy in El Salvador. George Will harks back to Woodrow Wilson to find that the cause of American problems, in general, in Vietnam, El Salvador, and Third World countries is the effort to force feed democracy on nations that simply are not ready for it. The United States pressed elections on Vietnam,

[2]*New York Times*, September 25, 1983.
[3]See for example Alexander Haig's testimony before the House Committee on Foreign Affairs, as reported in ibid., March 3, 1982.
[4]Reagan statement quoted in ibid., July 26, 1983.
[5]Ibid., July 31, 1983.

he warned, and Saigon "is now Ho Chi Minh City."[6] Henry Kissinger has emphasized different lessons. Never an admirer of the American democratic system, he proclaimed, upon accepting chairmanship of the commission on Central America, that "it is imperative [in dealing with problems there] that we avoid the bitter debates that characterized the Vietnam period."[7] Norman Podhoretz, editor of *Commentary*, adds yet another lesson; namely, that "fighting a war on the cheap is a sure formula for defeat." If in Central America U.S. military power is called for and we do not use it or use it halfheartedly, he notes, we will "reveal ourselves as a spent and impotent force."[8] More recently, and along the same lines, the Kissinger Commission Report evoked memories of Vietnam when it warned of the dangers of a stalemate in El Salvador. In words almost identical to those Kissinger used in his famous 1969 *Foreign Affairs* article on Vietnam, the report stressed that "the insurgency is winning if it's not losing, and the government is losing if it's not winning."[9]

On the other side of the political spectrum, liberal critics of Reagan's policies have gloomily forecast a replay of Vietnam in El Salvador. The Coalition for a New Foreign and Military Policy, responding to the president's "no comparison" statement, points to the long history of oppression in El Salvador and an unpopular regime backed by U.S. money and insists that the comparisons are all too obvious.[10] To George Ball, Johnson's in-house critic on Vietnam, El Salvador's "music and words sound like plagiarization. I have the feeling that we've heard it all before but in another setting."[11] Liberal journalist Tad Szulc warns that, if the United States persists in its present course in El Salvador, it will become bogged down "in an endless, Vietnam-style guerrilla war in the Salvadorean mountains and jungles," a "scenario for absolute disaster," he describes it.[12]

---

[6]George Will, "Woodrow Wilson's Ghost in El Salvador," *Herald-Leader* (Lexington, KY), July 31, 1983.

[7]*New York Times*, July 25, 1983.

[8]Ibid., July 24, 1983.

[9]Kissinger Commission Report, as summarized in *Herald-Leader*, January 8, 1984.

[10]*New York Times*, July 24, 1983.

[11]Quoted in Robert G. Kaiser, "El Salvador: A Rerun of Vietnam Movie?" *Courier-Journal* (Louisville), March 14, 1982.

[12]Tad Szulc, "El Salvador is Spanish for Vietnam," *Penthouse* 15 (September 1983): 58.

Outside the formal debate, similarly, discussion of El Salvador invariably begins with, or comes back to, Vietnam. When Congress discusses El Salvador, one legislator concedes, Vietnam is a "ghostly presence; it's there in every committee room, at every meeting."[13] Many of the top U.S. advisers in Central America, men like Ambassador John Negroponte and General Paul Gorman, are old Vietnam hands, and most of the U.S. military advisers served apprenticeships in Indochina. The programs being applied by American advisers often seem to be retreads of programs that worked in Vietnam or programs modified in the light of Vietnam failures.

The military brings to El Salvador an exceptional amount of Vietnam baggage. "All I want to do is win one war, that's all, just one," an adviser told a reporter, as though wars, like baseball, were tallied in win-loss columns. "It'll be like winning the world series for me." Another adviser expressed fear of a repetition of the final days of April 1975. "If the sense spreads that the U.S. will desert them," he says of the Salvadorans he is working with, "I don't know what they'll do. It's Vietnam all over again."[14] Among senior U.S. military officers, Adam Smith has written, Vietnam is a "silent obsession. It lurks in nuances and ellipses, even when the discussion is about something else."[15] They are unwilling to go through in Central America what they experienced in Vietnam. They are reluctant to see the army committed, as General Edward Meyer affirmed in the fall of 1983, unless the nation itself is committed.[16] The presence of Vietnam in the military mind was clearly manifested in September 1983 in the famous Freudian slip of Marine Corps commandant General P. X. Kelley who, before a committee of Congress, inadvertently used the word Vietnam when he meant to say Lebanon.[17]

---

[13]James McCartney, "El Salvador and the Ghost of Vietnam," Herald-Leader, May 1, 1983.

[14]New York Times, November 8, 1982.

[15]Adam Smith, "Will You Go to El Salvador?" Esquire 100 (September 1983): 12. See also Drew Middleton, "Vietnam and the Military Mind," New York Times Magazine (January 10, 1982): 34.

[16]See especially Richard Halloran, "Vietnam Consequences: Quiet from the Military," New York Times, May 2, 1983. This "lesson" is emphasized in the study by Harry G. Summers, Jr., On Strategy: The Vietnam War in Context (Carlisle Barracks, PA, 1981), a book which sets forth what has become the new conventional wisdom in the army.

[17]New York Times, October 2, 1983.

If the polls mean anything, the American public, at least partly because of Vietnam, has little stomach for any such commitment. Polls taken in the spring and summer of 1983 revealed that a solid majority of Americans (75 percent) saw the likelihood that U.S. involvement in El Salvador would turn into another Vietnam, and a smaller majority (54 percent) opposed sending troops even if the government was about to be defeated by leftist forces.[18]

Wherever one turns, then, discussion of El Salvador invariably refers back to Vietnam and discussion of Vietnam invariably moves forward to El Salvador. A political cartoon portrays President Reagan, waist deep in quicksand, rifle held above head, doggedly plunging forward, while a nervous Uncle Sam inches along cautiously behind. "Quit grousing!" Reagan orders Sam, "I'm telling you it's *not* Vietnam!" "It doesn't look like Munich either," a still wary Sam responds.[19] In her book *The March of Folly*, even Barbara Tuchman, who once said that the purpose of history was "not to instruct but to tell a story," sets out to find "lessons" from Vietnam and wonders how the United States can continue in El Salvador the "imbecility" it practiced earlier in Southeast Asia.[20] The discovery of lessons is not limited to Americans. A representative of the Salvadoran right wing, protesting American interference in his country's internal politics, exclaimed in frustration that El Salvador should "fight the war without the influence of foreign advisers who were defeated in similar conflicts and have nothing to teach the valiant Salvadoran soldiers."[21]

Since the two situations are so often joined, it is not only appropriate but also essential to determine the ways in which they are in fact similar and the ways they differ. On the surface, at least, the similarities seem obvious and compelling. Both wars occur in small, tropical, underdeveloped countries. In each case insurgents are attempting to overthrow an established government. Each insurgency is composed of a coalition of leftist groups in which Communists play a leading role.

---

[18]"Public Opinion on Central America," *Public Opinion* 6 (August–September 1983): 25; *New York Times*, July 25, 1983.

[19]Tony Auth in Detroit *News*, May 20, 1983.

[20]Gordon Wood, review of Barbara Tuchman's *March of Folly* in *New York Review of Books* 31 (March 29, 1984): 8.

[21]*Newsweek* 103 (January 16, 1984): 27.

Significant outside support comes from the major Communist power in the region and from the Soviet Union. The government in both cases comes from the right of the political spectrum, unrepresentative and unresponsive to the needs of many of its people, especially rural peasants, and it is therefore especially vulnerable to insurgency. It enjoys large-scale support from the United States. The wars themselves are remarkably similar in form. The insurgents rely on guerrilla tactics, ambushes, hit-and-run raids, and sabotage, from bases deep in the countryside. Government forces relying on U.S. aid and advice fight a 9-to-5 war, often indifferently and with indecisive results.[22]

Historical analogies are never exact, however, and these superficial similarities obscure a world of important differences. To start with the obvious, Vietnam is in Southeast Asia, its political culture derived to a large extent from China. El Salvador, only about one-eighth the size of Vietnam, is in Central America and is of the Hispanic political tradition.[23] At this point, the level of intensity of the war remains lower than it was in Vietnam almost from the inception of the insurgency there. So far, and despite their survival and successes, the Salvadoran insurgents do not seem to be in the same league with the Viet Cong.

There are much more important differences in the origins of the insurgencies, their composition, and the nature and extent of their "outside" support. War originated in Vietnam in 1945 as a nationalist revolution against French colonialism, and the second phase—the American phase—was an extension of that struggle. In El Salvador the revolution began in response to a narrowly based and reactionary regime that was totally unresponsive to the needs of a great majority of its own

---

[22]For several useful comparisons by journalists and scholars, see James McCartney, *Herald-Leader,* March 7, 1982; Don Oberdorfer, *Courier-Journal,* March 2, 1981; Robert G. Kaiser, ibid., March 18, 1982; Charles Mohr, ibid., August 21, 1983; and William M. LeoGrande, "A Splendid Little War: Drawing the Line in El Salvador," *International Security* 6 (Summer 1981): 45–47.

[23]For extended commentary on the importance and role of political culture in the Vietnamese revolution, see John T. McAlister, Jr., and Paul Mus, *The Vietnamese and Their Revolution* (New York, 1970); Frances FitzGerald, *Fire in the Lake* (New York, 1972); and David Marr, *Vietnamese Tradition on Trial* (Berkeley, 1982). For comment on the role of political culture in Central American revolutions, see Richard Morse, "Toward a Theory of Spanish American Government," in Howard Wiarda, ed., *Politics and Social Change in Latin America* (Amherst, 1974); and Eldon Kenworthy, "Dilemmas of Participation in Latin America," *Democracy* 3 (Winter 1983): 72–83.

people. Both wars in time became to some degree internationalized, but there is a crucial difference in the nature and
extent of outside support. In Vietnam the major source of
outside support was from the North Vietnamese who were
fanatically committed to liberating their southern brethren and
driving out the foreigners. China and the Soviet Union provided important assistance, but the Vietnamese dimension
was decisive to the outcome. External support in El Salvador
comes from Nicaragua, Cuba, and the Soviet Union, none of
which would appear to have the same level of commitment
as North Vietnam did in the earlier war.

It is extremely difficult to compare the respective insurgencies. In each case the guerrilla forces are made up of a
loose coalition of leftist groups led by hard-core Marxist-
Leninists. But the National Liberation Front of Vietnam appears
to have been much more tightly knit than the FMLN, a somewhat unwieldy and apparently divided coalition of five groups
including pro-Soviet Communists, Cuban-trained Trotskyites,
and Maoists. In Vietnam, moreover, there was nothing quite
comparable to the moderate leftists, Christian Democrats, and
Social Democrats who have joined the Salvadoran opposition.

Again, despite surface similarities, there are important
differences between the two governments. As narrowly based
as it was, the government of South Vietnam probably enjoyed
broader support than the narrow oligarchy which dominates
El Salvador, and there was nothing in Vietnam comparable to
the right wing and its death squads in El Salvador. Indeed, at
certain times the government of Nguyen Van Thieu would
seem a paragon of civil liberties compared to El Salvador. In
Vietnam the army more often than not was a tool of the government in power rather than a power in its own right, as
appears to be the case in El Salvador. The role of the Catholic
church is quite different. The church and its people represented the one secure base of support for the Diem and Thieu
governments in South Vietnam. In El Salvador it is badly split.
Like all historical events, then, Vietnam and El Salvador are
fundamentally different. It is reasonably safe to assume that
the revolutions and wars there will take different courses and
that whatever government emerges in San Salvador will be
different from that in Hanoi.

All things considered, the closest similarity may not be
the wars in Vietnam and El Salvador themselves but the way
in which the United States has responded to them. American

policies clearly reflect the same Cold War mind-sets and world views. In each case U.S. policymakers defined what began and, despite outside Communist support, remained indigenous struggles primarily in terms of the larger Cold War conflict. American involvement in Vietnam was thus justified in terms of preventing the Chinese, who at various times were or were not held to be Soviet proxies, from extending Communist domination over Southeast Asia. In El Salvador, President Reagan has said that the United States must draw the line in Central America against Communist "aggression" instigated by the Cubans who act as Soviet proxies. In each situation the domino theory has been employed to justify commitments to countries whose intrinsic significance is not obvious. The fall of Vietnam, it was argued, would set off a chain reaction which might have repercussions as far away as Hawaii or the Middle East. In the same way, we are told, the fall of El Salvador after the "loss" of Nicaragua could cause the loss of Guatemala, Honduras, Costa Rica, and even Mexico. And that might not be the end. "We are the last domino," candidate Reagan warned ominously in 1980.[24] In February 1965 and February 1981—the coincidence is eery—the United States issued White Papers, which might have been carbon copies, supporting these arguments. In each case the United States has made the outcome a test of its credibility. In each case, at one time or the other, administrations declared their intention to do whatever was necessary to save their client states from communism, and presidents assured a worried nation that they saw no need for combat troops.

At least at the outset in both cases, bold rhetoric was usually matched by cautious action, the pattern of involvement one of gradual escalation. First came economic and military aid, then a steadily growing stream of advisers, and with Vietnam, advisers were followed by combat troops. To keep things in some kind of perspective, it is worth noting that the fifty-five-man military advisory team now in El Salvador is smaller than the sixty-five-man Military Assistance and Advisory Group sent to advise the French in Indochina in late 1950.

American relations with its client states in Saigon and San Salvador are also hauntingly similar. We beg, plead, threaten, or cajole, and the governments go on much as before, making

---

[24]Quoted in LeoGrande, "Splendid Little War," p. 45.

occasional gestures to placate us but never exactly following our direction. Further, there is a marked similarity in the way the two armies respond to U.S. military advice.

The domestic debate in the United States is so similar that it cannot but evoke a sense of déjà vu. The official line emphasizes the importance of outside support for the insurgency; the opposition argues that it is indigenous. Critics stress that the government is reactionary and oppressive; the administration concedes it is not perfect but warns that the situation would be much worse if the Communists gain power. Washington contends that slow and steady progress is being made; its critics question such assertions. Most important, out of the domestic divisions in each case there emerges something of a standoff: the opposition prevents the government from doing what it thinks is necessary to win the war; it is not strong enough to force a withdrawal, however, and indeed most opponents are unwilling to shoulder responsibility for the loss of Vietnam or El Salvador. As a result, the United States year after year does just enough to perpetuate a bloody and destructive stalemate.[25]

Despite these similarities, there would appear to be one major difference, the importance of which is not yet clear. In the case of El Salvador, Vietnam already has happened, and it is very difficult to see how, in the light of this, it will happen again. Because there was a Vietnam, the media are much more skeptical and critical than they were in the early stages of Vietnam, even though television, in particular, could still be much more critical than it is. Congress is much more cautious, and it has consistently challenged Reagan's modest steps far more than it did the larger steps taken by Presidents Dwight D. Eisenhower and John F. Kennedy. Opinion polls indicate that the public foreign policy permissiveness of the 1950s and 1960s has been replaced in the wake of Vietnam by caution and fear. As noted earlier, the army is extremely fearful of becoming engaged in another "no win" conflict like Vietnam, whereas

---

[25]For commentary on this point, see Leslie Gelb, *New York Times*, July 24, 1983. The dilemma was neatly summed up by Representative Stephen Solarz of New York in the spring 1984 debate on Central America. "The American people do not want any more Cubas in Central America," he said, "but neither do they want any more Vietnams." Some congressmen might reverse the order of concerns. Solarz's statement was reported by the Associated Press, May 11, 1984.

in the 1960s, having passed out of the "never again" phase that immediately followed Korea, it was in a "can do" mood and ready to go to Vietnam. As a result, while American handling of El Salvador to date strikingly resembles earlier policy toward Vietnam, the fact that we have only recently gone through the trauma of Vietnam would appear to add a powerful restraining factor that did not operate in the years of escalation in Southeast Asia.

Given these similarities and differences, does the Vietnam analogy have value in dealing with the problems of Central America today? It is clear first, as Ernest May concluded of the period 1945–1965, that thus far history has been badly used. Each side in the current debate has been extremely sensitive to the Vietnam analogy, especially since Vietnam is so close and fresh in the popular mind. But the analogy has misled rather than guided, obscured rather than clarified. Conclusions on both sides have been based on superficial historical knowledge and faulty historical reasoning. Each side has blatantly abused history for partisan purposes; and each has demanded more than history can possibly deliver by asking it to forecast outcomes.

The Reagan administration stretches our credulity to the breaking point by asking us to believe that there is no comparison between El Salvador and Vietnam. The comparisons are all too obvious, and, more important, to say that El Salvador is not another Vietnam does not, as the president seems to wish, eliminate the need for further discussion. To reject the Vietnam analogy for analogy with Greece in the 1940s or the Dominican Republic in the 1960s, moreover, is the most blatant form of argument, by historical expediency, of selecting the example that has the desired outcome and using it.

The effort to apply lessons from Vietnam to El Salvador is equally misleading. It violates what David Hackett Fischer has called "the didactic fallacy," the attempt to extract specific lessons from history and apply them literally to contemporary problems without regard to the differences in time, space, and historical circumstances.[26] The lesson that we failed in Vietnam because we did not use our power decisively, and therefore in future situations like El Salvador we must apply it quickly and without stint, breaks down at several points. We cannot be sure first that a different application of American

---

[26]David Hackett Fischer, *Historians' Fallacies* (New York, 1970), p. 157.

military power in Vietnam would have produced better results; it might have provoked a nuclear war. The relevance of this lesson for the distinctly different situation in Central America is, in any event, open to question.

On the other hand, the opposition's ominous warning that El Salvador will be another Vietnam is as much an abuse of history as the administration's arguments and, indeed, as the so-called Munich analogy was for American involvement in Vietnam. It violates another of Fischer's fallacies, the "fallacy of the perfect analogy," the "erroneous inference from the fact that A and B are similar in some respects to the false conclusion that they are the same in all respects."[27] Vietnam and El Salvador are different in important ways, and it is highly unlikely that the outcome will be the same, namely, an unsuccessful effort to prop up a non-Communist government which cost 58,000 American lives and $150 billion. As Fischer suggests, each historical situation is unique, and we cannot make superficial comparisons and draw facile conclusions that, because such and such occurred before, the same or the reverse will happen this time.

Does this concede the administration's point that, since Vietnam and El Salvador are really not alike, we have nothing to worry about? No, it does not. A new Vietnam in Central America is obviously a worst case scenario; there are many possible outcomes to the current crisis, short of another Vietnam War, that could damage U.S. interests in significant ways.

Does rejection of the Vietnam analogy deprive the opposition of its strongest argument? On the surface it would seem so since Vietnam has such an emotional ring with the American public. When looked at from another perspective, however, the analogy may be a dangerous and self-deceptive argument for the opposition to employ. By focusing on the issue of whether we can succeed at an acceptable cost, we ignore what may be the more important question of whether we should be intervening in the first place. More significant, perhaps, as long as the president can show that El Salvador is not another Vietnam, he can do almost as he pleases there, and that leaves him considerable room to maneuver.

Even more important, the Vietnam analogy inhibits discussion of El Salvador and Central America on their own merits

---

[27]Ibid., p. 247.

and terms. Rather than indulging in the nondebate of whether El Salvador will become another Vietnam, we should be addressing the major issues in El Salvador itself. What is the nature of the struggle there? In what ways, if at all, does it threaten our vital interests? Can we morally justify intervention in support of the existing government? Can we tolerate doing nothing? What are the possible consequences of deeper involvement, including military intervention? All of these questions have been raised at one time or another, but we have never really confronted them in a systematic or sustained way.

Does this mean, then, that history has nothing to teach us, or, more specifically, that the Vietnam analogy is useless in dealing with our present dilemma in Central America? Obviously, this is not the case. History in general, and the history of American involvement in Vietnam in particular, have much to teach us, but we must use them with discretion and caution and not expect too much.

We could learn a lot that is of value from the study of the unique histories of El Salvador and other Central American nations, and from the study of our traditional relationships with these nations. Discussion of the current crisis in Central America thus far has been almost totally devoid of historical context, an alarming and perhaps dangerous omission given its importance. Such analysis would provide us with a much clearer picture of the origins and nature of the difficult and distinctive problems in each of the Central American nations. Understanding of our traditional role would make the United States more sensitive to the ways in which Central Americans view us. It might suggest a great deal about the extent of our influence there and the possible responses to programs we initiate.

Although history does not offer specific lessons, it can provide a desperately needed perspective on contemporary problems. From studying our involvement in Vietnam, for example, we can learn much about ourselves and how we deal with other peoples. The mind-set which got us into Vietnam is quite similar to that which the Reagan administration is operating from today and therefore is worthy of critical analysis. Many scholars believe that in dealing with the Vietnamese we consistently worked from a base of ignorance and cultural blindness. We should be sensitive to the same errors in our dealings with Central Americans today. Study of the interplay within the Moscow-Beijing-Hanoi triangle during the Vietnam War can shed light on, although obviously it will not foretell the direction of, the relations among the Communist nations in dealing with Central America.

When used cautiously and with due regard to its limitations, the Vietnam analogy may even provide guidance, if not outright lessons, that could be useful in handling specific problems in El Salvador. American relations with the Saigon government, for example, suggest, seemingly paradoxically, that the deeper our commitment the smaller our leverage in getting that government to take necessary actions for what we believe are necessary for its survival.[28] Policymakers should at least be alert to this possibility as our involvement in El Salvador and other Central American countries becomes more and more complex.

Above all else the Vietnam experience suggests the centrality of local circumstances in international conflicts. From the outset, American policymakers defined the problem in Vietnam in the context of the Cold War. To a considerable degree, however, local forces explained the origins, the peculiar dynamics, and the outcome of the war. By wrongly attributing the conflict to external forces, the United States drastically misjudged its internal dynamics. By intervening in what was essentially a local struggle, it placed itself at the mercy of local forces, a weak client and a determined adversary. What might have remained a localized struggle was elevated into a major international conflict, with enormous and fateful consequences for Americans and especially for the Vietnamese. The circumstances in El Salvador and Central America are different, and the outcome will certainly not be the same. But the point should be clear: we ignore local forces at our own peril.[29]

Without suggesting to us outcomes that are foreordained, the study of history might also teach us a healthy caution. "History does not teach lots of little lessons," historian Gordon Wood recently wrote; "it teaches only one big one: that nothing ever works out quite the way its managers expected or intended."[30] In the final analysis, however, one of the most important functions of history, or the historian,

---

[28]See Lawrence E. Grinter, "Bargaining Between Saigon and Washington: Dilemmas of Linkage Politics During the War," *Orbis* 18 (Fall 1974): 837–67.

[29]On this point, as applied from Vietnam to Lebanon, see Stanley Karnow, "Vietnam as an Analogy," *New York Times*, October 4, 1983.

[30]Wood, review of Tuchman in *New York Review of Books*, p. 10.

may be to expose the falseness of historical analogy. As a wise Englishman, James Lord Bryce, once put it, "The chief practical use of history is to deliver us from plausible historical analogies."[31] Let us study Vietnam and study it carefully and with an open mind. But let us be conscious that the purpose of our study is to gain perspective and understanding, not hard and fast lessons. With tongue planted firmly in cheek, the historian and Vietnam policymaker James Thomson once proposed that we learn one central lesson from Vietnam: never again "take on the job of trying to defeat a nationalist anti-colonial movement under indigenous Communist control in former French Indochina," a lesson of "less than universal relevance," he quickly and redundantly added.[32] Thomson obviously overstated for effect, but again the point should be clear. Each historical situation is unique, and the use of analogy is at best misleading, at worst, dangerous.

Writing in 1970 about the misuse of historical analogy in dealing with Vietnam, Fischer suggested that the problem had to be "studied and solved in its own terms, if it is to be solved at all."[33] Perhaps the best way to conclude this analysis of the use of the Vietnam analogy in the debate on El Salvador would be to paraphrase Fischer and change the point of reference. As valuable as an understanding of Vietnam may be to us, the problems of El Salvador and Central America can best be studied and solved in their own terms if they are to be solved at all.

---

[31]Fischer, *Historians' Fallacies*, p. 242.
[32]Quoted in Richard Pfeffer, ed., *No More Vietnams? The War and the Future of American Foreign Policy* (New York, 1968), p. 258.
[33]Fischer, *Historians' Fallacies*, p. 250.

Eldon Kenworthy

Central America: Beyond the Credibility Trap*

THE CURRENT CRISES in both Central America and the Caribbean evoke déjà vu for serious students of the region: Guatemala in 1954, Cuba in 1961, Santo Domingo in 1965, and Grenada in 1983. Have we not been here before? Exactly what is it that keeps bringing us back? Arguing the facts of these cases, then as now, seems increasingly pointless. Something systemic is going on and, until the syndrome is diagnosed, treating each isolated recurrence will get us nowhere. Within this essay we will focus on U.S.-Nicaraguan relations as well as search for the underlying trap, the perennial confusion, that gives validity to the Latin American aphorism: "They never remember while we never forget." They means us.

In a rarely called joint session of Congress in April 1983, President Ronald Reagan compared the current situation in Central America to the early dark days of the Cold War. "The countries of Central America are smaller than the nations that prompted President Truman's message," Reagan intoned, "but the political and strategic stakes are the same." Without bipartisan congressional support for a concerted U.S. response to this threat, "the region's freedom will be lost and our security damaged in ways that can hardly be calculated." For at stake not only is "the destabilization of an entire region from the Panama Canal to Mexico"[1] but also the transformation of this area into what Jeane Kirkpatrick, an architect of the president's policy, calls "a system for the projection of Soviet military power."[2]

---

*This article was originally published in *World Policy Journal* 1 (Fall 1983): 181–200 and is reprinted with permission of *World Policy Journal* and the author. The current version was updated to July 1984.

[1] "President Reagan's Address," *New York Times*, April 28, 1983.

[2] "Kirkpatrick on the 'Contagion,' " *Newsweek* 101 (March 14, 1983): 22.

These conclusions were embraced by Reagan's advisers long before he assumed the presidency. In the 1979 *Commentary* article that brought her to the president's attention, Kirkpatrick argued that U.S. credibility was on the line in countries as small and poor as Nicaragua.[3] And in *A New Inter-American Policy*, Reagan's campaign advisers on Latin America concluded that "the Americans are under external and internal attack. Latin America . . . is being overrun by Soviet supported and supplied satellites and surrogates."[4]

This theme was quickly taken up by the Reagan presidency. Secretary of State Alexander Haig informed Reagan in private: "Mr. President, this is one you can win,"[5] while on the record he told a congressional committee that Central America is "an area of vital interest to the American people," adding, "I know the American people will support what is prudent and necessary, providing they think we mean what we mean and that we are going to succeed and not flounder as we did in Vietnam."[6] The president has echoed this alarm from his first week in office down to his recent speeches. Addressing the nation by television in May 1984, he once again invoked President Harry Truman's 1947 speech and once again defined the issue as "the Soviet Union . . . aid[ing] and abet[ting] subversion in our hemisphere," as it has done in Vietnam, Kampuchea, and Afghanistan, among others. The Sandinista rulers of Nicaragua were characterized as "a communist reign of terror . . . not content to brutalize their own land. They seek to export their terror to every other country in the region."[7] Heading into his reelection campaign, the president gave no evidence of changing course on Central America. On this issue, noted *Washington Post* columnist Lou Cannon, " 'Let Reagan Be Reagan' is irrelevant. The truth is that there is no way to stop Reagan from being Reagan."[8]

---

[3]"Dictatorships and Double Standards," *Commentary* 68 (November 1979): 36.

[4]Roger Fontaine et al., *A New Inter-American Policy for the Eighties* (Washington, DC, 1980), pp. 52–53.

[5]Laurence Barrett, *Gambling with History* (Garden City, NY, 1983), p. 207.

[6]"Excerpts from Testimony by Haig," *New York Times*, March 3, 1982.

[7]Televised address of May 9, 1984, reproduced in *Realism, Strength, Negotiation: Key Foreign Policy Statements of the Reagan Administration* (Washington, DC, 1984), p. 135.

[8]"Polls or No Polls, Reagan Will 'Be Reagan' on Central America," *Washington Post National Weekly Edition*, May 28, 1984.

"What serious person denies that there is a vital interest in preventing the spread of Sandinista-style regimes in Central America?"[9] That rhetorical question by George Will, a columnist close to Reagan, contains the two key components of the administration's warning: Sandinista-style regimes and the vital interests of the United States. If one thinks of U.S. policy toward Central America as an equation, then together these two elements yield the conclusion that the United States faces a threat of major proportions.

If by Sandinista-style regime one understands Soviet satellite, then the first element has a high threat value. Multiplied by almost any definition of vital interests, the outcome justifies a strong U.S. response. But what if Sandinista-style really means a nonaligned nationalist, yet Marxist state, the rough equivalent, in our sphere of influence, of Yugoslavia in the Eastern bloc? Then the threat attached to this element shrinks. To arrive at a crisis calling for U.S. intervention, it becomes necessary to inflate the concept of vital interests; for instance, to argue that U.S. interests are compromised by such ineffables as blows to our prestige, or possible doubts abroad about our resolve to act decisively.

In point of fact, it is far from obvious that "another Cuba"—meaning another Soviet satellite nearby—would jeopardize U.S. vital interests. Cuba presently drains Soviet resources without being a military asset that could withstand U.S. pressure in the event of a major confrontation. That, after all, is the lesson of the Cuban missile crisis. If it had to, the United States could quickly "neutralize" any Caribbean or Central American nation. To say, then, that a Soviet-dominated Nicaragua would affect our vital interests already concedes a great deal to the new conventional wisdom which links U.S. interests more to the appearances than to the realities of power.

Even granting that concession for sake of argument, one is left with the question: What precisely is it about Sandinista-style regimes that threatens our vital interests? Critics have attacked the Reagan administration on one or the other of these two elements. Major U.S. allies such as Mexico, France, and Spain have challenged the White House's assessment of the Sandinistas and the Farabundo Martí National Liberation

---

[9]George Will, "Our Central American Myopia," Newsweek 102 (August 1, 1983): p. 76.

Front (FMLN), claiming that Washington misreads their nature and intentions. At home, high officials from past administrations, including those in policy roles during Vietnam, question whether U.S. vital interests are at stake when no opposing big power is intervening in Central America. Not until both elements are examined together, however, will we know whether the crisis in Central America is as momentous as the administration claims.

It will be argued here that neither element—not the intentions and capabilities of the Sandinistas and the FMLN, nor the concept of vital interests invoked by the administration—warrants the inflated value given to it by President Reagan. Vital interests will be emphasized, for this is the more elusive of the two and hence the factor most easily manipulated by this administration. Bringing the key concept of national interests back to earth is a prerequisite for breaking the pattern of intervention in Central America, to which Washington habitually returns. Bringing it back to earth means demystifying "credibility" and the "domino theory," concepts to be taken up later in this essay.

CENTRAL AMERICAN MARXISM

In striking the parallel with Truman's policy of containment, President Reagan echoed his predecessor's words: "At the present moment in world history nearly every nation must choose between alternative ways of life."[10] It seems that the president either does not perceive, or will not entertain, the possibility of a Central American government being both Marxist and nonaligned—that is, not a Soviet satellite or base. On this, Reagan follows his tutor on Latin America, Ambassador Kirkpatrick, who excels at fitting Third World realities into procrustean Cold War categories: either friend or foe; if friend, authoritarian and potential democrat, while, if foe, totalitarian in fact or tendency.

There is no place in this thinking for the type of regime the Sandinistas not only are but, if left alone, also will continue

---

[10]"President Reagan's Address."

to be: highly nationalistic and internally oriented Marxists presiding over a mixed economy in which U.S. trade and investment could continue to play a role, a regime not anxious to be embroiled in foreign disputes. There is no comprehension that Marxism is the form that rejections of the status quo have taken historically in Latin America. In theory, other forms are possible; some may be more desirable. However, as many Latin American clergy, nationalist leaders, and committed intellectuals attest, Marxism is the vehicle at hand there, just as liberalism is the vehicle here.

The possibility the president excludes is the Marxism found among the Socialist leaders of Greece, Spain, Portugal, Italy, and France, except for one characteristic. While Western political processes have roots in these countries, the same is not true of Nicaragua and El Salvador where elections have never allocated the power concentrated in military and economic elites. The commitment to fully free and competitive elections may be as tenuous among the Sandinistas and the FMLN as it is, for instance, among the leaders of Mexico; it is too soon to tell.

Democracy, however, should not be at issue in the present debate, for it is preposterous to argue that the vital interests of the United States are tied to Latin American governments being democratic. No U.S. administration, including this one, has acted on that premise. In its attempt to normalize relations with Chile, Argentina, and Guatemala, the Reagan White House has treated not only democracy but also human rights as issues largely internal to those societies. "Quiet diplomacy," not ostracism or interference, has been the administration line. As "Koreagate" reminds us, the isolation of domestic politics from foreign manipulation is a tenet that Americans of both parties understand and support. Thus, it is both inappropriate and inconsistent for Reagan suddenly to take on the task of democratizing Nicaragua, a task he equates with returning the Sandinista Revolution to its original "contract" with, of all entities, the Organization of American States (OAS).[11]

---

[11]In his letter to the Contadora mediators in July 1983, President Reagan seemed to make the establishment of democratic institutions in Nicaragua a U.S. requirement for any negotiated solution. In press conferences he has repeatedly stated that the Sandinistas broke a contract with the OAS by not holding elections, suggesting that this must be remedied before there can be peace in the region. How minor a role the OAS played in the Nicaraguan revolution can be seen in William LeoGrande, "The Revolution in Nicaragua," *Foreign Affairs* 58 (Fall 1979): 34–38.

What should be at issue in U.S. policy toward Central America are the foreign relations of nations on our borders. What credence should be paid the White House's contention that Nicaragua has become a "platform" from which Soviet military power will spread south to the Panamá Canal and north to the Rio Grande? Is Nicaragua a Soviet satellite and does its relationship to the Salvadoran left reveal a domino effect in progress?

Before reviewing the evidence, we must clear away the rhetoric. A favorite ploy of the president is to manipulate the word "American" so that his listeners are left thinking that all authentic Latin Americans share our values, including democracy and capitalism as we understand them. "Here in the Western hemisphere we are Americans from pole to pole," the president likes to say. "In the commitment to freedom and independence, the peoples of this hemisphere are one." If we are all Americans, there can be no contradiction between U.S. interests and the freely determined interests of the Nicaraguan people, for example. As a "fellow American," Reagan would know what Nicaraguans want and when their revolution has been betrayed. Within this rhetorical framework, capitalism is indigenous, socialism alien; U.S. military assistance is internal, East bloc assistance "a new kind of colonialism [that] . . . has established footholds on American soil."[12]

Thus, Latin Americans who profess Marxism and revolution merely by so doing alienate themselves from the hemispheric community. They have, in the president's words, "turned from their American neighbors and their heritage." Betraying their followers, Cuban, Nicaraguan, and Salvadoran leftist leaders have gone over to "the other side," a term Reagan appointees use synonymously with "world communism." From here it is but a short step to asserting that "the Soviets and the Cubans are operating from a base called Nicaragua," and that the Salvadoran left consists of nothing but "professional guerrillas" who are "dedicated to the same philosophy that prevails in Nicaragua, Cuba, and, yes, the Soviet Union."[13]

---

[12]"President Reagan's Address," and an earlier speech on the Caribbean Basin Initiative, "Text of the President's Address," both in New York Times, February 25, 1982.

[13]Statements of President Reagan made in the two speeches cited in note 12 above, in an address to the International Longshoremen as excerpted in the New York Times, July 19, 1983; and at his press conference of July 21, reported in ibid., July 22, 1983.

The link to the Soviet Union established, the president and his advisers then go on to count all the Cuban, Nicaraguan, and FMLN resources as projections of Soviet power, as if the Kremlin can channel these heterogeneous and nationalistic forces to the fulfillment of its goals. Fred Iklé, the Pentagon's number three policymaker, in testimony before Congress, raised the specter of the Soviets moving into Central America the way they did into Eastern Europe in the aftermath of the Second World War:

> If we deny arms, ammunition and money to those fighting the Cuban-backed forces, if our allies and U.S. banks keep sending more money to Nicaragua than to El Salvador, if we force those who wish to build democracy to share power with those bent on destroying it [a reference to congressional pressure for a negotiated solution in El Salvador], then the military strength that the Soviets and Cubans have assembled in the region is quite adequate to turn Central America into another Eastern Europe.[14]

In this hysteria that passes for realism, we are swept to the outer limits of what is possible, with no pause to consider where Central America is located in contrast to Eastern Europe or why Soviet leaders would want to pursue a course that would leave them vulnerable to U.S. countermoves in their own sphere of influence.

The case for the Sandinistas or the FMLN acting as extensions of the Soviet Union, either directly or through Cuba, does not withstand scrutiny. The pronouncements and behavior of both groups belie the charge, as do the pronouncements and behavior of Cuba and the USSR, neither of which has identified its vital interests with the survival of Central American revolutions. While extending aid, advice, and moral support, Cuban and Soviet leaders have clearly indicated to both the Sandinistas and the FMLN that every revolution must stand or fall on its own. From the moment the Sandinistas came to power, Fidel Castro has urged them to recognize the realities of geography and underdevelopment by staying on as reasonable terms with Washington as possible. Cuban and Nicaraguan negotiating positions have generated consternation among the FMLN, since these proposals and the example of

---

[14]"Pentagon Calls Soviet Arms a Threat," New York Times, March 15, 1983.

Grenada make clear just how much the guerrillas are on their own.[15] While it is undeniable that consultation and assistance flow among the three sets of leftist leaders, it has not been proven that they act in concert, much less that they sublimate national objectives to the geopolitical designs of the Soviet Union.

However much the Kremlin might like to stir up trouble for Washington in Central America, it must be careful not to break the tacit agreement that keeps the United States from going too far in Poland or in Afghanistan. The interests of the Sandinistas and the FMLN, on the other hand, lie in the opposite course, in demonstrating to Washington that their presence in this hemisphere poses no threat to a U.S. hegemony they know they cannot escape. It would only make sense for Central American Marxists to challenge U.S. hegemony if they were assured of Soviet backing when the predictable White House hostility came down on their heads, as happened in Guatemala in 1954, in Cuba in 1961, and most recently in Grenada. But the Kremlin has not extended to these revolutions anything like the promise it gave the Cubans in exchange for withdrawing Soviet missiles under Washington's pressure. For the Soviets, once was apparently enough.[16]

That Soviet and Cuban advisers are in Nicaragua is indisputable. Both in numbers and in roles, however, they are inferior to their U.S. counterparts in neighboring Honduras and El Salvador. Salvadoran guerrillas consult in Havana and maintain offices in Managua. Rightist Cuban and Nicaraguan exiles train in Florida and consult in Washington. Were we to assume this pattern to be proof of Castro or Reagan's control over such groups, we would have to hold our government in violation of both U.S. and international law. In fact, Title 18, Section 960 of the U.S. Criminal Code renders illegal even the provision of arms to any group attacking governments with which we are formally at peace.

---

[15]"Salvador Rebels Urged by Allies To Seek Accord," New York Times, August 5, 1983.

[16]Those close to the negotiations orchestrated by the Contadora countries—Mexico, Venezuela, Colombia, and Panamá—treat as well known the Kremlin's unwillingness to run risks in Central America. "Both the Sandinistas and the United States know nothing further can be expected [of the Soviets]," stated a Contadora politician regarding the support that the Soviet Union now gives Central American revolutionaries. "Latin Letter," Latin America Weekly Report, June 24, 1983.

An analysis of almost any revolution, including our own in the 1770s, reveals foreign participation. Central America is no exception. In quantity and sophistication, Washington arms its side in this region far better than any other outside power arms theirs. The central truth is that arms and advice do not buy the will and direction that are decisive in these situations. National upheavals, not putsches, are what we confront in Central America. The administration's elaborate White Papers and slide shows, in which isolated evidence of the flow of arms is extrapolated into sweeping generalizations, not only fail as science by violating the rules of inference but also reveal a monumental misunderstanding of revolutions as historical processes.

In its second White Paper, the Reagan administration made much of "the Sandinista military buildup," implying that this buildup could only serve offensive purposes, including the funneling of weapons to the FMLN.[17] The paper, however, omitted all mention of the now 15,000 Nicaraguan exiles led, for the most part, by past officers of Anastasio Somoza's National Guard, and their attacks on Nicaragua from U.S.-supplied bases in Honduras and Costa Rica. More than $75 million has been invested by the administration in this ostensibly "covert" operation set in motion in late 1981. By July 1983 the costs inflicted on Nicaragua included 600 killed and $70 million in economic losses. It is hard to take seriously the administration's proposition that the Sandinista arms buildup has nothing to do with these attacks, especially since CIA analysts report that 80 percent of the Soviet arms reaching the Sandinistas are defensive in character.[18]

In closed-door testimony to Congress, CIA Director William Casey maintains what President Reagan states publicly: the primary objective of the largest paramilitary operation mounted by the United States since the Vietnam War is to interdict arms passing from Nicaragua to El Salvador.[19] But in

---

[17]"Background Paper: Central America," released by the departments of Defense and State, May 27, 1983. Then Undersecretary of State Thomas Enders opposed the release of this document which tries to float sweeping conclusions on old and fragmentary evidence.

[18]CBS Evening News, August 4, 1983.

[19]For a synopsis of William Casey's testimony, see "Nicaraguan Aid Called Not Vital," *Washington Post*, February 21, 1983. In his April address to Congress, President Reagan said: "Our purpose, in conformity with American and international law, is

the nearly three years the operation has been in existence not a single shipment of arms has been intercepted by the Contras, and it is hard to see how they could achieve this purpose by overrunning villages, burning crops, and distributing "comic books" that instruct Nicaraguans in sabotaging their economy.

One scans the press in vain for evidence of significant arms traffic from Nicaragua to El Salvador over the past three years, despite extensive surveillance by U.S. naval, air, and ground units.[20] All along the administration has claimed that it cannot reveal its best evidence without jeopardizing intelligence sources. In June 1984, however, former CIA analyst David MacMichael stated that "there has not been a successful interdiction, or a verified report, of arms moving from Nicaragua to El Salvador since April 1981."[21] Plausible reports surface sporadically of canoes and backpacks moving medicines and ammunition, but for weapons and basic equipment, the Salvadoran guerrillas apparently rely on the Pentagon. Thirty to 40 percent of the military aid that the United States gives the Salvadoran military passes to the FMLN, either through battle losses or black market sales. While absolute numbers have changed, the Salvadoran army has remained three to four

---

to prevent the flow of arms to El Salvador, Honduras, Guatemala and Costa Rica." In a press conference held May 4, however, the president referred to the Contras as "freedom fighters" intent on restoring a revolution which the Sandinistas had betrayed. Thus, the stated reason for the "covert" action hardly seems to be the real reason. Perhaps because he is aware of this contradiction, Reagan prefers to dodge questions about the CIA operation, asserting that its covert nature rules out public explanation. Since March 1982, however, virtually every aspect of the operation has been leaked to the public including when it was approved, the amount of its budget, which Contra groups are included, and where their bases are.

[20]One of the most experienced reporters covering Central America, Alan Riding, wrote that "no significant weapons shipments have been intercepted on their way to El Salvador in the last two years." "U.S. To Put Radar System in Honduras," *New York Times*, March 12, 1983. Other reporters corroborate Riding's conclusion. See, for example, "Nicaraguan Aid Called Not Vital"; and "Salvador Rebels Reported To Get Little Arms Aid," *New York Times*, July 31, 1983.

[21]Several newspapers carried David MacMichael's statement. As revealing as what this former marine said, however—as the *New York Times* editorialized on June 18, 1984—is that the administration supplied no evidence to refute him. In its third White Paper issued at the end of that month, the administration seemed to soft-pedal the entire issue. Yet the allegation of significant arms flow from Nicaragua to El Salvador had been the major rationale (known as "reciprocity") for Washington's violating U.S. and international law by arming and directing the Contras against Nicaragua.

times larger than its opponents. Thus, Washington conceivably is doing a better job of arming each guerrilla than of arming each soldier.[22]

Finally, there is the question of whether Nicaragua has been drawn into the Soviet economic orbit. Cuba, as is well known, is a member of COMECON—the East bloc trading group—and the recipient of Soviet subsidies. The Reagan administration implies that the same is true of Nicaragua. Of all the medium- to long-term loans secured by the Sandinistas since they took power in July 1979 until March 1982, two-thirds originated in the West: Western Europe, Latin America (minus Cuba), and the international agencies. Seventeen percent came from East bloc nations (six from the Soviet Union, less than one from Cuba), and 10 percent from Libya.[23] No doubt these proportions have changed in the ensuing years which have seen stepped-up U.S. pressure on international agencies and on U.S. banks not to grant loans to Nicaragua. The World Bank, for instance, has apparently not approved any new money since February 1982, while the multilateral funding, totaling $213 million in 1979, fell to $22 million in 1983. For private investors, however, "it has been pretty much business as usual," according to an executive of a U.S.-based multinational.[24] This too will change as Washington puts the screws on American businesses operating there. In the wake of President Reagan's May 1983 decision to slash Nicaragua's sugar quota by 90 percent, that country's trade with COMECON also may rise from the 6 percent of the total registered in 1982.

---

[22]The 40 percent estimate comes from Salvadoran social scientists using information available in that country. Out of concern for their safety, no further identification will be made. While not as precise, American reporters interviewing both U.S. and Salvadoran military officials present the same picture: quantities of U.S. arms passing to the guerrillas either through battle or through black market sales. See, for example, "Nicaragua Buildup," New York Times, March 9, 1983. Senator Daniel Patrick Moynihan, ranking Democrat on the committee that oversees the CIA, on occasion has used the 30 percent estimate.

[23]"Widening the Search for Credit," Latin America Weekly Report, November 12, 1982. This pattern is corroborated by Michael Conroy's study "External Dependence, External Assistance, and 'Economic Aggression' Against Nicaragua," available from the Kellogg Institute of the University of Notre Dame (1984). Of loan commitments (not dispersals) from 1979 to 1983, according to Conroy, the East bloc nations accounted for one-quarter of the total. Nicaragua's sources of external aid are now more diversified than they were under Anastasio Somoza.

[24]"Nicaragua Outlook Worries Executives," New York Times, August 15, 1983. In 1982 the Sandinistas adopted measures designed to attract foreign investors.

The pattern is clear: should the Sandinistas turn to the Eastern bloc for trade, aid, and weapons, Washington will have no one but itself to blame. To interpret such a drift as the Sandinistas "betraying their revolution" or "showing their true colors," is what sociologists call blaming the victim. An inspection of the changes inside Nicaragua over recent years, then, reveals little to sustain the administration's charge that it is becoming a platform for Soviet expansionism. In speeches to their own people, Sandinista leaders continue to characterize their goals as "a free, democratic, pluralist and new society free of exploitation."[25] Progress has been made on drafting the laws and institutions needed to carry out elections scheduled for November 1984. Government officials continue to scan Western Europe for the political and economic support they need to maintain a nonaligned position. Soviet MiGs and missiles have not arrived, despite countless claims by the administration that they were on their way.

Most important, the Sandinistas continue to state their willingness to enter verifiable agreements with their neighbors and with Washington which will close Central American borders to arms shipments, prohibit the installation of foreign military bases, limit foreign advisers, and rule out certain offensive weapons. Cuba has made clear its willingness to enter such arrangements, while Mexico has offered to serve as a guarantor. In short, Nicaragua seems prepared to foreclose its becoming what Washington fears it already is: a Soviet satellite.

To date, the administration's response to these diplomatic overtures has conformed to the strategy set forth in a classified National Security Council document, approved by the president in April 1983: "Step up efforts to coopt negotiations issue to avoid Congressional mandated negotiations"; "adopt more active diplomatic campaign to turn around Mexico and the Social Democrats in Europe [persistent promoters of negotiations]. In the meantime keep them isolated on Central American issues."[26] Over the past three years the White House has presented itself as favoring negotiations, while

---

[25]Speech given by Daniel Ortega on the fourth anniversary of the triumph of the revolution, July 19, 1983, León, Nicaragua: "To Defend this New Society," *Nicaraguan Perspectives* 7 (Winter 1983): 39.

[26]"National Security Council Document on Policy in Central America and Cuba," *New York Times*, April 7, 1983.

behind the scenes it has sabotaged them. With the 1984 presidential campaign upon us and polls indicating public dissatisfaction with Reagan's inability to negotiate in Central America and with the Soviets over nuclear arms, these appearances may take on new luster. The underlying reality, however, is that the president and his closest advisers apparently cannot accept the legitimacy of a Marxist regime in Central America, no matter how "correct" its foreign policy.

Wayne Smith, recently the ranking U.S. official in Havana, notes three instances in which Washington failed to pursue Cuban overtures. Two opportunities arose in the early months of the Reagan administration, another in April 1982. To Smith's tally now must be added a fourth opportunity in March 1983 when Republican Senator Lowell Weicker was refused a hearing at home after private conversations with Castro in Cuba, and a fifth following Jesse Jackson's visit.[27] In July 1983, Castro told U.S. television he was willing to abide by a general agreement that would isolate El Salvador and Nicaragua from foreign arms and military advisers. While the White House noted that the proposal was constructive, it did nothing in response except to say that Cuban deeds, not words, were needed.

By one calculation, "Nicaragua's overtures were rejected at least eleven times by Reagan administration officials."[28] Two days after Sandinista leader Daniel Ortega made concessions on the question of multilateral versus bilateral negotiations, while reiterating Nicaragua's long-standing offer to join a verifiable ban on foreign bases and arms trafficking, President Reagan told a press conference that it would be "extremely difficult" to achieve peace in the region as long as the Sandinistas remained in power.[29]

In March 1982 the Mexican government presented Washington with detailed proposals for negotiating solutions to the interlocking crises of Central America, thereby meeting administration charges that previous Mexican suggestions had

[27]Wayne Smith, "Myopic Diplomacy," Foreign Policy, no. 48 (Fall 1982): 157–74; "In Brief," Latin America Weekly Report, April 15, 1983. See also Seweryn Bialer and Alfred Stepan, "Cuba, the U.S. and the Central American Mess," New York Review of Books (May 27, 1982): 17–22.

[28]"In Search of Results," Washington Report on the Hemisphere, August 23, 1983.

[29]Daniel Ortega, speech, July 19, 1983; the president's press conference, July 21, 1983. A synopsis of the Nicaraguan proposals is found in "Sandinista Proposals," Latin America Weekly Report, July 29, 1983.

been too vague. Polite inactivity followed. By year's end Mexico helped form the Contadora group to bring regional pressure to bear on Washington. The Reagan administration began its search for other forums more amenable to its control and, finding little Latin American cooperation, devised its own special envoy. Reported the *Washington Post*, "Reagan is privately impatient with the [Contadora] group's efforts for a regional peace settlement and is concerned that the effort may be providing world respectability to Nicaragua, which had advocated a similar plan."[30]

Meanwhile, the military escalation outlined in leaked National Security Council plans has been carried out. Washington has aided the Contras and initiated unprecedented land and naval maneuvers on Nicaragua's borders. Administration officials claim this pressure fosters negotiations by making opponents realize that the alternative is blockade, invasion, or both. If the Cubans and Sandinistas have made anything clear in the past, it is their reluctance to negotiate with a gun pointed too obviously at their heads. However much the Sandinistas and the FMLN may want to trade concessions for survival, they cannot trade away their nature; they cannot make themselves non-nationalist, nonrevolutionary, and non-Marxist. No amount of military threat will wring from them concessions that amount to self-destruction, yet Washington seems bent on asking for nothing less.

Mexico has long believed in the possibility of a negotiated solution that would protect the legitimate, vital interests of the United States. On this, other governments which the White House considers allied and democratic, such as Venezuela, Colombia, and Spain, concur. If Nicaragua does not wish to become what Washington finds unacceptable—namely, a Soviet satellite and a country preoccupied with foreign revolutions—a diplomatic solution should not be hard to find. Then why does the Reagan administration stall?

Negotiated solutions are binding on all parties. Agreements that rule out Nicaragua becoming a Soviet base also limit Washington's ability to unseat the Sandinistas. Pacts that isolate the Salvadoran conflict from outside manipulation would curtail Washington's role there too. It is important to

---

[30]"U.S. Show of Force Decried," *Washington Post*, August 15, 1983.

be clear about this. The Sandinistas offer to trade their "right" to become a Soviet satellite—a formal right, not an option that the Sandinistas have pursued—for their right to survive, unmolested by Washington inside their own borders. The Reagan administration's refusal to explore this bargain suggests it wants something more; namely, not to have to contend with Marxist governments in its sphere of influence.

The last objective is understandable. Yugoslavias are a thorn in any superpower's flesh. But is it an objective required by the vital interests of the United States? Should a prudent administration pursue this objective when, in so doing, it runs the risk of driving the Sandinistas into the Kremlin's arms— as with Cuba in the 1960s—without either the Sandinistas or the Soviets preferring that outcome? On the surface, it would seem that the Reagan administration is gambling with U.S. vital interests instead of ensuring them. To understand this paradox, we must turn to the second element in the administration's perception of the Central American crisis: how vital interests are defined.

THE CREDIBILITY TRAP

By most traditional definitions, U.S. vital interests would be compromised by the presence of a Soviet satellite in Central America, yet Washington seems uninterested in negotiations that would preclude that possibility and seems embarked on a course that may make such a possibility more likely. Thus, there are two possible conclusions. Either the Reagan administration does not know what it is doing in Central America or it has a conception of U.S. vital interests that rules out any Marxist state in this hemisphere no matter how innocuous its foreign policy.

The first alternative is not flattering to the American political process or its current national leaders. Reporters whose work requires continuous contact with top policymakers are loath to spell out what seems clear between the lines of their stories; that is, decisions are being made by people who neither know much about Central America nor care to find out. As Washington journalist Laurence Barrett substantiates, "Neither Reagan nor any of the three ranking advisers in the White

House during 1981 had been a practitioner or even medium-serious student of foreign affairs."[31] By mid-1983 the president had restored the conditions of 1981 by banishing the one learner among his top advisers on Central America, Under-secretary of State Thomas Enders. Control over Central American policy was returned to the man who shaped it in the early months of the administration, William Clark, initially the number two man at State and later the president's National Security adviser.

A college dropout with no previous experience in foreign affairs, Clark's primary credential is a loyalty to Reagan which was established when the president was governor of California. At his 1981 Senate confirmation hearings, Clark could not define Third World. "Seldom has a man so inexperienced become so powerful in helping to shape United States foreign policy," observed White House correspondent Steven Weisman.[32] Clark presided over National Security Council meetings which, according to the *New York Times*, rarely last more than one hour "because those present do not have much background beyond their briefing papers."[33] Interdepartmental consultation on CIA activities involving career professionals from the relevant agencies—the norm under previous presidents—were replaced by meetings of a handful of top political appointees, most with no previous experience of Central America and Africa, the targeted regions.

> As a general rule, officials said those at the meetings were given no advance notification that proposed covert operations were to be discussed. . . . [P]apers normally prepared by the C.I.A. were passed out at the meeting itself and then collected at the end of the meeting. . . . Mr. Reagan usually makes his decision at the table.[34]

"What's troubling me," a middle-level official confided to the *Washington Post*, "is that everything we're doing suggests we've thought out the consequences of our policy and know where we're likely to be down the road." With bureaucratic

---

[31]Barrett, *Gambling with History*, p. 219.
[32]"The Influence of William Clark," *New York Times Magazine* (August 14, 1983): 17.
[33]"Shultz After a Year in Office," *New York Times*, August 1, 1983.
[34]"Shift Is Reported on C.I.A. Actions," ibid., June 11, 1984.

understatement, he added: "I'm not sure that's really happened."[35]

This is an explanation, however, that an outsider finds difficult to pursue, so we turn to the second alternative. Is there a case to be made for viewing the existence of non-aligned Marxist states in this hemisphere as a threat to the vital interests of the United States? "Events that used to be local," wrote Henry Kissinger, now "assume global significance."[36] "It is always difficult to take any particular piece of property," a prominent student of U.S. diplomacy has said about foreign territory, "and say we couldn't live without it. Its importance stems from its being seen in a particular context as part of a chain of possible events."[37] The key words are "significance," "seen," "context," and "possible."

What matters is the perception that onlookers bring to a situation, not the situation itself. Perception is colored by memories and fears born of times and places distant from the event at hand. Central America is submerged in memories of Munich and Vietnam and in fears regarding world communism. Spatially, the ramifications of Central America reach as far as the Persian Gulf. "If we cannot manage Central America," Kissinger stated shortly before being named head of the president's Bipartisan Commission on Central America, "it will be impossible to convince threatened nations in the Persian Gulf and in other places that we know how to manage the global equilibrium."[38]

In Reagan's speeches the pursuit of credibility sounds like this:

> If Central America were to fall, what would the consequences be for our position in Asia and Europe and for alliances such as NATO: If the United States cannot respond to a threat near our own borders, why should Europeans or Asians believe we are seriously concerned about threats to them? If the Soviets can assume that nothing short of an actual attack on the United States will provoke an American response, which ally, which friend will trust us then? . . . The national security of all the

---

[35]"Aides Propound Scenarios," *Washington Post,* July 31, 1983.
[36]Henry Kissinger, *The White House Years* (Boston, 1979), p. 68.
[37]Ernest R. May, quoted in "When Is a Foreign Interest 'Vital'? " *New York Times,* August 8, 1983.
[38]"The Return of Kissinger," *Newsweek* 102 (August 1, 1983): 18.

Americas is at stake in Central America. If we cannot defend
ourselves there, we cannot expect to prevail elsewhere.
Our credibility would collapse, our alliances would
crumble.[39]

While one dictionary of political terms defines "credibility" as
the "degree to which a country convinces a potential enemy
of its strength,"[40] it is clear from both the Kissinger and Reagan
statements that allies also must be convinced. So too must
publics at home and abroad because, without trust in leaders,
a "credibility gap" will limit Washington's ability to take those
actions which it thinks impress foreign governments. Therefore, the audience is diverse and limitless; its attention must
be held. The image of strength and the will to use it must be
continuously recreated.

At first blush it is hard to conceive of any Central American nation presenting a test to U.S. credibility. The gross
national product of the poorest of these countries might not
greatly exceed the annual sales of one of our supermarket
chains. In territory, Oregon is larger than Nicaragua, El Salvador, and Guatemala combined. Central America's natural
resources are few and redundant, its populations poor, and
its markets small. American credibility is implicated in this
region not because of what these countries are but because
of where they are located. Central America lies inside the U.S.
sphere of influence. For a superpower not to intervene to
obtain at least the appearance of success within its own sphere
is thought to communicate incompetence or loss of nerve.
Allies and enemies in distant lands will think us weak if we
do not impose our will. It is precisely within a big power's
sphere of influence that it is always assumed to have the means
to do so.

The Kissinger Commission Report is explicit in stating that
revolution per se is not the problem, only the triumph of
forces "hostile" to us in a region which "the Soviet Union calls
the 'strategic rear' of the United States." According to the
report, this "would be read as a sign of U.S. impotence." Such
sexual imagery is not uncommon. In the 1980 inter-American
policy paper, we find that "Latin America, the traditional alliance partner of the United States, is being penetrated by Soviet

[39]"President Reagan's Address."
[40]William Safire, *Safire's Political Dictionary* (New York, 1978), p. 148.

power" and "sterilized by international Communism." Here, however, I wish to dissociate "hostile" from "Soviet." In the Kissinger report it does not matter that the hostile government is or is not independent of the Soviet Union; all that matters is that its hostility is expressed within a region that the Soviets, and others, view as our strategic rear.[41]

At issue, then, is not what is happening in Central America so much as how those events will be viewed by leaders and publics that "truly " count. That Salvadoran Marxists are nationalists not likely to subjugate their interests to Soviet interests, and that it is unclear which Soviet purpose would be served by its penetrating El Salvador, considering the costs, are matters less relevant to U.S. leaders than what people may think in Jerusalem, Manila, or Riyadh. Washington maintains its credibility when these relevant publics think Washington means business. Since our leaders anticipate how these audiences will react, the precise description of credibility becomes whether we have it when we think that they think that we mean business.

The pursuit of credibility renders Washington vulnerable to perceptions it cannot control. It is reminiscent of David Riesman's classic study of the American character in which the anticipated opinions of others overwhelm any internal sense of what counts.[42] With vital interests linked to credibility, we deliver choices over to distant and potentially misinformed others, in pursuit of an image of standing as confident and resolute as John Wayne. It is quite a paradox.

Moreover, vital interests have become attached to a "domino theory," which again, paradoxically, tries to project confidence and strength through an inordinate fear of the future. In an early interview, Clark replied "we do" when a reporter asked if the administration feared a domino effect in Central America. Were the Duarte government to fall in El Salvador, said Clark, "then Cuba has prevailed and then it is truly a step in their divine plan to go on to Honduras, Guatemala, Belize and then, a true threat to Mexico itself." Never has Cuba looked so awesome. Never has a domino—Mexico— shown so little concern for its fate, which may explain the

---

[41]*The Report of the President's National Bipartisan Commission on Central America* (New York, 1984), p. 111.

[42]David Riesman, *The Lonely Crowd* (New Haven, 1950).

disdain shown Mexico in the National Security Council document referred to earlier. More recently Clark asked, rhetorically, "When will Mexico and the United States become the immediate rather than the ultimate targets?"[43]

Revolutionary movements have existed in Guatemala and Nicaragua since the early 1960s and in El Salvador since 1970. They made little headway in the years when the Cuban Revolution was fresh and its techniques were exported. On the contrary, only when and where guerrilla forces have matched their strategy to the local situation, making common cause with nonguerrilla organizations, have they gained momentum. In Nicaragua, the only Central American nation to see this process end in victory, momentum came at a time when revolution was on the wane elsewhere in the hemisphere and rightist militarism was riding high. Repression inside these countries, not leftist victories elsewhere, is the better explanation if we must settle for only one.

Implicit in the domino theory is a fear of the future captured in Kirkpatrick's concern over President Jimmy Carter's noninterventionist response to the Nicaraguan Revolution. Without clear U.S. support for Somoza, Kirkpatrick argued in 1979, "Our enemies will have observed that American support provides no security against the forward march of history."[44] If Washington is working against the march of history, it may well fear dominoes. Our leaders usually profess the opposite, however.

How can the United States project an image of strength and self-confidence in the world by panicking at the uncertainties that characterize our time? A truly strong and confident nation can afford to wait and see and would focus on opportunities to shape positive outcomes. Implicit in the domino theory is a mentality mired in fear of the unknown, accompanied by an itch to strike preemptive blows such as in Grenada. Both these characteristics show weakness, not strength.

The pursuit of credibility in Central America, ironically but not surprisingly, has made U.S. leadership less attractive to many allied governments. All the major countries surrounding Central America have come to view Reagan's administration as irrational and dangerous. They may fear Washington,

---

[43]"For Haig Deputy, On-the-Job Training," *New York Times*, March 13, 1981; "The Influence of William Clark," p. 17.

[44]"Dictatorships and Double Standards," p. 36.

as one fears a drunken driver on the road, but their trust in U.S. leadership has waned. In May 1983, Brazil's rightist president, General João Baptista Figueiredo, made clear that, "if the United States decides to intervene, it will be without our support," a statement all the more significant as Brazil was the only nation to send a sizable contingent of troops to Santo Domingo when the United States intervened there in 1965. Later in the summer the leader of the Democratic Action Party, now returned to power in Venezuela, complained about "the unbearable paternalism of the United States and its apparent distrust of any Latin American with a sense of self-respect."[45] The current president of Mexico, more assiduously courted by Reagan than any other Latin leader, has criticized the president on numerous occasions, recently underscoring the obvious truth that "the military interventions and naval maneuvers of the United States have created a greal deal of irritation in Latin America."[46] Even the small Central American nations most threatened by Nicaraguan and Salvadoran radicalism—Honduras and Guatemala—are pulling back from Washington's "helpful" embrace.

At home, despite repeated appeals for "a truly bipartisan approach," the administration's Central American policies have brought demurrals from ranking military officers, leaks from the bureaucracy, and resistance from Congress. In June 1984 the House of Representatives took the unprecedented step of voting to stop all funding for a covert operation then in progress. Unable to convince the legislature, the administration has been forced to fund its military solution outside normal channels. Over one-half the military assistance to El Salvador has by-passed Congress. The General Accounting Office found "improper" use of public funds to carry out U.S. military projects in Honduras, while the CIA-Contra operation has continued beyond deadlines by which, according to previous administration assertions, its funding would have been exhausted.[47]

In Western Europe 500 politicians signed a statement critical of Washington's pressures on Nicaragua, while the governments of key U.S. allies continue to send economic and,

[45]"Brazil Lays Down Challenge to Reagan," *Latin America Weekly Report*, May 6, 1983; "Respect for Latins," *New York Times*, August 14, 1983.

[46]"Mexico Asks U.S. To Change Policies," *New York Times*, February 13, 1984.

[47]"U.S. Agency Assails Pentagon on Use of Latin Funding," *New York Times*, June 26, 1984; "President's News Conference," ibid., May 23, 1984.

in one case, military aid to the Sandinistas. Spanish Prime Minister Felipe González echoed the sentiments of other members of the Socialist International when he characterized the Reagan administration's involvement in Central America as "fundamentally harmful."[48] Washington's attacks on Nicaragua have earned it embarrassing censures by the World Court and by the General Agreement on Tariffs and Trade, undermining the U.S. claim to world leadership based on respect for recognized international treaties.

Scanning the globe for relevant audiences, it is hard to find evidence that confidence in Washington's leadership has grown in response to Central American policies designed to foster that confidence. The reason for this paradoxical outcome is not hard to find. A definition of national interests that gives prominence to credibility will do just what Kissinger says it will: convert nearly every crisis in the world into a test of vital interests. While those at the fulcrum of U.S. power may enjoy the heightened sense of importance this conveys, others at home and abroad find the proposition ludicrous and frightening. Among individuals, are not paranoia and megalomania the words used to describe this illusion that every event is either a threat or a challenge of vital proportions?

This conception of vital interests may suit a world power prepared to go it alone to get its way through intimidation and intervention, but this is not the kind of world power most Americans conceive their country to be. It may be for this reason that eight Gallup polls, taken from April 1983 to May 1984, reveal a public approval of only 27 percent for Reagan's handling of Central America; that is about as low as a sitting president is likely to receive on a specific issue.[49]

RAISING STAKES AND FORFEITING OPTIONS

Stretched to the limit implied by credibility, the concept of vital interests loses meaning for precisely the "serious persons" George Will was addressing in the statement quoted

---

[48]Diana Johnstone, "Leftists Fight World Bank Blockade," *In These Times,* August 10–23, 1983; "Covert Action Vote Approaches," *Update,* July–August 1983.

[49]"On Central America, Reagan Is Consistently Unpersuasive," *Washington Post National Weekly Edition,* May 14, 1984.

earlier. Especially when they suspect they may pay for defending those interests, reasonable and prudent people demand a clear definition of the stakes. The response of the Reagan administration has been to turn up the volume on alarms it has reiterated since taking office.

The president accuses the press of "hype and hoopla." Yet his administration has provided misleading White Papers,[50] called a rare joint session of Congress in which Central America was compared to the onslaught of the Cold War, and has dispatched thousands of U.S. troops to an area that could explode at any moment. What this administration has failed to do is explain just how the vital interests of the United States are threatened by nonaligned Marxist regimes in underdeveloped ministates.

In President Reagan's response, one sees credibility's final irony and deepest trap. To demonstrate "resolve" in Central America, the White House needs Congress to fund its policies and the American public to support them. The way the administration tries to elicit this backing is by magnifying the threat. Having portrayed the stakes as higher than they really are, the White House escalates the test it must meet to salvage its credibility. In short, it bootstraps itself into a crisis of higher stakes and diminishing options.

By 1984 the United States had arrived at a point it had reached before, notably in Guatemala in 1954 and in Santo Domingo a decade later. Then as now, a U.S. president spoke of "the first real Communist aggression on the American mainland."[51] Having thus defined the situation, Washington has limited its options. Either it prevails militarily through surrogate troops if it can, or at least under the banner of the OAS, or it finds a diplomatic solution that requires a reversal of the rhetoric, a difficult-to-finesse de-escalation of the situation.

---

[50]The credibility of the first White Paper, "Communist Interference in El Salvador" (February 1981), suffered under the scrutiny of the *Wall Street Journal*, among others. Documents were attributed to guerrilla leaders who did not write them, and the reluctance of the Soviet Union, apparent from a close reading of the text, was played down in the conclusions. In briefings before Congress no less than in its White Papers, the administration has tried to parlay fragmentary evidence into portentous generalizations, using dubious extrapolations. The House Intelligence Committee finally called the administration on these practices.

[51]"Excerpts from the President's Speech," *New York Times,* July 19, 1983. Apparently Reagan's speechwriters are ignorant of John Foster Dulles having proclaimed Guatemala the "first" back in 1954.

Washington chose the former course in all previous encounters with nonaligned leftist movements in this region.

Nicaragua today is not, however, the Guatemala, Dominican Republic, or Grenada of previous U.S. "successes." The army is not split and its people show no signs of deserting the Sandinistas in a situation defined as nationalism versus foreign imposition, the definition Washington gives to the situation by its actions. Dislodging the Sandinistas from Managua only means sending them back to the hills from where, five years ago, they defeated a well-armed U.S.-trained National Guard.

More indirect strategies for achieving U.S. victory, such as a naval blockade, require a degree of cooperation from surrounding countries that becomes more difficult to imagine with every passing month. Washington cannot now command the two-thirds vote needed for an OAS action.[52] Is the White House prepared to fire on Mexican convoys running a U.S. blockade? Would it force its warships through the Panamá Canal should entrance be denied by Panamá for lack of OAS sanctions? Is getting our way worth sinking an inter-American system still floundering from the Falklands-Malvinas War?

Compared to scenarios based on the Reagan administration's ability to prevail, whatever the cost, the diplomatic option is attractive. Pursuing it to a conclusion, however, is not a task easily performed by officials who see a Soviet satellite in every Central American Marxist movement, or who conceive U.S. credibility to be on the line whenever a Latin American country grows hostile or unpredictable.

Reflecting public skepticism, Congress plays an ambiguous role. On the one hand, it denies the administration the resources needed to impose swiftly a U.S. solution on Central America. On the other hand, it is conscious that a Democratic House in the spoiler's role offers a Republican executive an opportunity to salvage its credibility by "staying the course" while Congress takes the rap for "losing" Central America. "Who among us," the president pointedly concluded his 1983 speech to both houses, "would wish to bear responsibility for failing to meet our shared obligation?"

---

[52]According to the secretary general of the OAS, "all the governments here support the Contadora." "Orfila Looks at the O.A.S.," *Washington Report on the Hemisphere*, August 9, 1983. If it attempted to invoke the Rio Treaty against the Sandinistas now, "the U.S. would find it extremely difficult to garner the necessary 14 votes." "Three War Scenarios," *Latin America Weekly Report*, July 29, 1983.

Maybe no one in public life will blow the whistle; maybe no one trusts the American public to understand. Public reticence is still perceived as a "Vietnam syndrome," not as a realistic appreciation of the limits of U.S. power. If politicians have the courage to challenge present U.S. policy in Central America—its premises, not simply its execution—they will have reason and prudence on their side.

David F. Ross

The Caribbean Basin Initiative: Threat or Promise?

O N FEBRUARY 24, 1982, President Ronald Reagan, in an address to the Organization of American States (OAS), proposed a new economic program for what he called "the Caribbean Basin."[1] Known as the Caribbean Basin Initiative (CBI), this program has not yet been put into effect.[2] Legislative action by the U.S. Congress is required. This has not been forthcoming and is by no means a certainty.[3] Should the necessary legislation be adopted by Congress, the second step in the implementation of the program would be the acceptance of its provisions by at least some of the Caribbean Basin governments. Discussed below will be the question whether those governments would be best advised, in that event, to regard the proposal as a threat or as a promise.

Either twenty-seven or twenty-eight governmental units have been designated as the potential "beneficiaries" of the CBI. These include the five Central American republics (one of which has no contact with the Caribbean), plus Belize and Panamá; seven European dependencies in or bordering on the Caribbean Sea (Anguilla, Antigua and Barbuda, the British Virgin Islands, the Cayman Islands, Montserrat, the Netherlands Antilles, and Saint Kitts and Nevis); nine insular nations in or bordering on the Caribbean (Barbados, Dominica, the Dominican Republic, Grenada, Haiti, Jamaica, Saint Lucia, Saint Vincent, and Trinidad and Tobago); one European dependency outside the Caribbean (Turks and Caicos Islands); one

---

[1]Alfredo Vásquez Carrizosa, "Comentarios a los Trabajos de R. Roett y A. Lowental" [sic], *Relaciones Internacionales en la Cuenca del Caribe y la Política de Colombia*, eds., Juan Tokatlian and Klaus Schubert (Bogotá, 1982), pp. 85–89.

[2]U.S., Department of State, Bureau of Public Affairs, *President Reagan: Caribbean Basin Initiative*, Current Policy no. 370 (Washington, DC, 1982).

[3]Riordan Roett, "La Administración Reagan y la Cuenca del Caribe: Una Perspectiva General," Tokatlian and Schubert, *Relaciones Internacionales*, pp. 71–80.

insular nation outside the Caribbean (Bahamas); and two South
American nations outside the Caribbean (Guyana and Suri-
nam). The possible twenty-eighth one is Cuba. Excluded are
the larger nations bordering on the Caribbean (Mexico, Colombia, and Venezuela), dependencies of the United States
bordering on the Caribbean (Puerto Rico and the U.S. Virgin
Islands), and the French departments of Guadeloupe and Mar-
tinique. The list of twenty-seven has been published by the
U.S. Department of State, accompanying the text of Reagan's
address to the OAS and also as part of a background paper
issued the following month.[4] The list of twenty-eight is part
of the proposed legislation introduced in the Senate on
March 18, 1982 by Senator Robert Dole at the president's
request.[5] From this list the president could designate as beneficiaries any which had expressed a desire to be so designated;
were not "Communist" (the term is undefined); and had not
nationalized, broken contracts with, or otherwise discrimi-
nated against U.S. investors, without making amends.

What has been described as the "key proposal," or the
"centerpiece" of the CBI is "one-way free trade."[6] This means
that a designated beneficiary could export its products to the
United States duty free without having to make any reciprocal
tariff concessions to imports from the United States. The principal exceptions would be textiles and apparel, articles of which
less than 25 percent of the value was produced in CBI countries (including, for this purpose, Puerto Rico and the U.S.
Virgin Islands), and sugar in excess of the amount allowed by
quota. There also would be escape provisions to be activated
when U.S. firms could establish that their interests were seriously injured by duty free imports. Other provisions of the
CBI are less innovative, having been included in previous U.S.
foreign economic assistance programs. However, they would
presumably be focused more strongly on CBI-designated
beneficiaries than in the past. These include tax incentives for

---

[4]U.S., Department of State, Bureau of Public Affairs, *Background on the Caribbean Basin Initiative,* Special Report no. 97 (Washington, DC, 1982).

[5]U.S., Congress, Senate, S. 2237, *Congressional Record,* 97th Cong., 2d sess.,
March 18, 1982, pp. S 2421–S 2426.

[6]"Reagan Announces Aid for Caribbean and Assails Cuba," *New York Times,*
February 25, 1982.

U.S. investors, financial aid, and technical assistance. The supplemental financial aid requested by President Reagan was authorized by Congress in September 1982, and the technical assistance can be provided under previously existing authorizations so that these elements of the CBI already have been put into operation. In this sense it can be said that the CBI is in place and functioning. But its major elements—the "centerpiece" of duty free access to the U.S. market and the special incentives to U.S. private investment in CBI countries—remain conjectural.

THE CBI AS A PROGRAM FOR ECONOMIC DEVELOPMENT

One of the major purposes of the CBI, as expressed in Reagan's address to the OAS, is to assist the countries of Central America and the Caribbean through trade, aid, and investment "to earn their own way toward self-sustaining growth." It has political and military objectives as well, which it may be thought necessary to emphasize in order to gain congressional approval for those measures that seem to involve conflicts with U.S. economic interests.[7] From the point of view of the potential beneficiaries, however, it is as a development assistance program that the CBI is of greatest concern.[8] This development assistance program is based upon a particular ideological and theoretical perspective, partly enunciated explicitly by Reagan and partly implicit in the terms and provisions of the proposal.[9] Nations determining whether to seek the status of beneficiaries must therefore decide not merely whether they want economic development and whether they want aid but also whether the particular kind of development for which aid is offered is consistent with their own interests.

---

[7]"Reagan's Blueprint," *U.S. News & World Report* 92 (March 8, 1982): 20–22.

[8]"Mitterrand, in U.S., Backs Caribbean Recovery Project," *New York Times*, March 13, 1982.

[9]Abraham Lowenthal, "Elementos para el Análisis de la Política Exterior de la Administración Reagan," in Tokatlian and Schubert, *Relaciones Internacionales*, pp. 81–83.

1) Export-led Development

In one of the earliest of the modern analyses of the development process, Paul Rosenstein-Rodan suggested that to be successful a development program must proceed synchronously throughout the various sectors of the economy. This has become known as the "balanced growth," or, less elegantly, the "big push" theory of development. It aroused widespread opposition, not so much because the reasoning was not cogent but because the conclusion was disheartening. No nation—certainly no underdeveloped nation—could possibly muster the resources to advance simultaneously on all fronts. Therefore, most development strategies proposed since then have attempted to demonstrate that development induced in a particular sector, or group of sectors, can be transmitted to the rest of the economy, causing generalized growth which then helps to sustain the induced growth in the leading sector. When this happens the result is described as "self-sustaining growth," the term used by Reagan. The question is what makes an effective leading sector. One can argue plausibly in favor of basic industries, which come at or near the beginning of the productive chain—iron, steel, energy, and petrochemicals, for example—or in favor of light consumer products at the end of the chain. In a country whose labor force is engaged primarily in agriculture, it can be reasoned that agriculture, being there, is the place to start; or that manufacturing, being absent, is the most urgent need. A compelling case can be made for developing facilities to produce goods now being imported which are therefore known to have a local market, or for expanding export industries which generate foreign exchange that can be used to buy needed technology and capital. Specifically, the CBI is a proposal for export-led development.[10] The beneficiaries would benefit primarily by obtaining greater access to a foreign market, in some cases for their traditional exports but more importantly for new export industries, since 87 percent of traditional Caribbean-area exports already enter the United States duty free.

---

[10]"Experimenting Under the Sun," *Time* 119 (May 24, 1982).

2) Bilateral Development Assistance

A nation aspiring to economic development also must make decisions concerning external development assistance. Apart from the basic question of whether to seek such assistance or attempt to go it alone, there are other questions concerning the different kinds of assistance that can be sought. Financial assistance may be in the form of grants or of loans, may be directed to particular projects or to an overall foreign exchange deficit, or may come with or without any of a number of restrictive conditions. Nonfinancial assistance may be a transfer of technology or the concession of some trading advantage. Aid of whatever kind may come from one particular foreign country (bilateral aid) or may be assembled from a variety of countries (multilateral aid). Multilateral aid may be funneled through an international agency such as the World Bank, may be a package put together through bilateral dealings with two or more countries, or may come through a mutual self-help organization such as a regional common market. Not all choices are available to all nations, and a nation which is determined to obtain assistance may feel at a particular time that it has no choice whatsoever. There is always, however, the option of refusal. Patterns of development and international relations, once established, are often difficult to change. A nation desiring to establish a particular pattern but finding available only a type of assistance appropriate to another pattern might be well advised to delay its plans rather than to start off along the wrong path.

The CBI is an extreme form of bilateral assistance program. This point needs to be stressed because it has been obscured in several ways. First, despite the name, this is not a program for the Caribbean Basin but rather one for selected individual nations in that general area. The obscurity on this point is particularly dense because comparisons have often been made between the CBI and the European Recovery Program (Marshall Plan) of 1948.[11] Under the Marshall Plan, assistance was offered to the nations of Europe on the condition that they get together and formulate a common plan for European recovery. Those nations that were eventually excluded

---

[11]"A 'Basin' Marshall Plan," *New York Times,* March 3, 1982.

from the program were left out not because they were Communist but because they declined to integrate their economic systems into that of the European economic community. The CBI does not seek the formation of a Caribbean economic community but rather the opposite.[12] The participating nations would compete against one another for benefits. Those which were successful would become more closely integrated, not with each other but with the economy of the United States.

Second, the official U.S. pronouncements concerning the CBI, beginning with President Reagan's address to the OAS, have represented it as emanating from a consortium of nations, whereas it is in fact being offered exclusively by the United States.[13] Canada, Mexico, and Venezuela, later joined by Colombia, have indeed participated with the United States in discussions about the problems of the Caribbean area and have agreed to continue and, in some cases, increase their assistance to developing nations in that region. They have not, however, adopted either the standards or the forms that distinguish the CBI from other development assistance programs. Rather than contributing to a common pool of resources, they will select their own aid recipients in terms of their own perceived interests and offer their own kinds of help. They will provide, in short, not a supplement but an alternative to the opportunities available through the CBI.[14]

3) Private Foreign Investment

A third area in which fundamental decisions must be made by a nation embarking on a development program concerns the role to be played by private foreign investment. Like the others, this involves not a single question but several layers of questions. Should the private ownership of productive resources be allowed at all? If so, should their ownership be restricted to nationals, or should it be permitted to foreigners?

---

[12]Ricky Singh and M. S. Wallace, "The Caribbean: Circle of Crisis," *South* (January 1981): 21–25.

[13]"Western Hemisphere: Caribbean Basin Initiative Reviewed by Foreign Ministers," U.S., Department of State *Bulletin* 82 (May 1982): 64–68.

[14]Richard E. Feinberg and Richard S. Newfarmer, "The Caribbean Basin Initiative: A Bilateralist Gamble," *Foreign Policy*, no. 47 (Summer 1982): 133–38.

In the latter case, what precisely is the definition of "foreigner"? A Wisconsin dairyman who sells his farm, moves to Jamaica, and opens a milk-drying plant is not the same as the establishment of a branch operation in Jamaica by the General Foods Corporation. If direct foreign investment, however defined, is to be permitted, should it be permitted generally or restricted, as in Mexico, to certain types of productive operations? Should it, moreover, merely be permitted, or should it be promoted actively through such devices as tax incentives? There are obvious advantages to foreign investment for a developing nation: access to capital, technology, skills, and marketing channels are among the greatest.[15] The disadvantages are not so obvious, and the one most frequently cited may be spurious, a fact which tends to discredit arguments against foreign investment generally. The draining off of profits from the national economy to foreign owners is not likely to appear as a legitimate subject for complaint to disinterested and economically literate observers. The investment would not have been made in the first place without the expectation of profit, and would probably not have been made by foreign investors if national investors had been willing and able to exploit the opportunity. Of the total revenue generated by the enterprise, the appropriate question is not whether anything leaves the local economy but whether anything remains. Whatever does remain, even if it is only the wages of unskilled labor, is a net gain in terms of this kind of accounting.

The true drawbacks to foreign investment must be sought, rather, in terms of less tangible, or at least less quantifiable, effects. Opportunity costs, externalities, dynamic consequences, and self-determination are some of the principal areas in which they may be found.[16] Suppose that there is a choice between establishing a small factory with local capital and a large factory with foreign capital, perhaps a furniture manufacturing establishment, to pick an example in which economies of scale are not necessarily a significant factor. In the first place, the development agency is probably not aware that it is forced to make a choice at all. It does not typically

---

[15]Peter Johnson, "The Caribbean Basin Initiative: A Positive Departure," ibid., pp. 118–22.

[16]Sergio Aguayo and Cesáreo Morales, "El Futuro de la Cuenca del Caribe según la Administración Reagan," in Tokatlian and Schubert, *Relaciones Internacionales*, pp. 15–70.

prohibit or discriminate against local investment. If the opportunity exists, and local investors fail to take advantage of it, that is their choice and not the choice of government planners.

Such neutrality is an illusion, however, for two reasons. First, while the existence of a locally owned furniture plant would not inhibit the establishment of one by foreign investors, the existence of a foreign-owned one would probably prevent the opening, or compel the closing, of any such national operation. This follows from the advantages of foreign investment already cited. If the development agency says yes to the foreign investors, it is therefore saying no to any conceivable local investors, not merely those who are at present neglecting to seize the opportunity but also those who in the future might be ready to seize it. Second, a policy of passive nondiscrimination is actually a discriminatory policy between groups of different backgrounds. Since this is a new industry for the nation, there are no local investors with experience in the furniture industry, while the potential foreign investors are already furniture manufacturers merely looking for a better location to continue in a field where they are already successful. To equalize opportunity in such a situation requires an affirmative action program for local investors. It is not enough to open the door; you also must go out and look for people, show them where the door is, teach them how to operate it, and acquaint them with the benefits and challenges to be found behind it. Meanwhile, you must make sure that those who already possess this information do not fill all the spaces at the head of the line.

Development agencies commonly engage in a certain amount of such affirmative action, primarily because they find it politically advantageous to do so. They are often unaware that it is also economically advantageous. Because they are not only more difficult to get established but also tend to be smaller and less successful, local firms are likely to seem less desirable than their foreign counterparts as building blocks of economic development. The error lies in perceiving economic development as something to be assembled, like a building, rather than as an organic process.

The difference may be illustrated by continuing the example of the two furniture factories. The production of furniture, or virtually anything else, requires the bringing together of a substantial number of material and nonmaterial inputs. Some of these—manual labor and electric power, for example—will have to be obtained locally; others, such as machine tools and diesel fuel, will have to be imported. In between these extremes, there will be a great many, including technical and managerial personnel and sawmill products, which might either be obtained locally or imported, although not necessarily with equal facility. Potential local suppliers of material inputs are likely to have difficulty meeting the accustomed standards of the industry in terms of quality, uniformity, quantity, and the scheduling of delivery. Potential local technical and managerial personnel are likely to fall short of industry standards in terms of training and experience as well as in attitudinal and motivational factors. The local investor, and to some extent the immigrant foreign investor, will tend to do everything possible to overcome these difficulties. This is the market that he knows, and these people are his friends and relatives, associates and countrymen. For the corporate foreign investor, exactly the opposite situation prevails. Even with an honest intention to use local inputs whenever possible, "possible" will be understood to mean "just as good and just as cheap" as the accustomed inputs already available from outside the local market.

The significance of all this is that these are the linkages that are supposed to make it possible to transform an economic system by inducing change in one sector. Without these, a new manufacturing establishment is significant only for the jobs that it provides. This leads to two further questions: can foreign investment be attracted in ways that will induce it to establish linkages to the local economy; and what is wrong with merely creating jobs?

Governments which have become aware of the tendency of foreign investors to create enclaves rather than growth centers can and do in some cases impose requirements to counter this tendency. These include conditions that local personnel be trained within a specified time to take over jobs originally assigned to foreign supervisors and technicians, and that local sources of supply for imported inputs be found or cultivated within similar periods. This type of measure can be effective if the foreign investor has any reason to accept conditions which, from his point of view, are suboptimal. Such willingness could exist if the local market for the product were of significant size and could be entered only by local production in accordance with such conditions. On this basis, Mexico has had some success with this approach. Another reason would be that the nation possessed a rare resource which could be exploited only by acceptance of such conditions. The relevant resource in connection with manufacturing investments in the Caribbean region is cheap labor in close economic proximity to the United States. This could conceivably be used effectively in bargaining for the acceptance of conditions by foreign investors, as might the Caribbean market, but in both cases only if the nations involved agreed to a common bargaining position and adhered to it. The history of past efforts to establish regional, as opposed to national, economic policies in Central America and the Caribbean strongly suggests that such collective action is unlikely in the absence of strong external pressure. The CBI, with its exclusively bilateral approach, would be external pressure against the recognition of any community of economic interest in the Caribbean.

Under these circumstances the factory built by foreign investors rarely contributes anything to the local economy except production workers' jobs and payroll. Is this not, however, enough? Even if the branch plants of foreign manufacturing firms did nothing but reduce or eliminate unemployment, this would be a tremendous benefit in itself and moreover would buy time and free resources that could then be applied to finding other means of attaining self-sustaining growth. The short answer to this question is unfortunately not. The longer answer, which would explain the mechanisms and relationships involved, has not been sufficiently investigated, is not as yet well understood, and in any case is beyond the scope of the present paper. The facts, however, are unmistakable. Unlinked foreign manufacturing operations implanted in a less developed economy do not increase employment and often do the opposite. Traditional jobs tend to disappear more rapidly than nontraditional ones are created, and rural-to-urban migration of the labor force tends to exceed job creation in urban industry. Perhaps this has to do with the creation of expectations at a rate above that of the means for their fulfillment; perhaps it has to do with a distortion in the wage-price structure of the economy, or perhaps it has to do with something else not yet discovered. It seems to contradict the fundamental psychological assumptions underlying economic theory, but it would not astonish biologists. You cannot introduce a new element into an eco-system without affecting all the other elements and altering the entire system of interrelationships among them, often in unanticipated ways.

In sum, the CBI is a development assistance program based on a particular set of assumptions concerning what would be good for the Caribbean-area nations.[17] It assumes, in the first place, that they would be best served by a development pattern in which export industries are the leading sector. This is a plausible assumption, if only because the domestic mar-kets of these nations are quite small. It is a dubious assump-tion, however, since the vigorous development of export sectors in these same economies in the past has not in general led to self-sustaining growth. In the second place, it assumes that the nations of the Caribbean region would be best served by having their economies individually linked to the economic system of the United States rather than by their being linked to each other or to world markets generally. This is also both a plausible and a dubious assumption. It is plausible because the U.S. market is larger and more varied than any other, as well as being close at hand. It is dubious because the linkage of small and less developed economies to large, prosperous, industrial economies has not always worked to the advantage of the former. In the third place, it assumes that private U.S. investment has more to offer to the nations of the region than any alternative source or form of capital.[18] Like the others, this assumption is both plausible and dubious. It is plausible because U.S. private capital is plentiful and comes with access to the U.S. market. It is dubious because the establishment of linkages to the local economy has a low priority to, and is often contrary to the interests of, private foreign investors.

These three underlying assumptions of the CBI are identical with those underlying the Puerto Rican development program which has been in operation for forty years and which in that time has radically transformed the economy of this other Caribbean island, the least of the Greater Antilles. This has raised the question, addressed by Reagan in his announcement of the proposal to the OAS, whether Puerto

---

[17]"Caribbean Views Plan as 'Bold,' but Not 'Miracle,' " *New York Times*, Feb-ruary 25, 1982.

[18]U.S., Department of State, Bureau of Public Affairs, "US Interests in the Caribbean Basin," *Gist* (May 1982).

Rico's development would be adversely affected by making available generally in the Caribbean area advantages that up to now have been available to Puerto Rico alone.[19] That is clearly the question of paramount importance to Puerto Ricans. For the twenty-seven or twenty-eight potential beneficiaries of the CBI, however, the relevant question is quite a different one: do they want to undergo an economic transformation along the lines of the Puerto Rican model?

PUERTO RICO AS A MODEL FOR CARIBBEAN DEVELOPMENT

Puerto Rico's experience with economic development, based on private investment in export industries under a bilateral arrangement with the United States, has been ambiguous.[20] In its forty years of operation, the development program has been outstandingly successful by most conventional measures. What was, before the program got under way, a plantation economy, almost totally dependent upon sugar, tobacco, and coffee, has become one of those advanced economies—in terms of Colin Clark's schema—in which the agricultural sector is dwarfed by both manufacturing and services. More than 2,000 factories have been established, producing goods ranging from brassieres to petrochemicals. People who as young adults carried lard tins on their heads to bring water to their homes are now the grandparents in families which have not only piped-in potable water but also electricity, telephones, television, and a car in the driveway. If these are taken as indicators of economic development, then Puerto Rico has benefited from what is certainly one of the most successful development programs the world has ever seen. These achievements were made possible, moreover, by the fact that Puerto Rico, being within the U.S. customs system but outside the U.S. internal revenue system, could offer investors duty

---

[19]Baltasar Corrada, "The Caribbean Basin Initiative: Puerto Rico Will Benefit," *Foreign Policy*, no. 47 (Summer 1982): 126–28; Rafael Hernandez-Colon, "The Caribbean Basin Initiative: Puerto Rico—Partner or Victim?" ibid., pp. 123–25.

[20]Sidney Weintraub, "The Caribbean Basin Initiative: A Flawed Model," ibid., pp. 128–33.

free access to the American market, together with tax incentives not available on the U.S. mainland (essentially the same package of attractions that would be made available under the CBI).

By other measures, however, Puerto Rico's situation does not appear so enviable. Unemployment, as a percent of the labor force, has fluctuated but has never shown a long-term downward trend and is now about 25 percent, roughly what it was before the development program got under way. In absolute numbers, unemployment has increased substantially. In the fundamental sense, Puerto Rico has remained a plantation economy. Its products are no longer primarily agricultural but its people still produce virtually nothing capable of satisfying their own needs and depend for their subsistence almost entirely upon imports. Dependency upon ties with the U.S. economy is now far greater than when Puerto Rico was a sugar island.[21] Then, if the ties had been cut, sugar could have been sold on the world market. There would have been a severe financial loss involved, but survival would have been possible. Today, by contrast, the products are mostly components of U.S. manufactures, worthless except to the parent companies. The effects of this dependency are aggravated by the fact that to many multiplant firms the Puerto Rican operation can most conveniently be utilized as a cushion for the more fully integrated mainland operations. When sales decline, production cutbacks can be concentrated in the Puerto Rican plant, causing little damage to the firm's public image and labor relations at home. A minor recession on the mainland thus becomes a major depression on the island, while a mainland recovery must be strong and sustained before its effects are felt there.

Despite these serious problems, there can be no doubt that the standard of living in Puerto Rico has improved substantially under the development program. Relative to their Latin American and Caribbean neighbors, although not to their counterparts in the United States, the Puerto Ricans have become prosperous. The ties that bind this nation ever more tightly to the United States have been offensive and destructive to Puerto Rican culture and dignity, but they have driven

---

[21]Jenny Pearce, *Under the Eagle* (Boston, 1982).

off the specters of hunger and other forms of material deprivation. Except for a small band of militant nationalists, Puerto
Ricans appear to have toted the balance sheet in their favor.
In the early years of the development program, the dominant
political party maintained a studiously noncommittal stance
on the question of statehood versus independence, but its
principal leaders were known to favor greater independence
and eventual full independence. The second largest party was
outspokenly in favor of independence. The party approving
statehood, consisting mainly of sugar producers and their
hangers-on, was a poor third. Today, the defenders of the
status quo mainly favor eventual statehood, the party advocating statehood now has held the governorship for twelve of
the past sixteen years, and the *independentistas* barely elect
enough legislators to remain a viable organization.

Given this clear indication of approval by the Puerto Ricans
of their CBI-type relationship to the United States, based on
forty years of experience, how can there be any question that
a similar relationship would be equally acceptable to the people of other Caribbean-area nations? The answer is that the
strands that bind Puerto Rico in a relationship of dependency
to the U.S. economy include, but are not limited to, the terms
being offered elsewhere under the CBI. Tax incentives to
investors and duty free access to the U.S. market have indeed
radically transformed the Puerto Rican economy, but they are
not the forces that have driven away the specters of material
deprivation. Because of their peculiar status within the U.S.
system, Puerto Ricans are able to accept their chronic unemployment rate of 25 percent or more without severe suffering.
Even as second-class American citizens, Puerto Ricans participate in federally funded programs of aid to families with
dependent children; retirement pensions; unemployment
insurance; food stamps; public housing; grants-in-aid for education, highway construction, and public health; and many
other income-generating or income-supplementing activities
which elsewhere in the Caribbean region must be paid for, if
at all, entirely with local resources.

Perhaps of greatest importance, Puerto Ricans can emi-
grate without restriction to the U.S. mainland. Fully one-third
of all Puerto Ricans now living in the world live off the island.
Probably an even larger proportion of those living on the island

at any given time have in the past responded to relative economic opportunities by moving temporarily to the mainland and will do so again, or are receiving remittances from relatives living on the mainland. None of these provisions is included in the CBI package. In fact, both President Reagan and Secretary of State George Shultz have indicated that a reduction in immigration from Central America and the Caribbean is one of the benefits that they expect from the CBI.[22]

In brief, the significance of the Puerto Rican model for those nations considering how to respond to the CBI proposal is not that they are being given the opportunity to follow in Puerto Rico's footsteps. It is, rather, an opportunity to industrialize, urbanize, become totally dependent upon the vicissitudes of the U.S. economy and foreign policy, exchange a high rate of rural poverty for a high rate of urban unemployment, and, at the same time, participate in none of the attributes of Puerto Rico's status which have made this transformation tolerable there.

THE CBI: AN EVALUATION

Various difficulties confronting the CBI proposal have been pointed out by other commentators. The program will encounter strong opposition in Congress, principally because of the centerpiece of "one-way free trade."[23] The same provision would violate the General Agreement on Tariffs and Trade (GATT).[24] Both of these problems are political, rather than economic, and therefore outside the scope of this paper. The Reagan administration may be able to pass the program through Congress, and its position on the Law of the Sea treaty suggests that it would not be greatly troubled by the consequences of simply ignoring GATT. Other critics have suggested that, if adopted, the program would not best serve U.S. interests because our policy of combatting communism

---

[22]U.S., Department of State, Bureau of Public Affairs, *U.S. Approach to Problems in the Caribbean Basin,* Current Policy no. 412 (Washington, DC, 1982).

[23]"3 Caribbean Premiers Defend Reagan's Development Plan," *New York Times,* June 18, 1982.

[24]Aguayo and Morales, "El Futuro de la Cuenca del Caribe según la Administración Reagan," pp. 15–70.

by supporting repressive regimes is inherently self-defeating.[25] This may well be true, but it is also outside the range of this paper, which is concerned with the possible effects of the program on its recipients. Critics who have addressed the latter question have indicated that the program would be beneficial but of minor impact.[26] If they are correct about the degree of impact, then it is of no great importance whether the program is enacted or not, or whether it is, on balance, beneficial or harmful to its recipients. It is therefore this issue which most fundamentally demands resolution in any attempt to evaluate the probable effects of the program on the nations of the Caribbean region.

Analyses of the centerpiece provision of the CBI—duty free access to the U.S. market—emphasize the small range of U.S. imports from the affected nations that would fall under this provision. Eighty-seven percent of the total is already admitted duty free; another 3 percent consists of textiles and apparel, a category specifically excluded by Reagan; and another 5 percent consists of products subject to quota (principally sugar) and products ineligible because too large a proportion of their total value is produced outside the Caribbean region. This leaves only 5 percent which could be stimulated by duty free treatment. Of this small residual, more than 47 percent is beef, which is subject to only a 2 percent duty, the export of which from the Caribbean region is probably constrained more by productive capacity than by tariff protection. The remaining eligible products are of such small importance that even large percentage increases would be trivial in absolute amount.[27]

There are, however, two serious defects in this analysis. The first is the implicit assumption that only products already being sold by nations of the Caribbean region to the United States would be affected by tariff exemption. This assumption is consistent neither with logic nor with the relevant Puerto Rican experience. Logically, the greatest opportunities for investors created by a tariff exemption would be in producing

[25]Abraham F. Lowenthal, "The Caribbean Basin Initiative: Misplaced Emphasis," *Foreign Policy*, no. 47 (Summer 1982): 114–18.

[26]Richard E. Feinberg and Richard S. Newfarmer, "El Impacto Económico de la Iniciativa para la Cuenca del Caribe," in Tokatlian and Schubert, *Relaciones Internacionales*, pp. 91–113.

[27]Ibid.

goods subject to high tariffs, products for which U.S. producers have obtained protection and which therefore are not now being imported from the Caribbean region in significant amounts. This reasoning conforms to the experience of Puerto Rico where almost all of the new plants established under the development program undertook the production of goods not previously made there.

The second error is that the analysts have fallen into a trap set by Reagan in announcing his proposal. Despite rhetoric, this is not a plan for the development of the Caribbean Basin but rather a plan for the establishment of bilateral relationships with particular individual nations within the Caribbean region. Aggregate regional trade data, therefore, have little or no relevance. A couple of examples will make this obvious. Although beef is the principal dutiable and eligible export product of the region, most of the twenty-seven or twenty-eight nations involved do not export it at all. One of the reasons given by President Reagan for the region's critical need for economic assistance is its dependence on imported oil, yet 59 percent of total regional exports to the United States is accounted for by petroleum. What need to be analyzed are not the regional data but the data for each of the nations involved. The question to be addressed is not merely what do they now sell which they could sell more of if it were duty free but also what do they not now sell that they could produce and sell if it were duty free.[28]

Analyses of the investment tax incentives included in the CBI proposal also have failed to note that their true focus is not regional but nation by nation. For the region as a whole, political instability rather than taxation is the barrier to investment. Investors who fear the destruction or confiscation of their capital are not likely to be much influenced by considerations of profit maximization. Capital flight, instead of a sluggish inflow of capital, is the problem of the region when viewed in the aggregate.[29] Again, however, it is clear that this is the result of special conditions in particular nations whose data overwhelm those of the others. U.S. investors, with good

---

[28]U.S., Department of State, Bureau of Public Affairs, "Caribbean Basin Initiative," *Gist* (February 1982).

[29]Jonathan Sanford, *Caribbean Basin Initiative*, Issue Brief no. IB82074 (Washington, DC, 1983).

reason, are nervous about their assets in some Central American republics, and at various times in the past they have had just reason—in Trinidad, Jamaica, Haiti, Cuba, the Dominican Republic, the Bahamas, Anguilla, and Grenada, for example. Never, however, have U.S. investors been repelled from the Caribbean region as a whole.[30] Indeed, whereas local investment in El Salvador and Guatemala, for example, may well seek greater security by moving to Switzerland or Miami, U.S. investments are more likely to be shifted to another Caribbean nation just as they were to Puerto Rico and the Dominican Republic following the revolution in Cuba.

It must be concluded then that, while the CBI might very well exert a minimal effect upon the Caribbean region as a whole, its impact upon particular nations within the region could be significant. It is probable, in fact, that the fewer the nations which accept its terms and to which it is applied, the greater the impact on those nations. It is, moreover, one by one, rather than as elements of a regional system, that the nations of the Caribbean region must decide how to respond to the Reagan initiative. Whether it is to be regarded as a threat or as a promise cannot be determined on the basis of how it will affect the region in the aggregate, or the average nation within the region, but rather on the basis of how it will affect one's own particular nation.

The answer appears to be like that of a marriage proposal; it is a mixture of threat and promise. Willingness to accept the penetration of foreign investment will be rewarded by a higher level of statistically measurable income. A considerable loss of freedom will be involved. Absolute fidelity will be demanded but not offered reciprocally. Within a short time there will be a flock of dependents, unable to feed, clothe, and house themselves, and the higher income will never be quite enough to provide for their needs. The relationship, finally, will prove to be a great deal easier to get into than to get out of. It can be argued that marriages would never be contracted on the basis of a strictly objective comparison of costs and benefits, and that the only relevant question is whether a strong enough attraction exists between the two parties. Perhaps this is also true of the CBI proposal. For a

---

[30]U.S., Department of State, Bureau of Public Affairs, *Programs Underway for the Caribbean Basin Initiative*, Current Policy no. 442 (Washington, DC, 1982).

nation that wants to become one flesh with the U.S. economy, this offer may be the best one that can be expected, and the painful adjustments that would be required, along with the necessity of accepting a position of inferiority and dependency, may be a small sacrifice to make. For a nation that does not feel this attraction, the same sacrifice could be overwhelming.

Thomas W. Walker

Nicaraguan-U.S. Friction:
The First Four Years, 1979–1983

IN THE FIRST FOUR YEARS following the Sandinista victory in July of 1979, relations between the U.S. and Nicaraguan governments degenerated from a state of nervous correctness and guarded hope to bitter hostility bordering on war. This outcome, though certainly not inevitable, was far from surprising. Mutual distrust had existed from the start. In large part it was based in the strikingly different world views of the two sets of policymakers. The conventional wisdom among U.S. foreign policymakers is that Latin American social problems are simply a matter of underdevelopment and backwardness and can be solved by greater unregulated involvement in the world economy and by incrementalist social programs. Thus, for U.S. policymakers real social revolution is not only unnecessary, and perhaps even immoral, but also undesirable because in breaking old power patterns it opens opportunities for "Soviet-oriented Communist" penetration.

On the other hand, the Sandinistas, like a growing preponderance of young Latin American intellectuals, view the region's acute social problems as a product of an international economic system which misuses the means of production, generates income concentration, and creates and reinforces the position of an intransigent, tiny, privileged elite. For them, real social change cannot be achieved short of a violent social revolution which would alter the relationship between classes and allow a new government to manage the country's domestic and international economic life for the benefit of the majority. Thus, in 1978 and 1979, while the Sandinistas struggled to overthrow not only Anastasio Somoza but also the elitist system which he ran, the Carter administration reluctantly came to pursue a policy of promoting what many called "Somocismo without Somoza" which, while jettisoning the U.S. client-dictator, would have preserved old class relationships and political structures (such as Somoza's hated Nicaraguan National Guard and Liberal Party), while essentially excluding mass-based organizations such as the Sandinista National Liberation Front (FSLN).[1]

After the revolutionary victory, both sides sincerely tried to get along. For their part the Sandinistas knew that their country could ill afford to be excluded from the Western economic system. The Soviets, after all, had let it be known on a number of occasions that they were not willing to shoulder the expense of "another Cuba" in the Americas. For its part the Carter administration was aware of that fact, too, and apparently hoped that by being friendly and supplying aid it could co-opt the revolution from within and defuse it as the United States appears to have done with the Bolivian Revolution two decades earlier.

The Sandinistas, however, were much clearer in their revolutionary objectives than had been the Bolivian Nationalist Revolutionary Movement. Therefore, when the United States answered a Sandinista request for arms by insisting that such supplies be tied to U.S. training for the Sandinista People's Army, the Nicaraguans turned instead to the Socialist bloc for their weaponry.

The Carter administration's leverage in Nicaragua was further diminished by its unexplained failure to use its considerable influence to convince the government of Honduras to dismantle the armed camps in which thousands of Somoza's exiled National Guardsmen were menacingly housed a short distance from the Nicaraguan border. Finally, even the potential of foreign aid leverage was all but eliminated when Congress stalled a $75-million economic aid package for almost one year and ended up imposing a number of humiliating restrictions.[2]

It is intriguing to speculate how U.S.-Nicaraguan relations might have evolved had President Jimmy Carter been reelected.

---

[1]For additional description and analysis of U.S. policy toward Nicaragua in 1978 and 1979 see Thomas W. Walker, *Nicaragua: The Land of Sandino* (Boulder, CO, 1981); and William M. LeoGrande, "United States and the Nicaraguan Revolution," and Susanne Jonas, "The Nicaraguan Revolution and the Reemerging Cold War," in Thomas W. Walker, ed., *Nicaragua in Revolution* (New York, 1982), pp. 63–78, 375–90.

[2]Jonas, "Nicaraguan Revolution and the Reemerging Cold War."

Be that as it may, the inauguration of Ronald Reagan was a watershed. From then on, although apparent efforts at accommodation would occasionally surface, the dominant theme was confrontation. Preparing for the worst, Nicaragua engaged in a rapid military buildup as the Reagan administration accused it of being a totalitarian state and a platform for Soviet-Cuban directed subversion in Central America. Almost immediately there were rumors of a CIA plan to destabilize the Nicaraguan Revolution. Later, proof began to surface as CIA-backed counterrevolutionary forces—Contras—poured across Nicaragua's borders, engaging in various acts of terrorism from kidnapping and rape to sabotage and murder. By mid-1983 the confrontation had hardened with the arrival of thousands of U.S. troops in Honduras for joint exercises and with the stationing of marine-carrying U.S. ships off both Nicaraguan coasts. By that point few observers of Central America could still argue that a direct U.S. invasion of Nicaragua was out of the question.

The purpose of this study is to shed light on the process by which this diplomatic crisis took form. It will focus on U.S.-Nicaraguan relations under the Reagan administration and will look at military and economic dimensions and, to a lesser extent, areas such as diplomatic initiatives and the information/propaganda ideological conflict.

MILITARY

The Nicaraguan Threat?

From the outset the Reagan administration insisted that Nicaragua represented a two-pronged military menace. First, Washington argued that the Sandinistas had engaged in a massive arms buildup that was unrelated to its defense needs and therefore threatening to the stability of all of Central America. Second, from early 1981, when the State Department issued its famous White Paper on "Communist Support of Salvadoran Rebels," the administration maintained that the Nicaraguan government was playing a major support role in the Communist uprising in El Salvador.[3]

---

[3]"Text of State Department Report on Communist Support of Salvadoran Rebels," New York Times, February 24, 1981.

Support for the Salvadoran Rebellion. The charge that Nicaragua was materially aiding the Salvadoran insurrection is easy to deal with, not because massive proof can be presented to support one argument or the other but rather because existing evidence is so skimpy that no firm conclusion can be reached. From the start the Sandinistas freely expressed their moral support for the Salvadoran rebels. This is not particularly surprising. Similarly, they did not hide the fact that Salvadoran guerrillas enjoyed sanctuary in Nicaragua, as was also true for both Salvadoran and Guatemalan rebels in Mexico and, to a lesser extent, Costa Rica. But they repeatedly denied knowingly being a conduit for arms to those insurgents. It would be naive to accept blindly any government's word on such a controversial issue.[4] It must be noted though that in its first three years the Reagan administration had done an unconvincing job of documenting its arms-running charges against Nicaragua. The famous White Paper proved very little and was largely discredited within a very short while. As Wayne Smith, chief of the U.S. Interest Section in Havana from 1979 to 1982, later said, that document "became a source of acute embarrassment to the Administration, primarily revealing shoddy research and a fierce determination to advocate the new policy whether or not the evidence sustained it."[5] In the ensuing three years there were additional White Papers and a lot of rhetoric, but no hard proof.

To counter criticism about the lack of evidence, Reagan administration officials asserted that although they had ample proof they were unable to reveal it to the public for fear of endangering their intelligence apparatus. To add authenticity to their charges, they held several top secret closed sessions in which "sensitive" material was presented to carefully selected groups of Washington insiders and to the intelligence committees of both houses of Congress. The consensus coming out of those groups, including the Democrats controlling the House Intelligence Committee, was that the evidence was

---

[4]Americans need only think back to the deliberate falsehood generated by the U.S. government at the time of the U-2 incident in 1960, the pre-Bay of Pigs bombings of Cuban airfields in 1961, and the Gulf of Tonkin incident in 1964—to name just a few cases—to realize that deliberate lying is a normal, if regrettable, foreign policy instrument even of our own government.

[5]Wayne Smith, "Dateline Havana: Myopic Diplomacy," *Foreign Policy*, no. 48 (Fall 1982): 162.

conclusive against Nicaragua.[6] Given the propensity of U.S. politicians of both parties to want to avoid being painted "soft on Communism," especially in a period of increasing Cold War hysteria, such maneuvers failed to convince many observers.

The simple fact is that for arms from Nicaragua to get to El Salvador they would have to be transported by air, by water across the Gulf of Fonseca, or overland through Honduras. However, from early 1981, when some objective observers feel that there may have been some arms support from Nicaragua,[7] the U.S. government was unable to document any such traffic. The only arms-carrying plane ever captured turned out to be of Costa Rican origin. A much publicized sea invasion from Nicaragua early in 1981 turned out to be a hoax. In spite of a multimillion dollar CIA program designed explicitly to stop the alleged arms flow through Honduras, no arms whatsoever were intercepted. It is hard to believe that, if planes had been downed, boats seized, or overland smuggling parties intercepted, the Reagan administration would not immediately have held press conferences to present such obviously nonsensitive evidence. Since no such evidence was ever presented, it is only reasonable to conclude that the arms flow from Nicaragua to El Salvador, if it existed at all, was insignificant.

The Military Buildup. The charge that Nicaragua had created a military establishment which far exceeded the country's legitimate defense needs and therefore was designed for aggressive purposes is much more open to concrete investigation. It is undeniable that in the first four years of the revolution the Sandinistas significantly increased Nicaragua's armed strength. It is commonly estimated that by late 1983 the country had an army of around 25,000 persons (a substantial number of women serve in the Nicaraguan military) and a Popular Militia in excess of 60,000. Both the army and the militia were equipped primarily with Socialist bloc rifles (BZ-52s) and automatic weapons (AK-47s). Nicaragua also had imported a number of tanks, antiaircraft guns and missiles,

---

[6]"Haig and Salvador Official Meet; Nicaraguan is at Mexican Mission," *New York Times*, March 6, 1982; "U.S. Traces Nicaragua-Salvador Arms Trail," *Miami Herald*, March 12, 1982; "Covert U.S. Support of Nicaraguan Rebels 'Counterproductive,'" *Financial Times*, May 18, 1983.

[7]Alan Riding of the *New York Times* expressed this opinion to the author in a conversation in Mexico City in November 1982.

troop carrier trucks, and a few helicopters of Socialist bloc origin, as well as acquiring helicopters from the French. And, there were a few Soviet military advisers, some East German security personnel, and between 200 (if you take Fidel Castro's word) and 2,000 (if you prefer the Washington version) Cuban military advisers in Nicaragua.[8] In addition, a number of new military facilities were built, the Sandinistas talked for a while about importing Soviet and French jets, and several airstrips were lengthened in what Washington charged was preparation for the arrival of those planes.

All of this sounded ominous when taken out of context, but it is necessary to go deeper into the matter than was typical of the carefully staged media events organized by the U.S. government.[9] To understand the Nicaraguan buildup, it is imperative to examine: 1) the historical context, 2) the Carter administration policy and Reagan campaign rhetoric toward Nicaragua, and 3) the offensive and defensive capabilities of Nicaragua's military establishment.

HISTORICAL CONTEXT. The leadership which came to power in Nicaragua in 1979 was unusually well educated. Many individuals had a deep interest in history, both national and regional. Besides being painfully aware of the history of U.S. policy toward their own country, the Sandinistas were not unmindful of patterns of behavior that the United States had developed in the twentieth century in dealing with revolutionary, leftist, or merely populist governments in the hemisphere. From 1911 through the 1930s the Mexican revolution had stimulated the United States into heated rhetoric, a number of threats, and several military incursions. Later, a democratic attempt at reformist revolution in Guatemala (1945–1954) was destroyed by a destabilization program and

---

[8]The U.S. estimate may well be the least correct. Americans should remember that, immediately following the Grenada invasion of 1983, the U.S. claimed that there were well over 1,100 Cubans on the island, and that all were "well-trained professional soldiers" who had been "impersonating" civilians. The Cuban government, however, insisted that there were only 784 and that most were civilians. Eventually the U.S. government divulged figures and information which showed that the Cubans had been correct on both counts. See "In Wake of Invasion, Much Official Misinformation by U.S. Comes to Light," New York Times, November 6, 1983.

[9]The most dramatic and elaborately choreographed of these events was a television presentation by Bobby Inman of the CIA and John Hughes of the Defense Intelligence Agency on March 9, 1982. See "Transcript of Statements at State Department on the Military Buildup in Nicaragua," New York Times, March 9, 1982.

surrogate exile invasion armed, organized, and directed by the CIA.[10] As mentioned before, the ill-defined populist revolution in Bolivia (1952–1964) seems to have been co-opted and ultimately derailed by U.S. economic and military assistance and advice. The Cuban Revolution (1959 to date) has suffered CIA sabotage, economic destabilization, and a CIA surrogate invasion (Bay of Pigs, 1961). The right-wing military coup, which snuffed out a populist democratic government in Brazil in 1964, was the product, at least in part, of a U.S. destabilization program. In the Dominican Republic in 1965, a nearly successful revolt, aimed at returning that country to democratic rule, was blocked by direct U.S. military intervention. In the early 1970s a CIA destabilization program helped to create the atmosphere that stimulated Chile's U.S.-trained military to overthrow that country's elected leftist president.[11] All of these examples of "Yankee Imperialism" were very much in the minds of the Sandinista leadership when it came to office.

CARTER ADMINISTRATION POLICY AND REAGAN CAMPAIGN RHETORIC. Although the Carter policy toward the new government of Nicaragua seemed to be oriented toward cooperation rather than confrontation, there were matters in 1979 and 1980 which were highly disquieting to the Sandinistas. As noted earlier, the Nicaraguans were worried from the start by Washington's failure to convince Honduras to dismantle the encampments of exiled National Guardsmen just across their northern border. It is true that, until the CIA under Reagan started funding the former guardsmen, Somoza's vanquished troops presented no real military threat. However, during the literacy crusade of 1980, Nicaragua lost eight literacy volunteers to the terrorists operating out of those bases. In the same year the rhetoric of the Reagan presidential campaign offered scant cause for comfort. That summer the Republican national platform "abhor[red] the Marxist Sandinist takeover" in Nicaragua and promised to cut economic aid to that country. Early that year some of Reagan's top advisers produced

---

[10]For one of the best accounts of this matter see Stephen Schlesinger and Stephen Kinzer, *Bitter Fruit: The Untold Story of the American Coup in Guatemala* (New York, 1982).

[11]For ample documentation see U.S., Congress, Senate, Staff Report, Select Committee To Study Governmental Operations with Respect to United States Intelligence, *Covert Action in Chile,* December 18, 1975.

the famous "Santa Fe Document" which declared that World War III—a struggle between freedom and communism—already had begun and that the United States was losing in Central America for lack of decisive action.[12] During the campaign Reagan advisers continued to talk of the need for firm action in regard to Nicaragua; some even referred to the time-tested techniques of U.S. aid cutoffs, destabilization, and surrogate invasion.[13]

The hostile behavior of the Reagan administration immediately upon coming to power will be detailed later. However, given the historical context and developments of 1979 and 1980, the Sandinistas would have been foolish, indeed irresponsible, not to have modernized and beefed up their rag-tag armed forces.[14]

NICARAGUA'S OFFENSIVE AND DEFENSIVE MILITARY CAPABILITIES. Had Nicaragua, as the Reagan administration charged, become a military threat to the region? Was it an offensive power? Was it likely to threaten its neighbors? If one looks dispassionately at the matter, it quickly becomes apparent that Nicaragua's military might was essentially defensive, rather than offensive, in nature. Indeed, the Reagan administration was embarrassed in September 1982 when a subcommittee of the House Committee on Intelligence issued a staff report criticizing U.S. intelligence performance in Central America and noting in particular that, while U.S. intelligence services were publicly trumpeting Nicaragua's supposed offensive capabilities and intentions, there had been "classified briefings whose analytical judgments about Nicaragua's intentions were quite distinct from those that appeared implicit in the briefings on the buildup."[15]

That same month, before another committee of the House, Lieutenant Colonel John H. Buchanan, USMC (Ret.), gave his

---

[12]The Committee of Santa Fe, A New Inter-American Policy for the Eighties (Washington, DC, 1980).

[13]"Reagan's Advisors Step Up Search for the 'Responsible Right,' " Latin America Weekly Report (September 26, 1980): 5.

[14]Indeed, in an assessment of the situation just before President Reagan was inaugurated, I wrote: "As 1980 drew to a close, Nicaraguans had sound justification for devoting serious attention to matters of defense," in Walker, Nicaragua: The Land of Sandino, p. 121.

[15]Staff Report, Subcommittee on Oversight and Evaluation, Permanent Select Committee on Intelligence, U.S. Intelligence Performance on Central America: Achievements and Selected Instances of Concern, September 12, 1982, mimeographed.

assessment of the relative strength of the Honduran and Nicaraguan armed forces based on extensive interviewing and field research in both countries. His overall conclusion was that Nicaragua was in no position to attack Honduras; indeed, it would be "ludicrous" to do so. First he noted that the offensive capabilities of Nicaragua's Soviet-built T55 tanks were practically nil in the Central American setting. Buchanan pointed out that the administration's carefully staged public briefings had used nontopographical maps which allowed audiences to conjure up the image of Nicaraguan tanks rolling rapidly into neighboring countries. In reality, he noted, the terrain is such that to attack Honduras—the country which had screamed the loudest about the Nicaraguan menace—these tanks would have to stick to the Pan-American Highway. Under optimal conditions the trip would take ten hours. However, he further stated that the tanks would find it difficult, if not impossible, to negotiate the grade of some of the steeper parts of that winding mountain highway, and they would be operating virtually without air cover (Nicaragua had only a handful of antique aircraft) against the most powerful air force in Central America—that of Honduras. By the same token, Buchanan argued that it would be foolish for Honduras to invade Nicaragua since the Sandinistas had a well-motivated army and militia and an adequate network of antiaircraft guns and missiles which could neutralize Honduran air superiority.[16] In a phone conversation with Buchanan one year later, it was learned that, although additional weapons had been procured by both sides, the essential nature and relative strength of the military apparatus of the adversaries had not been altered.[17] To this it should be added that the Nicaraguans, under very explicit threat from the United States,[18] eventually announced that they had postponed plans to import Soviet-built jets.[19] France, which had promised to sell aircraft to Nicaragua, eventually backed down.

---

[16]Lieutenant Colonel John H. Buchanan, USMC (Ret.), Prepared Statement Before the Subcommittee on Interamerican Affairs, Committee on Foreign Affairs, U.S. House of Representatives, *U.S. Military Aid to Honduras,* September 21, 1982, mimeographed.

[17]Author's telephone conversation with John Buchanan, September 2, 1983.

[18]"U.S. Breathes Easier Despite Latin Turmoil," *Washington Post,* August 15, 1982.

[19]"Nicaragua Says Plans To Buy MiGs Postponed," *Washington Post,* November 19, 1982.

What about Nicaragua's 85,000-person armed forces? Did not those hordes pose a threat? In fact, as of the fourth year, the regular army was less than 25,000 strong, less than the combined Contra and Honduran army which Nicaragua faced on its northwest border. The Nicaraguan People's Militia, which was often misleadingly lumped by U.S. spokesmen with the regular army, was clearly not an offensive force. The *milicianos* were civilians of all ages and both sexes who received a few weeks of training, served occasional guard duty in their neighborhoods or places of work, and were ready in times of emergency to take up a weapon and defend the country. They were a low-cost defensive device. In 1983 they had been effective in helping to contain and repulse the Contra invasion, but they were not an army and they had almost no offensive capabilities.[20]

The U.S. Threat?

The question of whether or not the United States posed a military threat to Nicaragua is no longer a matter for debate. By 1983 there was massive evidence—much of it leaked from government sources—of the central and not so covert role of the Reagan administration in organizing large-scale counter-revolutionary military and sabotage activities against Nicaragua. In addition, it was public knowledge that the United States had poured armaments and advisers into neighboring Honduras, staged increasingly large and menacing joint military exercises just across Nicaragua's borders, and held threatening naval maneuvers off both of Nicaragua's coasts. Nor was it debatable that U.S. spy planes regularly violated Nicaraguan airspace. In addition, Nicaragua claimed that yankee naval vessels often penetrated its territorial waters. What is interesting and useful to examine, however, is the question of how and when all of this developed.

The earliest manifestation of the U.S. military threat was largely verbal. Within weeks of President Reagan's inauguration, the verbal attack on Nicaragua began. In February the

---

[20]The author attended militia training exercises in March 1981 and a swearing-in ceremony for a large group of *milicianos* in La Trinidad in December 1983.

famous White Paper on El Salvador attempted to link the insurgency in that country with Communist support from the Soviet Union and Cuba via Nicaragua. That same month came a blustering statement by Secretary of State Alexander Haig that the United States might have to "go to the source" to stop this subversion. Further, in the next few months there was talk that "various military contingencies" were being studied.[21]

At the same time there were symptoms of a more ominous U.S. threat. In March 1981, *Parade Magazine* carried a photo essay dealing with activities in a paramilitary training camp run by Cuban and Nicaraguan exiles in Florida.[22] The exiles themselves talked of the goal of "liberating" their homelands, and the author noted that these activities were probably "in violation of the neutrality act and subject to prosecution."[23] Soon it became apparent that this camp was only one of many scattered throughout the state, the Southwest, and California. When the Nicaraguan government formally requested the Reagan administration to disband these camps, some lame excuses were given but, in fact, the camps continued to function with impunity.

This raises the question of when precisely the CIA began to support covert paramilitary activity against Nicaragua. It is now fairly clear that "the company" was very active in Nicaragua from the waning months of the Somoza dictatorship onward. According to one source,

In 1978, with the [Somoza] dynasty nearing collapse, Jimmy Carter signed a 'finding' . . . authorizing under-the-table CIA support for democratic elements in Nicaraguan society, such as the press and labor unions. The Carter Administration correctly recognized that, with the Somoza regime crumbling, Cuban backed leftist forces would try to squeeze out more moderate elements. American financial support for Nicaragua's opposition forces has continued and it remains one of the many items on the CIA's yearly 'Classified Schedule of Authorizations.'[24]

---

[21]"Haig Voices Concern on Nicaragua," *Washington Post,* November 15, 1981.
[22]Eddie Adams, "Exiles Rehearse for the Day They Hope Will Come," *Parade Magazine* (March 15, 1981): 4–6.
[23]Ibid., p. 6.
[24]"A Secret War for Nicaragua," *Newsweek* 100 (November 8, 1982): 44.

Nevertheless, prior to the fall of 1981, there is only tantalizing circumstantial evidence of CIA involvement in paramilitary activities against Nicaragua. The undisturbed presence of mysteriously financed National Guard encampments in Honduras looks suspicious. So, too, are the terrorist raids conducted into Nicaragua by these forces throughout that period. The presence of exile training camps in the United States and the openness with which they operated following Reagan's inauguration reminded many observers of similar activities sponsored by the CIA prior to the Bay of Pigs invasion of Cuba. In addition, separatist activities among the Miskito Indians of Nicaragua's Atlantic coast increased in 1980 and 1981, stimulated in no small way by scare propaganda broadcast by the well-financed "Radio 15 de Septiembre" to Nicaragua's coast from across its borders. The Nicaraguan government charges that these activities culminated late in 1981 in a plot called "Operation Red Christmas,"[25] the purpose of which was to stage a rebellion on the Atlantic coast which, if successful, would have allowed Washington to shift its official recognition to a non-Sandinista government on Nicaraguan soil. Further evidence of suspicious paramilitary activity came when rebel Miskito leader (and one-time Somoza security agent) Steadman Fagoth turned out to be one of the survivors of the crash of a Honduran air force plane on December 28.[26]

In looking at U.S.-sponsored paramilitary activity against Nicaragua, we depart the realm of circumstantial evidence and enter one of cold, hard fact at the end of 1981. In December, in a statement that deserves an award for cynicism and irony, Secretary of State Haig informed the General Assembly of the Organization of American States that "the United States is prepared to join others in doing whatever is prudent and necessary to prevent any country in Central America from becoming a platform for terror and war in the region."[27] What is striking in retrospect is that President Reagan, only days earlier, had signed a CIA "finding" authorizing that agency to

---

[25]"Nicaragua: Sandinista Accusations of Reagan Destabilization," *Central America Report* (March 6, 1982): 70.

[26]"Its Borders Raided, Nicaragua Trains Civilians," *New York Times*, January 4, 1982.

[27]"Haig Urges Joint Action on Nicaragua," *Manchester Guardian/Le Monde*, December 13, 1983.

spend over $19 million to turn Honduras into precisely that type of a platform.[28] Earlier that year National Security Adviser Richard Allen had "set to work on a plan to harass the Sandinistas." Later, on several occasions, Undersecretary of State for Latin American Affairs Thomas Enders had reportedly discussed the need to "get rid of the Sandinistas."[29] On November 16 plans for covert operations against Nicaragua were presented to President Reagan at a meeting of the National Security Council.[30] These plans, which would soon become the CIA finding, "called for support and conduct of political and paramilitary operations against . . . the Cuban presence and Cuban-Sandinista support structure in Nicaragua."[31] Specific details included the training of paramilitary exile forces and the blowing up of bridges and power plants inside Nicaragua.

In 1982, as the Honduras-based, paramilitary campaign grew and became less and less covert, Reagan administration officials came to rely increasingly on the argument that the purpose of the whole operation was to interdict the alleged flow of arms to El Salvador, not to overthrow the Sandinistas. As Enrique Bermúdez, former National Guard colonel in command of the bulk of those CIA-organized Contras, said late in 1982: "We would never accept the role of American mercenary. It is not acceptable to us to carry out missions to interdict Cuban and Russian supply lines to El Salvador. We are Nicaraguans and our objective is to overthrow the Communists."[32] Indeed, Contra comments such as this, and the fact that as of late 1983 no arms whatsoever had been intercepted, indicate rather clearly that the explanation offered by Washington was either hopelessly naive or simply duplicitous.

Be that as it may, in 1982 and 1983 Honduras became a beehive of activity against Nicaragua. Over 10,000 counterrevolutionary troops were "recruited" (often by kidnapping, threat, or bribery), trained, armed, and disgorged into Nicaragua. (Americans can perhaps better understand this situation by imagining that a country infinitely more powerful than

---

[28]"U.S. Said To Plan 2 C.I.A. Actions in Latin Region," New York Times, March 14, 1982.

[29]"A Secret War for Nicaragua," p. 44.

[30]"U.S. Plans Covert Operations To Disrupt Nicaraguan Economy," Washington Post, March 10, 1982.

[31]Ibid.

[32]"Nicaraguan Exile Limits Role of U.S.," New York Times, December 9, 1982.

the United States has just sent more than 840,000 well-armed troops across its northern border.) Although they were unable to organize a civilian political infrastructure, or even to take and hold towns, the Contras were successful in sabotaging economic infrastructure and in carrying a campaign of terror to the civilian populations in border areas. In addition, there were bombing attacks by rebel air forces flying U.S.-donated planes out of bases in neighboring countries.

Most Contra activities were apparently coordinated from Tegucigalpa, Honduras, by U.S. Ambassador John Negroponte. Having played a key decision-making role in the latter part of the Vietnam conflict, Negroponte was reportedly "sent down there by Haig and Enders to carry out the operation without any qualms of conscience."[33] The second most powerful man in Honduras was Armed Forces Commander General Gustavo Adolfo Alvarez, a Cold War extremist whose power eclipsed that of titular civilian President Roberto Suazo Cordoba.

As of 1983 the U.S. contribution to the Contra campaign had been enormous. From the original allocation of a little over $19 million, the dollar expenditure had skyrocketed such that in the first half of 1983 alone the United States had reportedly spent over $90 million.[34] Other nations also had become involved. Argentine paramilitary advisers helped to train some of the "liberation" forces, and Israel chipped in by supplying the Contras with Socialist bloc arms captured from the Palestine Liberation Organization in Lebanon.

An important counterpoint to Contra activities was a series of increasingly large-scale joint military exercises in Honduras. The latest, "Big Pine II," featured the presence on Honduran soil of approximately 4,000 to 5,000 U.S. combat troops. The exercises which had taken place to that point served several functions. First, they offered a convenient cover for moving huge amounts of military equipment into areas bordering on Nicaragua. In at least two cases most of that equipment was apparently left behind to fall into the hands of the Contras. Second, they served as a shield to protect Contra forces in

---

[33]"A Secret War for Nicaragua," p. 45.
[34]" 'Contras' Lag: Nicaraguan Rebels Opting for Direct U.S. Role," *Washington Post*, July 31, 1983.

forays across the Nicaraguan border. It is no accident that upsurges in Contra activities coincided neatly with such exercises. Finally, they tended to alarm the Sandinistas, thus stimulating them to spend increasingly large amounts of scarce resources on defense.

The U.S.-sponsored Contra campaign against Nicaragua was notably unsuccessful if the prime objective was to unseat the Sandinistas. As noted above, these "freedom fighters," as Reagan called them, were unable to capture and hold a single Nicaraguan town, the obvious reason being that they enjoyed little support from the Nicaraguan people. It was not that everyone was happy with the Sandinistas. The deteriorating economic situation had caused significant discomfort which, in turn, had generated discontent. However, the fact that the main force of the Contras—the Nicaraguan Democratic Forces—was commanded exclusively by former National Guard officers, and that many of the soldiers themselves were ex-guardsmen, made support for the rebels unthinkable to most Nicaraguans. Furthermore, the brutal behavior of all Contra forces, including the one commanded by Sandinista defector Edén Pastora in the south,[35] had violated the most basic tenet of guerrilla warfare: guerrillas must cultivate, rather than alienate, their potential civilian base.

Nevertheless, the covert operations against Nicaragua did have several results which were probably viewed as positive by Reagan officials. First, they caused the Sandinistas to infringe somewhat on civil liberties, thus tarnishing the revolution's image and diminishing its appeal as an alternative model for development. Increased Contra activities on the Miskito coast late in 1981 triggered the forced relocation of Indians away from the border areas. Later, after stepped-up Contra incursions throughout all of the border regions; the destruction of key bridges; attacks on the oil refinery; and the appearance in the U.S. press of reports detailing the CIA finding of December 1981, the Sandinistas reacted by imposing a state of emergency which curtailed certain civil liberties, notably freedom of the press. In both instances—the Miskito relocation and the imposition of the state of emergency—the Reagan

---

[35]"On Nicaraguan Border, Villagers Arm for War," New York Times, December 14, 1982.

administration enjoyed a propaganda bonanza. Administration officials conveniently neglected to mention, however, that many societies restrict civil liberties in time of emergency, as, for example, the U.S. imprisonment of over 100,000 American citizens of Japanese descent during World War II and the British use of preventive detention in Northern Ireland.

The other favorable by-product of Contra activity, from Washington's point of view, was the cost of this harassment to Nicaragua. Late in 1981 an insider in the State Department reportedly boasted that the United States intended to "turn Nicaragua into the Albania of Central America," that is, poor, isolated, and radical.[36] There is no doubt that the Contra campaign had a destabilizing effect on the Nicaraguan economy. Besides resulting in the death of upwards of 1,500 citizens in 1982 and 1983[37] (in the United States an equivalent loss would be 126,000 dead), the Contras caused millions of dollars worth of damage to infrastructure and crops and necessitated a significant transfer of funds from social services into the military. All of this helped significantly in the goal of economic destabilization.

In sum, whereas it is highly dubious that Nicaragua presented any appreciable military threat to its neighbors—much less to the United States—Washington, using Honduras as a springboard, had organized a massive operation against the Sandinistas which had inflicted considerable hardship, loss of life, and damage.[38] What is more, several thousand U.S. troops in Honduras and an even larger number of marines in a flotilla of ships off both Nicaraguan coasts were firm evidence that the U.S. threat would not soon diminish. It is not surprising that there was a very real concern in Nicaragua that the next shoe to fall would be a direct invasion by regular Central American and U.S. troops following some sort of fabricated incident like the infamous Gulf of Tonkin almost two decades earlier.

---

[36]From an interview conducted in late 1981 by a political scientist with a State Department insider. Neither party wished names to be used.

[37]This is my own rough conservative estimate generated by projecting from data presented in "U.S. Promoting War in Central America," *Manchester Guardian/Le Monde,* November 14, 1982; and "Nicaragua Offers To Join in Talks on Regional Peace," *New York Times,* July 20, 1983.

[38]"Washington Fiddles While Central America Burns," *Mesoamerica* 2 (July 1983): 2.

ECONOMIC

Economic conflict between the United States and Nicaragua also merits investigation. Was the Nicaraguan Revolution economically threatening to the United States or vice versa?

The Nicaraguan Threat?

There was very little evidence as of mid-1983 that the Nicaraguan Revolution, or the economic model which it adopted, was a real threat to U.S. economic interests. In spite of the impression which the ordinary citizen would garner from the U.S. media or from Reagan administration pronouncements, Sandinista economic policy was remarkably moderate and measured. In the domestic sphere, Nicaragua's economic planners doggedly insisted on preserving a large private sector. Undoubtedly, the Sandinistas benefited from the negative economic lessons of the Cuban Revolution in which "guerrilla economics" and oversocialization of the economy had resulted in chronic productivity problems. For this and other reasons, the economy was only partially nationalized in Nicaragua. As in Costa Rica a couple of decades earlier, the banking and insurance industries were immediately nationalized. In addition, all properties owned by the Somozas and their accomplices, as well as all abandoned or decapitalized assets, were confiscated. This still left 50 percent to 60 percent of the productive capacity in private hands, a proportion similar to that of Brazil, Mexico, and other Latin American countries. What is more, since local entrepreneurs, panicked by the specter of impending communism, often refused to invest in the reactivation of their own enterprises, the Nicaraguan government for a couple of years actually spent proportionately more of its scarce resources on reactivating private production than it invested in the confiscated "Area of People's Property." It was possible that the persistently uncooperative behavior of a large segment of Nicaragua's propertied classes might eventually cause the government to jettison its attempt to preserve a mixed economy. As of late 1983, however, the domestic economic model being pursued

was hardly unique and certainly not the type of radical economics that should have been disquieting to economic
moderates.

The same also could be said for the international dimension of Nicaragua's economic behavior. Take, for instance,
the attitude toward the $1.6-billion international debt inher-
ited from Somoza. The Sandinistas could easily have argued
that they had no moral obligation to repay much of that money
since it had been borrowed for the benefit of the dictator and
his accomplices rather than the nation as a whole. Instead,
the Sandinistas honored their previctory promise to try to pay
off the loan. Unable to pay according to the original schedule,
they renegotiated the debt and until March 1983 did not miss
a single payment.

Sandinista policies toward foreign investment were hardly
radical either. There had never been much foreign investment
in Nicaragua. However, little of what existed was confiscated
in the wake of the Sandinista victory. Rather, the Sandinistas
negotiated with American companies, often giving them very
favorable terms in order to encourage them to stay. A notable
example would be that of the banana exporting firm, Standard
Fruit and Steamship Company. Speaking of a contract which
Standard renegotiated with Nicaragua early in 1981, the company's vice-president and financial officer bragged openly,
"We're doing exactly what we did before. They're making the
concessions."[39] As late as the end of 1982, Nicaragua was still
making concessions in its economic regulations in an effort
to encourage foreign investment.[40]

One aspect of Nicaragua's foreign economic policy which,
on the surface, might have seemed a legitimate cause for worry
for U.S. policymakers was the Sandinistas' oft-proclaimed goal
of "diversifying dependency." The Nicaraguans knew that the
idea that a tiny country such as theirs could ever have a completely, or even relatively, self-contained economy was ridic-
ulous. However, when they assumed power they were not
happy that the country's economy was primarily dependent
on, and therefore vulnerable to, one country, the United States.
They therefore worked to increase the number of countries

[39]"Castle and Cooke Unit and Nicaragua Agree on Banana Production," *Wall
Street Journal*, January 13, 1981.
[40]"Nicaragua Eases Rules on Foreign Investment," *New York Times*, December
8, 1982.

with which Nicaragua traded and from which it secured loans and aid. Generally, they achieved a fairly balanced four-legged relationship with the United States, Western Europe, the Third World, and Socialist countries. Given the vast market that the United States represented and the relative accessibility, quality, and price of its industrial products, it was highly unlikely that Nicaragua would ever voluntarily shut itself off from an economic relationship with the "colossus of the North."

The U.S. Threat?

While the Nicaraguan Revolution posed little economic threat to the United States, the same could not be said in reverse. From February 1981 onward the Reagan administration pursued a multifaceted and very visible policy of economic destabilization toward Nicaragua. By the time Reagan came to office in 1981, the Nicaraguan economy was already in serious trouble. The destruction of infrastructure caused by the war, the huge and unfair debt inherited from the Somozas, and significant declines in the world market value of virtually all of the country's principal export commodities had created a situation in which Nicaragua was in urgent need of economic support. Instead, from President Reagan it got a concerted program of economic sabotage.

The first step was the U.S. decision early in 1981 to cut off economic aid and to deny Nicaragua credit for the purchase of wheat. Although Libya soon announced a $100-million loan and the Soviet Union and several Western countries agreed to supply wheat, this move had great symbolic importance given U.S. influence in Western financial circles.

The aid and credit cutoff was followed by an effort, on the part of the Reagan administration, to block loans to Nicaragua from the multinational lending agencies. The three most important institutions of this type for Latin American countries are the International Monetary Fund (IMF), the Inter-American Development Bank (IDB), and the International Bank for Reconstruction and Development (the World Bank). The United States frequently has used its predominant position in the IMF to reward and punish Latin American governments. However, the Nicaraguans had decided early on to avoid dealing with that institution since its guidelines for loans were

seen as profoundly inimicable to policies of social redistribution. Furthermore, the fact that the IMF had granted a loan
to Somoza just two months before his overthrow had particularly galled the Sandinistas. However, Nicaragua did apply
for assistance from both the IDB and the World Bank, and
through these organizations the United States was eventually
successful in punishing the defiant Sandinistas. In the IDB the
United States holds an absolute veto over expenditures of
funds from the Special Operations Fund (FOE). From 1981
onward not a single Nicaraguan request for FOE support was
approved. The other type of IDB allocations—those drawn
from ordinary funds—requires only a simple majority for
approval. However, since the United States is allocated 34.5
percent of the vote, based on its monetary contribution, it
blocked most Nicaraguan loan requests of this type by simply
working in concert with a minority of conservative Latin American countries. Accordingly, with the exception of a $35-million
loan for Nicaraguan dam construction in mid-1982 (passed
because virtually all Latin American countries were furious
over the U.S. role in the Falklands crisis) and a very small loan
approved one year later, the United States succeeded after
1981 in torpedoing all ordinary IDB loans to Nicaragua. Similarly, in the World Bank, Washington apparently used political
pressure in 1982 to see that a confidential Country Program
Paper on Nicaragua turned out to be quite negative.[41]

Since 1982 the World Bank has turned down Nicaraguan
requests for support for a number of projects ranging from a
water supply system, roads, and the literacy program to storm
drainage and low-income housing. The excuse given by the
United States for opposing such loans was that the Sandinistas
had pursued "inappropriate macroeconomic policies."[42] Ironically, Nicaraguan macroeconomic policy, with its emphasis
on a mixed economy, was not markedly different from that of
several Latin American countries—Brazil, Mexico, Costa Rica—
for which the United States offers enthusiastic support in the
IDB and the World Bank. Moreover, Nicaragua's implementation of sewerage and health projects, funded by international organizations, was better than average and, in some
cases, exceptionally good.

---

[41]"Nicaragua Supported for $30 Million Loan," ibid., February 3, 1983.
    [42]"U.S. Using IDB Muscle Against Sandinistas," Washington Report on the
Hemisphere, September 6, 1983, p. 1.

Although the United States frequently had its way in both the IDB and the World Bank, it did so against the will of the majority of the member nations. The representatives of several nations, including West Germany, Great Britain, and Italy, described U.S. action as "an attempt to evade [the] ideal" of the IDB. The representative of Bolivia, Paraguay, and Uruguay—hardly radical countries—commented that "we consider it undesireable in an institution such as this one or the World Bank for decisions to be made on the basis of political motives in economic disguise."[43]

In addition to blocking loans from multinational lending agencies, Washington was active, though not notably successful, in attempting to persuade other countries to cut off aid to, and trade with, Nicaragua. Diplomats from West Germany and the Netherlands reported this type of pressure on Western European nations that supported Nicaragua.[44] The Europeans, however, generally stood fast against these machinations. The hidden hand of the United States also may have been behind the Venezuelan decision in 1982 to stop supplying Nicaragua with oil. It apparently had something to do with Mexico's mid-1983 decision to cut off temporarily oil supplies until Nicaragua made payments on its Mexican debt (previously, Mexico had been quite lenient on payments from Nicaragua).[45] Mexico soon dropped its hard position, and most Latin American countries refused all along to join in the U.S.-promoted boycott of Nicaragua. Remarkably, even Nicaragua's Central American neighbors decided to continue normal economic relations with the Sandinista government.[46]

Perhaps of more significance was the U.S. decision gradually to curtail its own trade with Nicaragua. Prior to the Sandinista victory, the United States was that country's leading trading partner. Within weeks of coming to power, the Reagan administration cut off Nicaraguan access to American wheat. Later came a threat to stop the import of Nicaraguan beef. In October 1982, Standard Fruit Company suddenly pulled its banana-buying operation out of Nicaragua. Since, as noted

---

[43]"U.S. Faulted for Veto of Nicaraguan Loan," *Washington Post*, July 2, 1983.

[44]"4 Central American Nations Refuse To Join a U.S. Boycott of Nicaragua," *New York Times*, September 26, 1983.

[45]"Mexicans Pressing Nicaragua on Oil," ibid., August 13, 1983.

[46]"4 Central American Nations Refuse To Join a U.S. Boycott of Nicaragua," ibid., September 26, 1983.

earlier, the same company had crowed loudly about the con-
cessionary agreement it had reached with the Sandinistas in
1981, its precipitous departure in 1982 was viewed with considerable suspicion. This blow was followed in May 1983 by a
White House decision to cut the quota for the importation of
Nicaraguan sugar by almost 90 percent, from 58,000 tons to a
mere 6,000 tons. Other related acts included the issuance by
the State Department of a "traveler's advisory" on Nicaragua
in 1982 (an apparent attempt to curtail tourism), the closing
of six Nicaraguan consulates in June of 1983 (most trade had
been conducted through those offices), and the refusal that
same year to sell spare parts for computers made in the United
States.

Still another aspect of economic destabilization was CIA
covert support for "moderate"—that is, legal but antirevolu-
tionary—forces in Nicaragua. As already noted, President Carter's 1978 CIA finding authorized support for the opposition
press and independent labor unions. There are no hard data,
but it can be assumed that such support was accepted and
continued through the remainder of the Carter period and
into the Reagan administration. The only significant opposition paper is La Prensa which, after most of its staff resigned,
dedicated itself from the spring of 1980 to slanted, alarmist
attacks on the revolutionary system. This behavior undoubtedly did much to erode private sector support for the reconstruction process and to discourage reinvestment in Nicaragua.
Another "democratic" force targeted for support by the Carter
finding was the labor unions associated with the traditional
political parties. These, too, contributed to economic destabilization by staging a number of strikes until the right to strike
was suspended late in 1981.

Finally, it must be noted that the CIA's Honduras-based
paramilitary operation against Nicaragua was also an important
element of economic destabilization. In the first place it
resulted in the destruction of economic infrastructure and
impeded the cultivation and harvesting of crops. According
to Junta Coordinator Daniel Ortega, infrastructure losses in
the first half of 1983 alone amounted to an estimated $70 mil-
lion.[47] The CIA-sponsored Contra threat also was damaging to

---

[47] "Nicaragua Offers To Join in Talks on Regional Peace," ibid., July 20, 1983.

the Nicaraguan economy in that it necessitated large and otherwise unnecessary expenditures on defense.

Given this elaborate, multifaceted program of economic destabilization on top of other impressive problems such as the huge Somoza debt, the loss of economic infrastructure incurred during the revolutionary war, significant drops in the price of Nicaragua's principal export products, and two natural disasters in 1982 (flooding and drought), it is small wonder that Nicaragua's economy was severely strained by late 1983. What is remarkable is that it was still functioning. What was particularly frustrating and infuriating to scholars who had studied Nicaragua closely was the smug, conventional wisdom which had become generalized in the Western media and even among part of the scholarly community (which apparently had not bothered to investigate the matter very closely) that the macroeconomic difficulties which that country was experiencing were due primarily to radical, "Marxist" economic planning and government bungling.

IDEAS AND WORDS

Another area of conflict between the United States and Nicaragua was in the realm of words and ideas.

The Nicaraguan Threat?

Officials of both the Carter and Reagan administrations expressed worry about the Marxist overtones of the Nicaraguan Revolution. Most of the Sandinistas were indeed Marxists. They had never made any attempt to hide that fact even during the insurrection. This meant that they had a different view of free enterprise, class, democracy, and revolution than did their counterparts in Washington. However, what many North Americans failed to realize was that Sandinista Marxism—like that of many, perhaps a majority of young Latin American intellectuals—was in no way imported or imposed from abroad. Rather, it flowed naturally out of a reality in which unbridled dependent capitalism meant poverty for the many and privilege for the few, electoral "democracy" was simply a device used on occasion by the privileged classes to manipulate the uneducated masses into legitimizing and perpetuating their dominant position, and revolution appeared to be the only way to break the otherwise immutable social, economic, and political structures of class exploitation. Above all, the Sandinistas were nationalists concerned with uplifting the human condition and dignity of the common citizen and with restoring sovereignty to the country.

The Sandinistas also used rhetoric heavily laced with buzz words—"imperialism," "capitalist exploitation," "bourgeoisie," "proletariat," "liberation," "vanguard"—which, though appropriate in their own setting, tended to unnerve North American decision makers having little contact with, or understanding of, Central American reality. These same individuals were further alarmed to be told over and over that the new Nicaraguan "national anthem" included a section calling upon Nicaraguans to "fight against the yankee, the enemy of humanity." In fact, these words were not part of the national anthem but rather the FSLN battle hymn which, like all such hymns, is a historical artifact and therefore over time could lose its jingoistic import just as the Marine Corps hymn, with its unfriendly reference to Mexico and Tripoli, is now a historical curiosity rather than a cause of offense to Mexicans and Libyans.

Given Sandinista rhetoric and ideology it was easy, though very incorrect, to argue that the new leaders of Nicaragua were nothing more than puppets of the Soviet Union. Tragically, such arguments overlook a number of incontrovertible facts. First, the Sandinistas achieved their victory over the Somozas in spite of, rather than with the assistance of, the local Soviet-oriented Communist Party, the Nicaraguan Socialist Party (PSN). The individuals who originally founded the FSLN in 1961 had actually broken away from the PSN in disgust when it became clear to them that the Communists were neither revolutionary nor nationalist. From then until just before the Sandinista victory, the PSN had decried Sandinista efforts as ill-advised and premature. As late as the winter of 1978–79, they worked actively to obstruct a Sandinista victory by being the only supposedly mass-oriented party willing to go along with a U.S. scheme to arrange a mediated settlement between Somoza and his conservative opposition. It is true that Cuba, along with Costa Rica, Venezuela, and Panamá, assisted the Sandinistas in procuring arms, but there is no evidence that the Soviets favored revolution in Central America at that time.

There are other problems with the Soviet puppet argument. After the Sandinista victory, the Soviet-oriented PSN came to play only an extremely marginal role in the new governmental system. The Soviets, though willing to provide arms and some economic assistance, have refused to give Nicaragua any hard currency.[48] Nicaragua abstained rather than voting with the Soviet Union on certain key issues in the United Nations such as Afghanistan and the Korean Airline incident. Nicaragua retained very good diplomatic relations with a variety of non-Communist countries ranging from Sweden and Spain to Nationalist China and Brazil. Finally, far from adopting either socialism or communism, the Sandinistas retained a mixed economy in which the bulk of productive activity remained in private hands.

Perhaps a more real threat presented by the Sandinistas to the United States in the realm of ideas was Nicaragua's role as a model. After their victory in 1979, the Sandinistas were immensely popular throughout Central America. Indeed, their triumph undoubtedly gave hope to the oppressed and impoverished majority throughout the region. Therefore, even though it is unlikely that the new government sent any significant amount of arms to insurgents elsewhere, the Sandinista victory itself may have served as a sort of stimulant for the upsurge in guerrilla activity which took place in Guatemala and El Salvador in the following year. For some in Washington even such an unwitting role in promoting the spread of revolution was unacceptable. Small wonder that the United States, as will be detailed below, mounted a massive disinformation campaign to discredit the Nicaraguan model.

The U.S. Threat?

One of the standard tools which the U.S. government uses to destabilize chosen enemies is "disinformation," the deliberate dissemination of distorted or false information in order to discredit the target government. Disinformation was used against the governments of Guatemala (1954), Brazil (1964), and Chile (1973), to name just a few of the well-known cases.[49] It also was used in Angola in the mid-1970s and, according to

---

[48]"Nicaragua Gets a Loan To Meet Interest Debt," ibid., December 14, 1982.
[49]See notes 10 and 11 above.

"several lower-ranking State Department officers with experience in the country," was being employed in El Salvador as of late 1983, in an effort to "convinc[e] the civilian population that the guerrillas, not the Army, are the real bad guys."[50] Disinformation is promoted at various levels. The CIA often does the dirty work of originally generating false and distorted information and seeing to it that it is seeded in U.S target country, and third country news media. Once such material has appeared in the media, it is then possible for public officials, from press secretaries on up to the president himself, to denounce the target country saying that "we are informed that," or "it is reported that." This apparently relieves the public official of the moral burden of deliberately and directly telling an untruth. Once enough disinformation has appeared in the media, public officials can then routinely talk in generic, nonspecific terms of the evils of the target regime or group.

It is reasonably clear that Nicaragua was a prime target of CIA disinformation. The Sandinistas had made that charge for some time. Late in 1983 even *Newsweek* observed that the CIA had been "spending an estimated $80 million" in the effort against Nicaragua which included "masterminding a variety of propaganda activities to destabilize the Sandinistas."[51] The disinformation, however, was not targeted just at Nicaraguans. For the dozens of North American scholars who had done serious research in post-Somoza Nicaragua, there was a striking difference between what they had seen in that country and what their friends and relatives back home were hearing from the U.S. government and mass media.[52] In the United States, Sandinista Nicaragua was described in general terms as a Marxist, totalitarian, police state which, while massively abusing the human rights of its own citizens and mishandling the economy, was actively assisting Communist revolution in El Salvador and building a huge military establishment to destabilize its other neighbors. The Sandinistas had betrayed the original objectives of the revolution and had turned their country into a Soviet satellite.

---

[50]"America's Secret Warriors," *Newsweek* 102 (October 10, 1983): 39.
[51]Ibid.
[52]The worst distortion seemed to be coming out of the most "mass" of the mass media: *Reader's Digest,* large circulation news magazines, and television news on the three major networks. Some more serious daily newspapers such as the *New York Times* and the *Washington Post* were relatively, though by no means completely, free of disinformation.

It is impossible here to detail the high degree of falsehood and distortion in each aspect of these charges, but some examples will illustrate the point.[53]

THE MISKITO "MASSACRES." Late in 1981, in response to "Operation Red Christmas," the Nicaraguan government moved 8,500 to 10,000 Miskito Indians out of the sparsely populated northern border areas along the Rio Coco. These evacuations were involuntary and involved the subsequent destruction of buildings and property in the deserted villages. However, the move was carried out for both security and humanitarian reasons. Miskito Contras operating out of Honduras were recruiting Nicaraguan Miskitos, often at gunpoint, to join the Contra army. In the process they had killed dozens of uncooperative Miskitos as well as some Sandinista soldiers. In western Nicaragua the evacuation was treated as a humanitarian rescue operation. Nicaraguan doctors and young people volunteered to assist in the overland exodus, and relocation villages were supplied with the latest in tropical, low-income housing.

In the United States, however, quite a different picture was presented. In January, Alan Romberg, State Department spokesman, announced that 170,000 Miskito Indians had fled the border zone,[54] and the *Washington Post* reported a charge by the Honduran Defense Ministry that Sandinista soldiers had invaded Honduras and had massacred 200 Miskito refugees.[55] In fact, there never had been 170,000 Miskitos in all of Nicaragua and only about 3,000 to 5,000 had gone into exile in Honduras.[56] In addition, a subsequent investigation by the UN High Commission on Refugees resulted in a joint declaration by that institution and the government of Honduras that, in reality, no massacre had taken place on Honduran soil.

This was not the end of the matter. In March 1982, *Time* ran a dramatic story about the plight of the Miskitos, in which it now located the famous "massacre of the 200" in Nicaragua.[57] United Nations Ambassador Jeane Kirkpatrick declared

[53]For information on Nicaragua through the fifth year of the revolution see Walker, *Nicaragua: The Land of Sandino* (2d ed., 1985); and Thomas W. Walker, ed., *Nicaragua: The First Five Years* (New York, 1985).

[54]"Nicaragua Denies American Charges of Repression," *Miami Herald*, January 31, 1982.

[55]"Border Attack Reported: Honduras Says Nicaraguans Killed 200," *Washington Post*, January 3, 1982.

[56]Ibid.

[57]"Moving the Miskitos: Nicaragua Uses Brutal Force on Its Proud, Once Friendly, Indians," *Time* 119 (March 1, 1982): 22.

that Nicaragua was the worst human rights violator in the hemisphere and likened Sandinista behavior to the Nazi genocide of the Second World War.[58] Not to be outdone, Secretary of State Haig produced photos from France's Le Figaro which allegedly depicted Sandinista troops burning heaps of Miskito bodies.

The dramatic allegations of genocide against the Miskitos also turned out to be a wild distortion of reality. To Haig's embarrassment, the Gamma photographer, who actually took the Le Figaro photo of Red Cross workers disposing of corpses during the Nicaraguan insurrection four years earlier, soon surfaced to denounce the misuse of his work.[59] In addition, after extensive investigations on the ground in Nicaragua and Honduras, major human rights monitoring organizations (Amnesty International, the Inter-American Commission on Human Rights, and America's Watch) concluded that, while in their judgment there had been some isolated cases of unexplained disappearances of Miskito prisoners in outlying areas and one instance in which a Sandinista officer appears to have overseen the reprisal execution of several dozen Miskito prisoners in the village of Leimus in December 1981, there was no generalized program of execution, let alone genocide. Indeed, Amnesty International stated that, although the Sandinistas had infringed on some human rights in dealing with the Miskitos, "reports of shootings of civilians and other deliberate brutality during the transfer were later shown to be false, and government medical and other civilian personnel assisted residents during the transfer."[60]

CUBAN-NICARAGUAN AID FOR SALVADORAN GUERRILLAS. Another subject about which the American people have received

---

[58]"Nicaragua: Sandinista Accusations of Reagan Destabilization," Central America Report (March 6, 1982): 70.

[59]Council on Hemispheric Affairs, press release, "Miskito Atrocity Stories Termed 'Grossly Exaggerated' and 'Groundless,' " March 5, 1982, p. 2.

[60]Amnesty International, "Nicaragua Background Briefing: Persistence of Public Order Law Detentions and Trials" (London, 1982), p. 8. For additional coverage of Nicaragua's human rights performance, in general, and that relating to the Miskitos, in particular, see Amnesty International, Prepared Statement of Amnesty International USA on the Human Rights Situation in Nicaragua Before the Subcommittee on Human Rights and International Organizations, U.S. House of Representatives, September 15, 1983 (mimeographed); Inter-American Commission on Human Rights, Organization of American States, Report on the Situation of Human Rights of a Segment of the Nicaraguan Population of Miskito Origin (Washington, DC, 1984); and America's Watch, Human Rights in Nicaragua (New York, 1984).

distorted information is the question of alleged Cuban-Nicaraguan support for the Salvadoran guerrillas. The striking lack of evidence behind the Reagan administration's claim that Nicaragua had served as a conduit for the flow of arms from the Socialist bloc to the guerrillas in El Salvador has already been noted. There also were some remarkably contrived stories that Cuba and Nicaragua were actually sending personnel to El Salvador to help in, or coordinate, the guerrilla effort. For instance, on October 19, 1981, when the administration was attempting to convince Congress to approve additional aid for the government of El Salvador, Rowland Evans and Robert Novak published a column in the *Washington Post* which asserted, on the basis of "unimpeachable" sources, that 500 to 600 Cuban troops had passed through Nicaragua to El Salvador where they had helped sabotage a bridge over the Rio Lempa.[61] As it turned out, the story had originated with the Salvadoran government, which is hardly an unimpeachable or reliable source and which appears "to have been instructed to 'leak' the information by U.S. intelligence operatives."[62] Nevertheless, even though the report—clearly a hoax—was never directly confirmed by Washington, the column was "reportedly cited . . . in briefings."[63]

A couple of comically clumsy attempts at disinformation regarding alleged Nicaraguan personnel support for the Salvadoran Revolution occurred the following spring. At that point, the Reagan administration was attempting to prove that "Nicaragua and Cuba were directing the guerrilla operation in El Salvador."[64] In early March, Secretary of State Haig made "a dramatic announcement . . . to a House subcommittee that evidence of outside interference in El Salvador could be seen in the capture of 'a Nicaraguan military man' helping direct the insurgency."[65] To Haig's embarrassment, the prisoner subsequently escaped to the Mexican embassy where officials confirmed that Ligdamis Gutiérrez Espinosa was simply a nineteen-year-old student at the University of Nuevo León in

---

[61]"Bridge Over the Rio Lempa," *Washington Post,* October 19, 1981.

[62]"Evans and Novak's New Version of Discredited 'White Paper,' " *Washington Report on the Hemisphere,* December 1, 1981, p. 5.

[63]Ibid.

[64]"Haig and Salvador Official Meet; Nicaraguan is at Mexican Mission," *New York Times,* March 6, 1982.

[65]Ibid.

Monterrey and had been arrested as he attempted to enter El Salvador legally on a trip from Mexico to his homeland during the Easter recess.[66]

Undaunted by that episode the intrepid Haig went on to an even greater public relations debacle on March 12. On that occasion he flew another nineteen-year-old Nicaraguan, Orlando José Tardencillas, from a Salvadoran prison to Washington for a televised press conference, "on the expectation that he would back up U.S. charges that Cuba and Nicaragua [were] supplying, training and directing leftist insurgents fighting El Salvador's civilian military junta."[67] Instead, Tardencillas, who freely admitted that he had been fighting with the Salvadoran guerrillas, insisted that he had been doing so as a private individual, and that the statements he had made in El Salvador and was expected to repeat in Washington implicating his government and that of Cuba were false, having been extracted through torture and threat of death. Claiming that he had been sentenced to death through a court-martial in El Salvador, he maintained that U.S. officials had promised him asylum if he would agree to the news conference.[68] Toward the end of this event, he said: "I am aware of what is happening and very clear of what awaits me. I know whose hands I'm in. I'm a revolutionary and one of the risks is death. I am willing to accept it."[69] Although State Department officials at first did not know whether the prisoner would be returned to El Salvador, and almost certain death, Washington ultimately decided to cut its losses and release him to the Nicaraguan embassy.

These are but a few examples of what appears to have been a campaign mounted by Washington to discredit the revolutionary government of Nicaragua. Other cases of obvious distortions and fabrications relate to stories of Sandinista attacks on the Catholic church, the government's attitude and policy toward the private sector, the alleged persecution of Nicaraguan Jews, and Sandinista abuses of human rights in general.

---

[66]Ibid.; "Nicaraguan Comments on 'Mercenaries,' " *Washington Post*, March 19, 1982.

[67]"State Department's Guerrilla Recants," ibid., March 13, 1982.

[68]"Nicaraguan Given Hero's Welcome," ibid., March 16, 1982.

[69]"State Department's Guerrilla Recants," ibid., March 13, 1982.

DIPLOMACY

Another dimension of the Nicaraguan-U.S. conflict which merits attention is diplomatic behavior. How has diplomacy been used by the two parties? Has it been employed to reduce the possibility of violence? Has either side, or both, genuinely been interested in seeking a peaceful negotiated settlement?

On the surface, it would appear that the two sides had made efforts at a peaceful solution. In matters like this, countries rarely allow themselves to appear to be obstacles to peace. Both governments have presented negotiating positions and, on occasion, officials from both sides have sat down to talk with, or at, each other.

Whereas Nicaragua has appeared to be interested in going beyond rhetoric, the United States has seemed quite unconcerned with actually carrying the process through to a diplomatic solution. In 1981 the Nicaraguans proposed to Honduras that the two countries cooperate in setting up a joint border patrol. This would have served the dual purpose of restraining any arms flow that might have existed across Honduran territory from Nicaragua to El Salvador and diminishing the then rather minor terrorist activities which former National Guardsmen were mounting against Nicaragua from bases in Honduras. Although Honduras initially showed some interest in the idea, it eventually backed down and accepted the U.S. position that any settlement in the area should be multilateral rather than bilateral. Under pressure from France and Mexico, later from Mexico and Venezuela, and finally from the Contadora countries (Colombia, Mexico, Panamá, and Venezuela), the United States made several gestures to indicate interest in a negotiated settlement. But when Nicaragua made concrete proposals and requested serious negotiations, there was silence and a lack of follow-through from Washington.[70]

In fact, it was clear that the United States was simply not interested in any settlement that would have left the Sandinista Revolution intact. Washington's real attitude toward negotiations is most vividly betrayed in a leaked top secret document published verbatim in the *New York Times* in the spring of

---

[70]A number of articles in the *Washington Post, New York Times,* and *Miami Herald* document the history of this diplomatic dance.

1983. This document, which was prepared by the National Security Planning Group (the president and his most trusted foreign policy advisers) in April 1982, is entitled "U.S. Policy in Central America and Cuba Through FY 1984."[71] Although it deals with many matters, its references to negotiations are difficult to misread. In describing the "current situation," its authors stated: "We continue to have serious difficulties with U.S. public and congressional opinion, which jeopardize our ability to stay the course. International opinion, particularly in Europe and Mexico, continues to work against our policies." Later, under "policy implications," these planners declared that the administration should "step up efforts to co-opt negotiations issue to avoid congressionally mandated negotiations, which would work against our interests." These sentences speak for themselves.

WHY?

As of late 1983 it was clear that the United States, not Nicaragua, was the threatening party. While paying only lip service to the concept of negotiation, the Reagan administration had mounted a massive economic, propaganda, and surrogate military assault on Nicaragua. The obvious concluding question is why. Was this sort of behavior in the national interest? If not, in whose interest was it?

I would argue that Reagan's policy toward Nicaragua was actually contrary to real U.S. national interests; Nicaragua offered neither a military nor an economic threat. The United States could easily coexist, if it wanted to, with systems such as that of Sandinista Nicaragua. Since the Soviets were willing to make only a very limited commitment to Nicaragua, the Sandinistas needed U.S. trade, technology, and economic assistance. Their moderate combination of social Catholicism and pragmatic nationalist Marxism was hardly threatening, even in an ideological sense. Also, it is not illogical to expect that socially responsible regimes such as that of Nicaragua, by uplifting the standard of living of the majority, would eventually turn into better trading partners for the United States

---

[71]"National Security Council Document on Policy in Central America," *New York Times*, April 7, 1983.

than the socially irresponsible, anti-Communist dictatorships that the United States so often ends up supporting in the region.

In fact, Reagan's policy toward Nicaragua, although dysfunctional in terms of real U.S. national interests, was symptomatic of a defect in Washington's approach to foreign policy which has plagued the United States for decades. To be specific, U.S. policy often responds more to domestic political pressures than to objective international reality. While often ill informed on the specifics of world affairs, the American public has been steeped in the rhetoric of the Cold War for almost forty years. Since the United States is a democracy, this, in turn, shapes the behavior of candidates, elected officials, and career foreign service personnel. In practice it is safer in foreign affairs to be conservative and to employ a Cold War frame of reference. Liberals in the foreign policymaking apparatus were burned during the McCarthy era in the 1950s and again suffered seriously under the Reagan administration. Similarly, politicians employing easily digestible Cold War rhetoric have tended to prosper, while those who have attempted to explain and deal openly with a more complex, and actually less threatening, reality have frequently gone down to defeat. As a result, from the time of President Dwight Eisenhower onward, U.S. policy in Central America has exaggerated the Communist threat while downplaying or ignoring the tremendous social and economic inequalities perpetuated by the anti-Communist regimes this nation has supported. President Reagan's policies toward Nicaragua were simply a more extreme version of an old and dysfunctional pattern.[72]

---

[72]The wording of much of this paragraph is from Presbyterian Church (USA), *Adventure and Hope: Christians and the Crisis in Central America: Report to the 195th General Assembly of the Presbyterian Church* (Atlanta, 1983), p. 100. The author wishes to thank the Presbyterian church for its kind permission to publish this material, which he wrote while part of the UPCUSA Task Force on Central America, here under his own name.

Policy Options

Daniel Oduber

Is Peace Possible in Central America?

CENTRAL AMERICA is more and more in the news. Before 1978 we lived in permanent political and social upheaval but very little was known about us outside the area. Recently, hostilities have increased and our troubles are becoming more important to the news media all over the world, especially since our struggle has been described as part of the East-West conflict. Central Americans had no voice when politicians and journalists reinterpreted the nature of our conflict. However, we must now view it from a totally different perspective than from that which our peasant or city worker would have comprehended. As a Central American, I will try to analyze the situation.

Central America today is formed by seven independent nations. Some years ago this region, which had formed part of the Spanish colonial empire, included only five countries: Guatemala, El Salvador, Honduras, Nicaragua, and Costa Rica. We have always had good relations with Panamá, but Panamá was, and is, closer to South America, having been a province of Colombia until 1903 when the United States decided that it should become an independent state to provide a suitable contract to build an interoceanic canal. Even today Panamá is closer to the Andean countries than to Central America, but we would be very happy if they decided to be closer to us. Belize is another independent nation with a more Caribbean than Central American mentality, in spite of the fact that a majority of its population is composed of Mayan Indians. British rule, and consequently British institutions, have been the strongest force in Belize. Of the five Central American republics that once were dominated by the viceroyalty of Mexico and the captaincy general of Guatemala, four provided strong and cheap labor after independence for the colonizers and

193

feudal lords. Costa Rica, however, had neither Indians nor minerals and so it was left to its own fate.

The Spanish crown and the Spanish church sacked Central America, but the brutality was more obvious in countries with mineral wealth or large Indian labor to exploit. The *conquistadores* first, the colonial power second, and the landlords after them built a feudal society that still struggles to survive in these four countries. Since the middle of the last century, the European powers, and later the United States, were eager to fill the vacuum left by the Spanish. By the conclusion of the Second World War, the United States was the only major power in the area. Unfortunately, on practically no occasion did the United States ally with the newly emerging forces in these countries. On the contrary, it was continually a partner and strong ally of the heirs of feudalism.

The ideals of the Second World War caused a great wave of enthusiasm in Central America, and a weak middle class began to emerge which created social organizations based on social justice, economic development, and political democracy, as preached and promised by the great powers which had won the war against totalitarianism, tyranny, and murder in Europe and the Pacific. Central Americans believed this message and organized regionally, with the aim of helping rebels and patriots against dictators. In many instances, U.S. statesmen allied with us, but in general they either did not care or were openly allied with the feudal interests and armies that protected these interests.

Since 1945, Central Americans began making contacts among Latin Americans and leaders in the U.S. trade unions, universities, civic organizations, the Senate, and the House of Representatives to fight for democracy in the hemisphere. In Havana in 1950, the first organization was formed. Hubert H. Humphrey, Wayne Morse, Clifford Case, Ernest Gruening, and other senators were there. Little by little other leaders in the United States backed the Central American cause. We no longer believed that we were fighting alone. The struggle in the hemisphere, and specifically in Middle America, had many different nuances, and it was soon learned that no two countries could be freed in the same way. Rafael Trujillo in the Dominican Republic, Fulgencio Batista in Cuba, Marcos Pérez Jimenez in Venezuela, Gustavo Rojas Pinilla in Colombia, Manuel Odria in Peru, Anastasio Somoza in Nicaragua, and others in El Salvador, Honduras, and Guatemala had to be analyzed separately and treated individually.

These forces that favored democracy and freedom had to be supported by public opinion in the hemisphere and later in democratic Europe. Examining the first thirty years from 1945 to 1975, one can easily determine why, in the majority of cases, the United States was accused of supporting dictators. Sometimes, as with Cuba, it was only at the very end of the struggle that U.S. foreign policy showed a certain amount of acceptance of the armed struggle against the dictator.

At this stage, more people in the area were educated and had traveled abroad. The electronic revolution had permitted great masses of people to become better informed. With more roads, electricity, radio, and television, protest against the United States increased slowly, and it became known as the ally of repressive and brutal regimes. Progressively the hemisphere reacted against the United States; old legends of American imperialism were revived, this time with greater insight. Cuba became Communist in 1960 and immediately decided to back Communist minorities in the area. Ideology, weapons, training, and money were provided, with the result that dictators became more ruthless, massacring even educated democratic leaders who had long records in the struggle for democracy and who had absolutely nothing to do with these Communist minorities.

Preoccupied in the 1960s and 1970s with Vietnam and Watergate, the United States took Central America for granted, and it "resolved" the problem simply by backing military dictators on the erroneous assumption that strongmen trained in American military schools were the most capable of forming governments that could stop communism. These military groups, with few exceptions, became avid money-makers, forgot all about democracy or social change, and not only alienated the politically aware middle class but also eliminated it physically by imprisonment, exile, or murder.

At the end of the 1970s, Central America's populations, eager for change, had only one alternative: military governments or idealistic guerrillas who promised that change. It is important to remember that most Central Americans knew nothing about the Cold War with its sophistic alternatives, capitalism, or communism. It is also important to remember that they knew nothing about democracy because they had never experienced it. The only reality they faced was death, hunger, or displacement. In four Central American countries, over 150,000 people have died since 1978, and ten times that number have been displaced from their homes. That means, in terms relative to the U.S. population, 1½ million people killed and 15 million displaced, all in only five years.

Can you really believe that these people are fighting and suffering genocide because they are the defenders of a democracy they never knew, or a private enterprise that always ignored them? No, they are fighting for something they cannot express in words or ideologies. They are fighting for a piece of land, or even a piece of bread, and now for a day of peace in their own huts. Their fight is emotional against humiliation and brutality. The groups that first exhibit political solidarity win the confidence of these downtrodden majorities. These groups convince them to fight for a political system that might guarantee them respect and security for their families. They deeply resent the brutal authority that has predominated for over four centuries. Neither will they accept a regime of the type preached by the Leninists, which means another form of totalitarianism. Unfortunately, the more vivid representative of continuing brutal domination is the armed "thug" who threatens the lives of average Central Americans and their families. These thugs are not the Leninist commissars but the armed sergeants trained in the United States.

What kind of leaders arose in this struggle? As mentioned before, since the 1950s dedicated and devoted democrats have led the struggle against repression and injustice. Parties began to form more in the European tradition than in that of the United States; that is, in the tradition of the Social Democratic or Social Christian parties of Europe. International organizations were brought into America to strengthen party bonds with Latin America and the Caribbean. The Socialist International, the Demo-Christian International, and the Liberal International came to fill the vacuum and took advantage of the old concept of party organizations in the area. Youth organizations, trade union federations, and even incipient peasant organizations began to work internationally. According to party lines, I belong to the Socialist International, which has been in contact with Socialist and Social Democratic parties in the region. You will be able to understand our political reality more easily if I tell you that I recently attended the ninetieth anniversary of the Civic Radical Union in Córdoba. This party just won the elections in Argentina and opened a new era with the presidency of Raúl Alfonsín.

In our group you can count PRI (Partido Revolucionario Institucional) of Mexico, the Socialists of Guatemala, the MNR (Movimiento Nacional Revolucionario) of El Salvador, the Liberals of Honduras, and the PRD (Partido Revolucionario Democrático) of Panamá. We are continually working together with European Social Democrats such as Mario Soares of Portugal, Felipe González of Spain, François Mitterrand of France, Bettino Craxi of Italy, Willy Brandt of Germany, and Olaf Palme of Sweden. As pointed out, we have the backing of some prominent U.S. politicians and social leaders in promoting this party activity aimed at political and social change in Central America, South America, and the Caribbean.

In the last twenty years other small groups, inclined toward Leninism and revolution and inspired by Fidel Castro's Cuba, decided to begin armed struggle against dictatorship and injustice. In the Central American isthmus we recognized these forces, and in many cases had contacts with them, arguing endlessly in favor of democracy. Unfortunately, people of these countries have not believed in democracy because in this region it has always meant faked elections, corruption, and brutality. Cuba helped in their training and recommended not only armed solutions but also Leninist institutions for future governments. Their many armed cells were small in comparison with other social organizations fighting for change. Their influence has been felt more in the last two decades since our most important democratic leaders have been killed, tortured, or exiled by army men, paramilitary groups, or death squads.

The war began in the 1960s. In those days the opposition was formed mainly by our democratic leaders with their popular organizations, and no one paid attention to the small Leninist groups that were preparing the underground insurrection in the cities and in the mountains. If one studies the recent history of Guatemala and El Salvador, to mention only two countries, the list of assassinations is almost incredible. In ten years almost no political or social leadership groups have been spared: professors, trade unionists, priests, teachers, politicians, students, and even nuns and one archbishop were killed or simply disappeared in the same manner that we are learning today was used in Chile and Argentina. As a result, our movements were left without leadership, and when our efforts succeeded, as in the case of Nicaragua, it was the Leninist leadership, which had gone underground, that took over the government and the army.

During all these years the United States was openly allied with the repression, in spite of great and noble efforts by many individual Americans who believed we were offering the right solutions. In Nicaragua, U.S. officials backed tyranny and corruption for forty years. In El Salvador and Guatemala, business interests were more important for the United States than anything else, and in recent years highly placed U.S. officials have praised murderous and corrupt military governments as the best allies the United States can have.

From this brief analysis, it can be understood how Leninist leadership has been able to gain control of and dominate the legitimate protest and opposition in several of our countries, while democratic leaders have been without the necessary support or, in so many cases, have been eliminated. Although we are friends of the United States, how can we defend its policies during the greater part of the last forty years? With this background is peace possible in Central America? Is it possible to work with patience and through dialogue, or is the only alternative a military solution? Political leaders of different ideologies have been meeting recently in many European countries, the United States, and Latin America to discuss the possibilities of peace. The most active international groups in the area, the Social Democrats, Liberals, and the Demo-Christians, decided to work together for peace through dialogue, thus backing the Contadora effort. What is the Contadora Group?

During Jimmy Carter's presidency, the treaties of the Panamá Canal were revised by his administration and the Senate. Panamá was a very small country to be left alone, so both the Security Council of the United Nations and many inter-American organizations were mobilized to help the negotiations. I had long discussions with President Omar Torrijos about the need for a task force of Latin American leaders to coordinate activities and act as a friendly go-between group with Washington.

I was then president of Costa Rica and, with Carlos Andrés Pérez, president of Venezuela, Luis Echeverría, president of Mexico, and Alfonso López Michelsen, president of Colombia, we convened on Contadora Island close to Panamá City to

begin working. Later President José López Portillo of Mexico
and Michael Manley of Jamaica joined the group to complete
the work. There were difficult negotiations among friends and
allies. However, the treaties were revised and the Senate
approved them, with the result that Panamá remained a good
and reliable friend of the United States. Had it not been for
those negotiations, Panamá would have become embittered
and the youth of that country would have made this failure
an issue for rebellion against the United States. We believed
then that negotiations were possible on all controversial issues
between the United States and the Central American countries, and our group became known as the Contadora Group.

The war of liberation in Nicaragua was supported by the
same group, and the heroism and sacrifice of its people is
well known. The last stages of the Nicaraguan war were conditioned by a total alliance of all opposition forces—Communist
and democratic—and ideologies were left aside. Even in the
final days of the war, Communist groups of indoctrinated leaders—proletarians, GPP (Guerra Popular Prolongada), and ter-
ceristas—were small in this combined effort to overthrow the
regime. The only outside country that helped to the very end
was Cuba and, through Cuba, other anti-U.S. countries.

At the beginning of 1979 the government of Venezuela
changed hands, and the new administration did not want to
continue military support of the rebels. Panamá was weak and
without material resources and Costa Rica could only lend
territory. In desperation, even democratic leaders turned to
Cuba and its friends who had not yet given much assistance.
And so the glorious internal warriors of the struggle in Nicaragua were led by small bitterly anti-U.S. groups. We think
that appropriate help and a presence in Nicaragua after the
victory would have created a different political situation than
the one we face today. As it was, these anti-U.S. groups controlled the new army at the end of the war, and they slowly
became the major force in the new regime. Also, most of the
democratic forces ignored our plea for massive support of this
regime.

With the victory in Nicaragua, rebel forces and clandestine groups in El Salvador and Guatemala were encouraged to
begin their own struggle. Salvadoran and Guatemalan rebels
began to contact us just after Somoza was defeated. We always
claimed that a peaceful solution was possible and that a rash
and immature approach not only was defeated beforehand

but also would hurt Nicaragua by making impossible the peace it needed to stabilize its regime and reconstruct the country. We met many times in Panamá with General Torrijos and with the principal members of the Contadora Group and other representatives of friendly parties. We were aware that our democratic leaders were still the main targets of the thugs in those countries, and that few of our leaders had been spared from imprisonment or death. This meant that the more radical groups were left to pursue the revolution.

Nevertheless, we continued searching for peaceful solutions and democratic goals in Central America. In 1979 and 1980 we patiently participated in many meetings with opposition representatives of El Salvador and Guatemala, including guerrilla leaders, and with U.S. government officials and representatives who were seeking a peace proposal for El Salvador. Since those days the U.S. government has decided that its presence in the negotiating groups was negative, and that it was better to leave negotiations in the hands of Latin Americans. González, Pérez, Torrijos, and many other friends participated actively in these efforts until the 1980 election was held in the United States.

The last days of the Carter administration were vital for the consolidation of a peace plan, and it was finally ready at the beginning of December 1980. It was presented, via the American embassy in Tegucigalpa, to the guerrilla and political leaders in El Salvador. Suddenly, they changed. Afraid of the new administration just elected in the United States, Castro and his friends in the area opted for a "final offensive" which, they said, would be a military victory for the rebels. Our efforts of two years had failed and the war continued. On January 9, 1980, the guerrilla leaders of El Salvador communicated to General Torrijos that the final offensive would begin the next day. They anticipated victory before the beginning of the Reagan administration.

They did not succeed, however. The population did not support them, and the army did not split as they had expected. A stalemate set in. The deaths in battle and the political assassinations increased. The new administration in the United States portrayed the civil war in El Salvador as a confrontation between East and West and depicted Nicaragua and Grenada as the beachheads of the Soviet Union in the neighborhood of the United States. We Central Americans had another perspective. The Nicaraguan government was allied with friends of the USSR and its satellites, and Nicaragua was helping the rebels in El Salvador who had chosen the Cuban way to change society and were vindictive and vociferous against the United States. In its origins, the Salvadoran Revolution was directed, helped, and sustained by Nicaragua. But, where democracy really exists and functions, we are not afraid of communism or Marxism-Leninism. In Mexico, in spite of the difficult circumstances that the government faces, communism is weak. That is also the case in Costa Rica, Colombia, Venezuela, and the Dominican Republic. Where democracy really works and the people vote in free elections, democratic parties are by far the strongest. The only way out, then, is to begin to build a real and stable democracy which can be achieved only through dialogue and a great deal of patience.

For this reason, several years ago Contadora reappeared, this time with the full backing of the presidents of Mexico, Colombia, Venezuela, and Panamá. Costa Rica was left out due to its problems with Nicaragua. This was seen as the best way to achieve a Latin American solution for the Central American war. An important aspect of the Contadora effort is that Latin Americans have to prove that they can solve their own problems among themselves; otherwise, the permanent U.S. intervention and paternalism cannot be blamed on the United States but on our own incapacity to achieve peaceful solutions. Once Contadora began to work again, it received support from all over the world: the United States, the USSR, China, the countries of Europe, the Vatican, Latin America, and Japan. Early in 1984 a meeting of the Central American foreign ministers in Panamá produced documents approved unanimously. This event shows progress in understanding and, more important, in talking together.

Weapons inventories, withdrawal of military advisers, and nonintervention in neighboring states go together with the implementation of human rights, electoral processes, and the building of democracy. It is no easy task after 163 years of the type of independence that these countries have had, but we have to convince the U.S. government that intervention, military solutions, or paternalism are not going to produce solid results. On the contrary, such continuous actions will keep Central America in permanent civil war.

Suppose that the Nicaraguan government were overthrown after thousands of deaths and infinite destruction. What would happen? The defeated groups, well armed and trained, would certainly go to the mountains to continue the war as guerrillas. If the rebels of El Salvador could obtain a military victory, as they anticipated in 1980, the defeated groups, encouraged by neighbors, would continue the conflict end-lessly. There is no middle path between war or peace. War in Central America cannot be won by anybody, in spite of what military experts and myopic politicians keep saying. Peace is the only way out, and peace has to be built through dialogue, accepting pluralism, and letting Central Americans handle their own problems.

There is a subtle intervention coming from outside the region, instigated by the enemies of the United States. As any great power throughout history, the United States has the right to defend its borders, and the area of Central America and the Caribbean is of great strategic importance to it. However, we believe that the experience of the United States with Mex-ico and Canada has shown that restraint and respect are the most important aspects of their relations with their neighbors. Permanent respectful relationships with all the countries of the area are the basis of understanding and peace.

Ideological pluralism is the basis of democracy. Inter-nationally the same principle applies. If we have democratic governments we can have peace, but, in order to build democ-racy, we need justice and education. Each one of the countries in Central America and the Caribbean has a different history and social structure. We must help one another, and we are doing it, patiently, in order to build modern and efficient systems of government that can provide democratic processes and respect for human rights.

Having a constitution that forbids the existence of an army, Costa Rica cannot provide advice in military matters. Central Americans have been struggling to build a fair society in which an army is not needed. Disarmament in many of these small countries of our region is one of our major goals, and we feel this can be obtained slowly with the help of the Con-tadora Group and the cooperation of the Western Hemi-sphere. Although social revolt in Central America has been used recently by the enemies of the United States to make a case against that country, it is not an ideological war.

Seen in a world perspective it is a very minor war, as are many others in the world today where enemies of the United States take advantage of local troubles to discredit American foreign policy. We believe that an open and clear backing of peaceful solutions, such as the ones we have been seeking, will facilitate the achievement of peace and democracy and will permit a permanent and respectful relationship among sovereign democracies in the area. Modern technology shows that military perspectives have to be modernized and based on solid political bases. Extremism fails. The banners of freedom, human dignity, and justice should be given back to democratic leaders in Latin America as has occurred in the last decade in the Dominican Republic, Panamá, Ecuador, Peru, and Argentina where military governments have been replaced by civilian rule.

The five foreign ministers of Central America met recently in Panamá under the guidance of the four Contadora countries and, on January 8, 1984, signed, in the name of the governments of Costa Rica, El Salvador, Guatemala, Honduras, and Nicaragua, a document that established the mechanisms to execute the agreements already approved in September 1983. These are assigned to three areas: security, politics, and socioeconomics. Unanimously the foreign ministers agreed to accept a supervised inventory of military installations, weapons, and other materiel in order to freeze and reduce them to achieve a military balance; list the foreign military advisers and similar groups with the aim of eliminating them; observe strict nonintervention in other countries; and to stop the arms traffic by determining areas, ways, and means to establish a total control. In the political field, each country committed itself to justice, liberty, and democracy; respect for human rights; modernization of electoral instruments to guarantee a real popular participation; the creation of effective democratic parties; to set dates for the electoral processes; and guarantee the participation of all political groups existing in each country. They also proclaimed the need to sustain permanent dialogue among governments. Finally, in the economic and social areas, an effort must be made to change unfair structures, promote social justice, and develop more productive economies.

A technical group, under the Contadora Group organization, is given the immediate task of implementing these norms, and three commissions, one for each area, are given the responsibility to make the necessary studies, legal proposals, and recommendations as well as to set to work immediately and present results not later than April 30, 1984. Each commission is formed with representatives of the five Central

American countries, but it is the Contadora Group of countries that will make them work.

All this was done in one year, and wars that could not be stopped were slowed. If we examine this effort carefully, we deduce that peace is possible if we continue to assert these lines of thought. Every country in the world is backing this effort, but there are still many politicians who would like war to continue and military materiel to increase without giving a thought to the suffering and the people killed and displaced. Peace can be obtained if we win the minds of citizens of all countries, of organized institutions in each country, of world-wide international organizations, of media representatives, and, more than anything else, of the few men in this area who now have political power and the authority to make decisions. A society flourishes when men respect one another's ideas; countries must learn about each other's ideologies. This is possible only with dialogue and through understanding. If we do this, patiently, peace is possible in Central America and in the world.

Abraham F. Lowenthal

The United States and Central America: Reflections on the Kissinger Commission Report

THE REPORT of the President's National Bipartisan Commission on Central America—the Kissinger Commission Report—is a significant contribution to national consideration in the United States about how to deal with revolutionary change in our border region, but it is a disappointing and ultimately unsatisfactory one, destined more to stimulate further controversy than to resolve it. The report comprises an analysis of Central America's turmoil and of U.S. interests there, a proposed program of U.S. actions for protecting our interests, and an attempt to build a national consensus to support the recommended measures. On each of these dimensions the report falls short.

The report's discussion of Central America's turmoil combines skewed history with flawed assessments. Its background section mostly skips over the interventionist record of the United States in Central America and therefore fails to take adequately into account the intense nationalism that fuels today's crisis. The report deals with the politics of contemporary Central America, as if democracy and stability were the norm there, and thus portrays death squads and leftist insurrectionaries as extraneous elements, not recognizing that they are at the heart of the region's tragedy.

The report's discussion of the leftist revolutions in Central America is revealingly incomplete. Having laid the groundwork for understanding the steady rise of insurgent movements in the 1970s, the report suspends its well-crafted analysis of the gathering preconditions for revolution and jumps into extended discussion of Soviet and Cuban involvement. To be fair, this section confirms what nonadministration analysts have been saying: the Soviet-Cuban involvement in Central America was limited and hesitant during the very years that the revolutions gained momentum. Nowhere does the report account for the strength and resilience of the Sandinista movement or El Salvador's FDR-FMLN, but it deliberately conveys the impression that external Communist agents are to blame. The entire approach to Central America's civil wars is cast not in terms of the region's own dynamics but of U.S.-Soviet confrontation. The report talks, for instance, of the "insurgencies we confront." It treats Central America's profound internal war as something that could be largely resolved by expanding U.S. military and economic aid.

The report's discussion of U.S. interests in Central America adds little or nothing to previous official formulations. It may be revealing that the commission did not include its statement of U.S. interests up front, where it might have attracted attention, but rather buried its main articulation in the body of the document, on page 37. There, seven U.S. interests are advanced: 1) "to preserve the moral authority of the United States," 2) "to improve the living conditions of the people of Central America," 3) "to advance the cause of democracy," 4) "to strengthen the hemispheric system," 5) "to promote peaceful change," 6) "to prevent hostile forces from seizing and expanding control in a strategically vital area of the Western Hemisphere," and 7) "to bar the Soviet Union from consolidating either directly or through Cuba a hostile foothold on the American continents in order to advance its strategic purposes." It is not clear why the sixth and seventh interests are distinguished in this listing; in practice, the report treats the takeover by hostile forces of Western Hemisphere nations as necessarily implying or involving the danger of Soviet strategic advance. What is most striking is that the report walks away from the conclusion that flows from its own listing of U.S. interests: that the single-minded U.S. pursuit of the final objectives—to prevent Soviet involvement—is today having the effect of undercutting all other aims. It is undermining the moral authority of the United States, extending and deepening wars that worsen the region's economies, retarding the prospects for democracy and peaceful change, and further dividing the tottering inter-American system. That trade-off is the painful nub of our Central American quandary.

The Kissinger Report proposes a massive increase in economic and military assistance; the establishment of the new regional Central American Development Organization, with the United States as its center; efforts to support the region's democratization; social and economic projects, including a Literacy Corps and thousands of scholarships for study in the United States; stepped-up pressures against the Sandinistas; and declared support for the diplomatic initiative of the Contadora nations (Mexico, Panamá, Venezuela, and Colombia), coupled with explicit rejection of the idea that negotiations should lead to a sharing of power among the contending parties in El Salvador.

Taken in its entirety, which is how the Kissinger Commission urges its readers to approach the report, what is recommended is a major increase in U.S. involvement in all aspects of Central America's struggle. Implemented as a whole (which is unlikely to happen, thanks to Congress), the effects of the Kissinger Report would be primarily to step up U.S. military aid and to involve the United States more fully in the military struggle, for many of the other recommendations are either trivial or mutually inconsistent.

The report's section on strengthening Central American democracy, for instance, is remarkably thin. After some standard support for aiding local self-help groups, the report immediately turns to endorsing the binational centers operated by the U.S. Information Agency because they "provide valuable insights into the advantages of personal freedoms in the United States," as if that would bring democracy to the region. The report's main economic recommendation—that some $8 billion in U.S. aid be provided to Central America over the next five years—is based on dubious assumptions. The report presumes, in calculating how much U.S. aid will be required, that the destruction of Central America's infrastructure, because of civil wars, will have ended; posits a decline in international interest charges; assumes that substantial foreign investment will be made in Central America; and ignores the inflationary and other distorting effects of military aid. The report also shies away from the one measure—opening the U.S. market to Central America's exports—that the commission's sole economist, Carlos Díaz Alejandro, sees as the only significant hope for improving the region's development prospects.

The report's lucid discussion of the pervasiveness of social inequity in Central America and its effects on political polarization is contradicted by the assumption that providing more military aid to the guardians of the status quo will somehow contribute to social change. The report's recommendations for promoting social change are limited, if not ironic. Its bold endorsements of a Literacy Corps to teach Central Americans to read and of a massive college scholarship program are astonishing, if somewhat impractical, tributes to Cuban policy through the sincerest form of flattery.

Also, the support noted for the Contadora process is luke-cool, at best. The professed U.S. support is undermined by clear opposition to the substance of the Contadora approach: the acceptance of the Sandinista regime and the promotion of negotiated power sharing in El Salvador.

To be sure, the report contributes significantly in several respects to the gathering national discussion about what to do in Central America. It makes it clear, for instance, that economic injustice and political oppression are at the heart of Central America's turmoil, and that sustained reforms will be needed to remove these causes of continuing insurrection. The report portrays Soviet policy toward Central America as gradualist and ambiguous, not reckless, aggressive, and confrontational. The report provides some legitimacy, albeit grudgingly and somewhat contradictory, for the notion that the United States can accept revolutionary regimes in its border region. It shows that moderate to conservative persons, who do not otherwise challenge the Reagan administration's approach, find the activities of the Salvadoran government difficult to accept and consider the record of Guatemala's rulers absolutely anathema. It makes it clear, as well, that a broad consensus exists in this country that Cuban activism is part of the problem in Central America, and that Soviet and/or Cuban bases would be regarded as unacceptable by the American body politic. The report provides a number of creative suggestions for ways the United States could help Central America develop, if and when conditions in that region change.

These are important contributions, and the Kissinger Commission should be commended for them. But the commission did not succeed, despite its artful use of all the standard devices, at producing a significant consensus on the tough issues facing the United States in Central America.

The report addresses both sides of the crucial question whether the United States, in its border region, can accept a revolutionary regime, even a Marxist-Leninist one, if the regime forswears military alliance with the Soviet Union and denies to the Soviets the opportunity to establish bases and other offensive facilities in this hemisphere. At some points the report avows that the United States can accept "indigenous revolu- tion" in this region as long as it is truly indigenous. At another point the pale of acceptability is limited to "indigenous reform." In many other passages the report suggests that revolutionary regimes in this area are bound not to be indigenous, and that the consolidation of a Marxist-Leninist regime in Nicaragua would pose a permanent security threat. The exact nature of that threat is nowhere clearly stated, however. In one impor- tant passage, the report directly states that the possibility of Soviet bases being established is "not the sole or even the main security concern." Just at the point where an unambig- uous explication of the security challenge would surely have been logical, the report trails off into vagueness.

The report waffles on other key issues. It explicitly states in one fascinating paragraph that its members did not attempt "a collective judgment" on whether the United States should support the Contras' efforts, for instance, but then makes it clear that some signers regard this support as vital, while others regard it as entirely unacceptable. The report's one notewor- thy stand—its insistence that support for El Salvador be con- ditioned on that country's improving its dismal record on human rights—is vitiated by a footnote from Henry Kissinger and two of his colleagues (which says, in effect, that they agree with this "conditionality," unless the Salvadoran regime really needs the assistance) and also by language elsewhere in the report emphasizing that the government of El Salvador needs assurance that it will not lose U.S. aid. A recommendation that multilateral economic assistance to Central American nations be conditioned on their meeting agreed standards regarding reforms and other measures to use the aid effectively is qual- ified into near meaninglessness by suggesting that the United States could maintain bilateral programs to such countries "regardless of performance." Practically every major propo- sition in the report is qualified elsewhere in the text by a counterstatement. In short, there is much less to the Kissinger Report's consensus than meets the eye.

The vision that the Kissinger Report holds out as the aim of U.S. policy in Central America is a peaceful, democratic, reform-oriented, prosperous, stable, and congenial set of neighbors. The fundamental problem is that this goal is surely a mirage. Central America's nations are mostly conflict-wracked, repressive, polarized, economically depressed, unstable, and harboring deep resentments toward the United States. Wholehearted adoption and sustained implementation of the Kissinger Report's recommendations could not change this grim reality. On the contrary, part of the problem for the United States lies in the paradox that an increased U.S. presence tends to heighten the very nationalist and revolutionary sentiments that make Washington uncomfortable. A national consensus to achieve the unattainable does us little good, especially when the pursuit of the mirage makes the goal recede further away.

What already has been said is enough to establish why the Kissinger Report probably will fail in its main political task to build a coalition in support of an agreed upon policy. Because the report takes a bow in almost every direction, it does not really stand up for any policy. Because it proposes unrealistic, costly, and predictably ineffective expansions of the current approach, its ultimate effect is likely to be to leave the debate about where it was before. The American people, and the Congress, are unwilling to endorse President Ronald Reagan's underlying approach to Central America but have been unable to change or challenge the policy effectively.

The commission should be criticized, ultimately, for failing to do what a presidential commission is preeminently qualified to do: to compare broad and realistic options for U.S. policy. The commission does not appear to have given serious consideration to any alternative for U.S. policy to the administration's settled, and unsettling, course. The report argues that the case can be made for doing nothing in Central America (although this case is never presented) or for doing a lot, but not for doing "too little." By this rhetorical twist, proposals for doing something different from what the administration is doing are set aside as too little and are thus summarily dismissed. The Kissinger Commission did not set forth alternative options for U.S. policy and therefore lost the chance to build a consensus behind a new policy with a greater chance for support and success than the administration's established approach. That is the Kissinger Report's most disappointing aspect.

What are the options for U.S. policy toward Central America? I believe there are four. One is essentially the established policy of the Reagan administration, reinforced by the Kissinger Report's dominant thrust: to support the government and security forces in El Salvador, Guatemala, and Honduras; to provide them with economic and military assistance; to hold out for a military victory of the current anti-Communist regimes, however distasteful some of them may be, against leftist insurgencies; to attempt to strengthen the legitimacy of these regimes by pushing them to hold elections and to curb flagrant repression; and to harass, subvert, intimidate, and perhaps overthrow the Sandinista regime in Nicaragua. That the Sandinista regime is resisting attack, and that the FDR-FMLN in El Salvador is clearly stronger than it was three years ago, suggests that this U.S. strategy is not working, but the Kissinger Commission argues that a more sustained and expanded version of this policy will ultimately bear fruit; if we double or triple the investment, it will ultimately pay off.

It is possible that several years of sustained and escalated counterinsurgency warfare, accompanied by massive economic and military aid, will eventually wear down today's leftist movements in Central America, at least for a time. It is more probable, however, that increasing U.S. involvement in support of the current regimes in Central America will further polarize the region and help intensify its civil wars, push left-nationalist movements into even closer alignment with Cuba and the Soviet Union, further fragment the United States internally, and undermine the confidence of European and Latin American allies in the political judgment of the United States. The Kissinger Report did not effectively address any of these costs of the current policy, nor did it squarely face the likelihood that the Central American regimes will continue to lack legitimacy at a time when escalating U.S. involvement may be called for.

The second policy option, hinted at by several passages and recommendations of the report but certainly not its dominant thrust, would be for the United States to involve itself deeply in Central America's turmoil but in clear pursuit of basic change rather than in defense of the status quo. This approach, which Tom Farer has called "managing the revolution," would imply much more intense U.S. efforts to restructure the armed forces in Central America and to disband the death squads, to impose measures of agrarian reform and to undertake other broad structural changes, and to help bring reformist governments to power in the region—in short, long-term efforts to transform the very nature of Central American society. This stance, going far beyond what the Kissinger Report recommends in the direction of progressive interventionism, no doubt appeals to those noble impulses in the U.S. tradition that John F. Kennedy aroused. Even the restrained version of this option that peeks through the report at various spots seems to most experienced observers an idea whose time has passed. The United States by now realizes that it does not know how to manage other countries' revolutions. It may be able to bolster or to nurture local efforts, but it cannot effectively impose basic change, and interventionist efforts to do so will backfire. The American people, moreover, are unlikely to sustain for long a messy and disappointing attempt to remake Central America in the face of serious obstacles. Stepping up U.S. intervention in Central America—even if the focus could be socioeconomic and political, not military, and even if the animus were reformist rather than anti-Communist—is likely to lead to a much more costly U.S. role than the American public will, or should, sustain.

A third possible course for U.S. policy would be to scale down involvement in Central America, commensurate with this region's limited real importance to this country. With respect to some problems, former Secretary of State Dean Acheson once mused that the best advice is "don't just do something; stand there." A new administration could reject the Reagan view of Central America as a test of U.S. resolve and a place to "draw the line" and concentrate instead on defending concrete U.S. interests where they are directly threatened. If the United States had the self-confidence to stand back from Central America's turmoil and to concentrate its energies, attention, and resources on some of the tough problems we face—economic decline, resource scarcities, nuclear dangers, environmental decay, narcotics trade, and terrorism—the result might be to spare both the country and Central America much grief.

There also would be severe costs to adopting this more passive stance toward Central America, both in terms of national self-esteem and of international perceptions. For the United States just to back away from its declared interest in Central America's fate would send powerful signals that Washington is not to be trusted. The Reagan administration, to be sure, has been caught to some extent in a "credibility trap" of its own making: raising the declared stakes in Central America to justify a high level of U.S. involvement and then upping the ante in view of the high stakes until it seems as if the international image of the United States depends not on our strength but on making impossible dreams come true in El Salvador. The Reagan administration's lamentable excesses should not make us lose sight of the fact that neither the U.S. public nor our international allies would respect a U.S. decision simply to write off Central America which is too close to home, physically and psychologically, to treat it as unimportant.

There is a fourth and better way, however. It is to define much more carefully what our vital interests are in Central America and to pursue those interests vigorously while shying away from unnecessary involvements. The core interest the United States has in Central America is to assure that no bases, offensive facilities, or strategic weapons are introduced by the Soviet Union or on its behalf into the border region of the United States. This is true not only, or even primarily, because such weapons or facilities would be directly threatening to U.S. security, for in today's world the difference proximity makes is less than it used to be. Nor is the main reason for U.S. concern that having to cope with hostile bases would distract or tie down U.S. military resources otherwise available elsewhere, although there is some validity to this argument. Rather, the strong U.S. interest in excluding Soviet offensive weapons and facilities arises largely because, in a world where perceptions are themselves realities, the inability of the United States to keep direct security threats out of its immediate vicinity would be generally regarded as a sign of weakness. That point is one well understood by U.S. leaders and the American public, by Latin Americans of all tendencies, and by the leadership of the Soviet Union; it is the stuff of international power politics.

It should be possible, given the shared assumptions and interests of all the parties, to reach international agreements that would prevent Central America and the Caribbean from becoming a locus for Soviet offensive bases, facilities, or weapons. Such an understanding between the United States and the Soviet Union has been in place with regard to Cuba since 1962 and has been effective; a region-wide agreement in which all parties were involved would be much more likely to endure. The United States should actively and diligently pursue negotiations with all the relevant actors that would lead to an international understanding to keep foreign bases and offensive weapons out of the Caribbean Basin. The Contadora nations could take the lead in these negotiations, but Washington must make it unmistakably clear that the United States seeks such an accord.

As the reciprocal of its continued insistence that Central America and the Caribbean constitute a permanent security zone for the United States, it would be appropriate for this country to take a sustained interest in these regions' economic development and political evolution. It should do so, however, on terms that respect the sovereignty of their nations and that recognize that their internal dynamics will be much more important in shaping their future than either U.S. or Soviet involvement. General programs to provide access to the U.S. market for all these nations make sense as the most effective and least interventionist way to support regional economic growth. So do economic assistance programs for those countries able to use help effectively and where U.S. involvement will not contradict core values at the heart of U.S. society. These programs should be long-term and low-key. They should not be expected to assure the political loyalty of these countries in any immediate sense, and they should be offered as an incentive toward peace by making them contingent on regional negotiations. These programs should reinforce the peace process in Central America, not substitute for it.

The United States, like other great powers before it, finds it difficult to accept autonomous and even hostile nations in its border region. The reasons for this difficulty have less to do with "national security" than with "national insecurity," the psychopolitical discomfort accompanying the loss of control of something we are used to controlling. That is true even though the significance of what has been controlled is less than it used to be and even though the costs of retaining control are mounting, for old axioms and habits of thought change slowly.

An approach to Central America that focuses sharply on what is still important to control and what is still feasible to control—that is, the military predominance of the United States in its own sphere—would help this country achieve the kind of consensus which the Kissinger Commission sought but failed to create. It would enable the United States to restore and preserve its credibility and self-confidence rather than tying them to losing causes. It would allow the United States to accept Central America's future rather than to frustrate itself in perpetual pursuit of hegemony lost. Finally, it would permit the United States to concentrate more fully on other problems in the Western Hemisphere and beyond. The time has come to regain a sense of national perspective and purpose. It is time to move from sterile partisan debates on Central America to a truly bipartisan policy based on full national consideration of what is at stake there and what is not.

Conclusion

George C. Herring and
Kenneth M. Coleman

Beyond Hegemony: Toward a New Central American Policy

THE ESSAYS printed here comprise a ranging critique of U.S. policy toward Central America under Jimmy Carter and especially under Ronald Reagan. The authors generally agree that Washington has defined the problem wrongly. During the era of the Cold War, many local and regional conflicts have quickly become internationalized, and in Central America the Soviet Union and its allies have sought to exploit the growing turmoil. The present crisis in Central America has its roots primarily in the political, social, and economic inequities that have long afflicted the region, problems to which the United States, through its quasi-imperial role in many of the countries, has contributed. The changing role of the Central American Catholic church, as elaborated by Kathleen Blee, makes clear the extent to which new forces are at work in the area. The Reagan administration thus errs grievously in portraying the current strife as instigated, controlled, and directed by the Kremlin.

The U.S. stake in the region also has been distorted. The administration repeatedly has claimed that U.S. vital interests would be threatened by additional Communist takeovers in Central America. For the most part, however, these interests have been defined only vaguely in terms of geography and credibility, with the administration warning that acquiescence in Marxist triumphs so close to home would tarnish the prestige of the United States and drastically weaken its influence throughout the world. Some of the contributors to this volume concede that U.S. strategic interests would be endangered by the establishment of a Soviet satellite in Central America. They do not view the Sandinistas in Nicaragua or the FMLN in El Salvador as mere instruments of Soviet policy, and they agree that the emergence of a Marxist government in any of the Central American countries would not necessarily lead to a Soviet satellite. Eldon Kenworthy specifically attacks the notion of credibility as a basis for policy, warning that "a definition of vital interests that gives prominence to credibility and dominoes will . . . convert nearly every crisis in the world into a test of our vital interests."

The contributors generally concur that, having defined the problem incorrectly, the Reagan administration has developed solutions that have been notably unsuccessful, in some cases counterproductive, and that hold out the possibility of a major conflict. Kenneth Coleman contends that in El Salvador and Guatemala, and possibly in Honduras as well, the United States is pursuing a course that, if traditional patterns hold true, may ensure the result it is trying to prevent. Historically, he asserts, the greater the extent to which centrist reform elements have been excluded from power the more likely revolution is to succeed. By contrast, the greater the role played by such elements the more likely that revolution will be rendered irrelevant.

Focusing on the specific case of Nicaragua, Thomas Walker argues that the United States must bear primary responsibility for a confrontation with the Sandinista government which has assumed increasingly dangerous proportions in the last few years. Since that government took power in Nicaragua, and especially since Reagan took office, Walker contends, Washington has pursued a policy that has been consistently hostile and provocative. It has rejected diplomatic overtures proposed by Nicaragua and the Contadora nations. It has mounted a massive program of "disinformation" to discredit the Nicaraguan government and a program of economic destabilization to undermine it. Most important, it has helped to organize and has provided generous support to a not-so-covert war waged by counterrevolutionaries against the Sandinista government. In short, the administration has set as its goal nothing less than the overthrow of the revolutionary Nicaraguan government.

George Herring challenges the notion popular among many critics of U.S. policy that the administration is rushing headlong into another Vietnam, a position other contributors to the volume might reject. Conceding the similarities between the revolution in Vietnam and those in Central America, and in particular the similarities between U.S. responses to both, he argues that each historical situation is unique and that facile historical analogies are poor guides for the present and future. Herring also stresses that because Vietnam happened it is unlikely to occur again. Although he rejects the Vietnam analogy used by opponents of the administration, he does not concede Reagan's point that, because Central America is not Vietnam, the president's policies there deserve support. Indeed, Herring contends, the Vietnam analogy may be a highly dangerous argument for critics to rely on because, as long as President Reagan avoids a commitment that approaches the magnitude of Vietnam, he retains considerable room to maneuver.

The authors also agree that some administration measures proposed for Central America, but not yet implemented, are based on flawed assumptions and may have disastrous results. Among other things, the Kissinger Commission Report calls for a major expansion of an already massive military assistance program. Additional large increments of military assistance of the sort that has been poured into El Salvador and Honduras may further polarize conflicts within the individual Central American countries. Such military aid and the use of Honduran and Costa Rican soil for counterrevolutionary efforts have inflamed traditional Central American rivalries between Nicaragua and its neighbors and have drawn a previously peaceful Costa Rica reluctantly into the turmoil. In addition, continued significant increases in the U.S. presence in the region, as Abraham Lowenthal points out, are likely to stimulate further in Central America the very nationalist forces that the United States has always had difficulty controlling.

As Billie DeWalt and David Ross make clear, moreover, the Kissinger Commission's proposals for major economic assistance programs, and President Reagan's earlier proposals for a "regional" program of economic assistance, are similarly flawed and likely will not have the salutary effects claimed by Washington. DeWalt affirms that no type of economic assistance will accomplish anything until the agrarian problem resulting from concentration of land ownership is addressed head-on. Ross challenges the notion that export-based development of the sort proposed in the Caribbean Basin Initiative will provide an answer to Central America's problems. If past experience is a guide, he suggests, such development will not promote self-sustaining growth, and for any gains registered through the program the Central Americans will pay a high price in terms of their growing dependence on the whims of the U.S. market. Basing his conclusions on the record of the Alliance for Progress in the Kennedy years, Walter LaFeber, in even more dramatic fashion, warns that such aid programs, as proposed by the Kissinger Commission Report, will widen the already yawning gap between rich and poor and make further revolutions inevitable.

The authors disagree fundamentally on the reasons why U.S. policy has been so misguided. Thomas Walker attributes the problem primarily to the American political system, an ignorant mass public, steeped in the rhetoric of the Cold War, which has rewarded at the polls politicians proclaiming simplistic anti-Communist slogans and penalized those who seek to deal with international issues in all their complexity. Kenworthy blames the problem on the ignorance and ideological bent of the policymakers themselves, especially those in the Reagan administration. Going beyond the Cold War, or the personalities in any given administration and treating the problem from a broad historical perspective, LaFeber, by contrast, finds the fault resting with the requirements of a capitalist system that has looked upon Central America and other less developed regions primarily as outlets for U.S. exports and investments.

Whatever the precise cause, the authors agree that the methods employed by the United States are based on false assumptions. Most are also in agreement with Lowenthal that the proclaimed goal of U.S. policy—a stable, democratic Central America—flies in the face of history and of a Central American political tradition and culture which has been volatile and undemocratic.

It is always easier to indicate what is wrong with a set of policies than to propose alternatives, but criticism bears with it an obligation to do just that. A first essential step, one toward which the authors hope this volume may contribute, is to reshape the current debate on the crisis in Central America. Political debates are inevitably colored by recent history. As Herring points out, much of the debate on Central America has taken place so far in the context of Vietnam, an analogy which is at best misleading, at worst highly dangerous as a basis for policy. What has been missing is a sensitivity to the unique histories of the individual Central American nations; the often stormy relations among them; and their traditional, quasi-imperial relationship with the United States. We could begin in no better place than by trying to inject into the debate a greater appreciation of the historical context from which the Central American crisis has emerged.

It is also necessary to examine more closely and more critically the administration's portrayal of the conflict in Cold War terms. The Soviet Union and Cuba undoubtedly have played important roles in the emerging conflict in Central America, and the Sandinista government has supported the revolution in El Salvador. Much more precise discussion is needed, however, as to exactly what these roles have been and how the interests of the various Communist nations coincide and conflict. At the very least, the administration's simplistic rhetoric needs to be exposed for what it is. Perhaps more than anything else, the people of the United States need to understand, as Daniel Oduber so eloquently puts it, that Central Americans themselves are "fighting for something they cannot express in words or ideologies. They are fighting for a piece of land, or even a piece of bread, and now for a day of peace in their own huts."

Careful assessment of U.S. interests in the region is in order too. Thus far, these interests have been assumed and stated rather than defined, and it is urgent that they be defined with precision. What are these interests, specifically? Do they involve the protection of U.S. industries and the nation's traditional economic role in the region? Are they essentially strategic? Should Washington's primary concern be the prevention and elimination of Marxist governments, or is it enough, as Lowenthal suggests, to prevent Soviet bases and satellites? What about the abstract notion of credibility? Is it a valid basis for policy, or, as Kenworthy insists, is it a handy but entrapping device to build support for policies that have been hit upon instinctively?

The authors of this volume believe that the United States must drastically revise its traditional economic and political approaches to Central America. It has been tilting at windmills, while ignoring or failing to see the fundamental problems of the nations of the region. These problems have deep roots in the colonial and early independence eras of Central American history, as Michael Webb points out. Thus, prescriptions formulated from alien ideological perspectives can prove facile.

The United States usually has held that "marketplace solutions" to development problems are best for all countries, but other solutions are possible and may be preferable. It is imperative that the United States stop trying to export its own economic system, a product of a unique set of conditions that cannot be duplicated in Central America. It may be able to help others adapt pieces of its system to their needs, but it must leave them free to choose for themselves the total economic package they want.

This is especially important where the Hispanic concept of the social function of property is an important part of the culture. According to this concept, property is held conditional upon the fulfillment of state-stipulated obligations to society.[1] Such traditions may point in the direction of state socialism, but there is reason to believe that, once the social obligations of property ownership are redefined by Central American states, a major role for private ownership will remain.[2] Whatever the case, U.S. support for panicky property owners, who resist fulfillment of their social obligations, prevents Central Americans from addressing their own problems by time-honored Hispanic concepts that are not necessarily socialist. The United States must leave the creation of new economic systems to the Latin Americans, restricting itself to an unobtrusive advisory role.

Development programs in Central America also must confront the region's fundamental problems of employment, land tenure, and income distribution. These problems are interconnected, and each contributes to the failure to attain a high standard of living. Poverty in Central America is, to a large extent, the result of too few jobs. In the rural areas, land is increasingly controlled by only a few owners, leaving the predominantly rural population no means to earn a decent living. Some peasants migrate to the cities, while others work out tenuous short-term arrangements. Neither of these solutions works well and the worst poverty remains rural poverty.

---

[1]See Charles W. Anderson, *Politics and Economic Change in Latin America* (New York, 1967), p. 57.

[2]Joseph Collins, *What Difference Could a Revolution Make?* (San Francisco, 1982), pp. 31–50.

In addition, urbanization has outstripped the capacities of new industries to absorb the people coming from the countryside, these mechanized and capital-intensive industries creating relatively few jobs. Improvement in public health in the postwar era also has led to a population boom that intensifies the employment problem.

To deal with this issue, the United States must tolerate, indeed encourage, genuine land reform. Once the rural poor have moved to the city, they are not easily induced to return, and, since industrial employment is unavailable for two-thirds of the migrants, governments must address the problems causing the migration in the first place. One of the best things the United States can do to help Central Americans resolve fundamental agrarian problems is to turn a deaf ear to property holders when land reform is undertaken. For the United States to do nothing would permit the Central Americans to do something. Ideally, the United States should even support land reform financially when such help is requested.

The United States could be more tolerant of those governments that seek to improve the welfare of their citizens through collective measures. Socialized medicine, agricultural cooperatives, and state-owned banking systems are not necessarily indications of the emergence of Soviet-style governments. On the contrary, adoption of these methods may simply indicate that other governments realize that they cannot ensure enough jobs to guarantee that individuals will be able to pay for necessary services.

The United States could encourage Central American governments to experiment with diverse methods for urban job creation and enhancement. In doing so, it must accept the fact that such experiments will usually require an expanded role for the state. The fundamental moral appeal of existing guerrilla movements is not so much their vindictiveness against the rich as their commitment to see that everyone who wants will have a job that pays a decent wage and provides a sense of doing something important for society. That is a powerful appeal to urbanites who labor at low wages in the service sector or to *campesinos* who have struggled a lifetime with no more than seasonal employment. The United States therefore must be willing to go beyond conventional methods of economic assistance and make loans to cooperatives and other collective institutions. The Inter-American Foundation, an agency created by Congress to assist the truly poor in Latin America and the Caribbean, might be made an instrument for reconstruction and development through the support of cooperatives which do not violate basic U.S. economic principles. Encouragement for the Catholic church's efforts to create base communities also can help to facilitate necessary change.

Politically as well as economically, while remaining faithful to its own values, the United States must adopt a profoundly different attitude toward revolutionary change. It should speak mainly with the moral authority of its actions, befriending genuine democracies such as Costa Rica and maintaining a decent distance from governments that are undemocratic.

Furthermore, while exercising discretion in the company it keeps, Washington can strengthen democracy by its behavior toward those with whom it disagrees. Disagreement expressed with respect will reflect the ethos of democracy. Maintaining a firm commitment to human rights will call for even greater discipline. There will be occasions when it will have to be made clear that regardless of economic or political ideology we cannot have warm relations with regimes that violate basic human rights. This standard must be applied to governments of the right and the left. In general, the United States should downplay its public judgments of others, letting its message come from the initiatives taken in some cases and not taken in others.

Most important, we must accept revolutionary change when it is inevitable. We cannot be true to our values by trying to hold back political upheavals in other countries. When change by peaceful means has been systematically denied, it is useless to insist that change occur peacefully or not at all. The United States also must realize that revolution in Latin America will inevitably include a strong element of Yankeephobia and must be prepared to let it pass quietly and patiently. If it responds with panic or hostility, it will merely confirm the old distrust, provoking more belligerency in regimes it should be trying to conciliate.

The United States does have important security interests in Central America. The establishment of Soviet bases, or the introduction of strategic weapons in this hemisphere, would pose distinct dangers. The best way to protect legitimate security interests in the region is not to threaten others. Rather, it is to reassure revolutionary regimes that we will respect their autonomy as long as they pose no danger to us. We must make clear that socialism per se does not threaten our security.

If revolutionary regimes move toward socialism, we should accept that, retaining an open mind about how democracy can best be expressed. We should be willing to consult with those who wish to democratize their societies, but, if revolutionary regimes do not wish to consult with us, that is their right. If, on the other hand, they overtly and blatantly deny democratic values, they should expect to find us cool toward them. By "cooling it," the United States will make it less likely that revolutionaries will turn to the Soviet Union for assistance. If revolutionary regimes know that we will not attempt to overthrow them and that we will feel threatened only if they turn to the Soviet Union, they should be less likely to move in that direction. The key is to provide assurances that we can accept revolutions which pursue economic and political models that differ from ours.

In the specific case of Nicaragua, numerous steps should be taken to begin to defuse a conflict that has become increasingly dangerous. A quiet cessation of the clandestine support for the Contras is obviously a first essential move, and it should be followed by easing the formal and informal economic sanctions that have been imposed over the past four years. Congressional pressure in this direction is well conceived and should be heeded by the White House. Beyond these tangible measures, we should have the honesty to admit, in retrospect, that the Somoza regime we supported for forty-five years was blatantly undemocratic, and the regime we have condemned in recent years has developed policies that have contributed significantly to the welfare of the people of Nicaragua. At some point in some way we must make clear that the Nicaraguan Revolution has a right to exist, whether or not we like the political and economic institutions it has created. We must leave to the Nicaraguans the shaping of their own economic system.

In a still broader sense, the United States should begin a quiet retreat from the role of hegemonic power, the delineator of acceptable behavior by others. A useful first step would be to support the Contadora initiative. The fact that Mexico, Panamá, Colombia, and Venezuela have taken the lead in seeking a regional peace is itself highly significant and worthy of U.S. encouragement. The United States could greatly facilitate their efforts by ending its support for the Contras in Nicaragua and by endorsing government opposition talks in El Salvador which look toward power sharing. Beyond that, it should back in every way possible the Contadora proposals to promote regional disarmament, respect for human rights and economic justice, the establishment of democratic processes, and especially nonintervention. It is essential to recognize, as Oduber has put it, that peace must be built "through dialogue, accepting pluralism, and letting Central Americans handle their own problems."

As we write in the summer of 1984, the future remains foreboding. The United States is less secure in its own hemisphere than it was four years ago, not so much because of the spread of revolutionary movements but because its own policies have dangerously raised the level of violence. Nicaragua may yet prove to be more democratic and less socialist than might be expected, and the confrontation with the United States may ease. José Napoleón Duarte may be able to mediate the conflict in El Salvador, thereby averting a full-scale civil war and possible U.S. intervention. Such outcomes seem at best uncertain, and major challenges for U.S. policy probably lie ahead.

Our purpose here has been to offer a critique of existing policies and to propose alternatives, with the modest hope of contributing to the current debate on Central America. With Oduber, we continue to believe that peace is possible. We fear that if changes in policy are not soon introduced, however, the United States will plunge more deeply into the Central American morass with fateful consequences for itself and the people of the region.

Index